Sandra,

Thank you for all you do to make small businesses successful!

Tony E Keck
2/19/2015

Start *Grow* Sell

*A Primer for Starting, Growing and Selling
Your Government Contracting Business*

By

Tom Keith

&

Ryan Keith

Copyright © 2015 by Tom Keith and Ryan Keith

All rights reserved. This book or any portion thereof may not be reproduced or used in any manner whatsoever without the express written permission of the publisher except for the use of brief quotations in a book review.

ACKNOWLEDGEMENTS

Thank you to all of those that have helped us out along the way, both in our personal and professionals lives. There are too many to thank all of you individually, however, we would like give a special thank you to Mona Neff for putting up with us and helping us so much through the process of writing this book.

DISCLAIMER

This book includes information that was current at the time of writing. We have done our best to be current and accurate, but websites and business and government contracting processes change constantly. If you find out-of-date links or information, please contact us at *info@TheUnconventionalStrategist.com*, and we will update in the next edition. This book is based solely on our personal experiences. We are not providing legal advice — we are sharing the story of our business model.

CONTENTS

INTRODUCTION 1
STRATEGIC PLANNING or PLANNING STRATEGICALLY ... 3
WHAT FOLLOWS 9

PART 1: START YOUR COMPANY 13

CHAPTER 1: BASICS FOR HOW TO START YOUR COMPANY 15
CHAPTER 2: STARTUP PREPARATION FOR GOVERNMENT CONTRACTING 33
CHAPTER 3: TAXES 45
CHAPTER 4: BUSINESS PLANNING 63

PART 2: GROW YOUR COMPANY 91

CHAPTER 5: ESSENTIAL STEPS TO ENSURE LONG-TERM GROWTH 93
CHAPTER 6: NETWORKING 107
CHAPTER 7: UNDERSTANDING CONTRACTS 121
CHAPTER 8: WHAT'S ALL THIS ABOUT REQUESTS FOR PROPOSALS 133
CHAPTER 9: THE PROPOSAL PROCESS 161
CHAPTER 10: GENERAL SERVICES ADMINISTRATION (GSA) SCHEDULES 169
CHAPTER 11: WRITING WHITE PAPERS 183
CHAPTER 12: TARGETING YOUR FIRST CONTRACT 191

CHAPTER 13: CONTRACT RESPONSIBILITIES ………..... 203
CHAPTER 14: TIME AND LABOR CHARGING …………… 213
CHAPTER 15: DEFENSE CONTRACT AUDIT AGENCY …. 221
CHAPTER 16: HIRING ……………………………………… 227
CHAPTER 17: HIRING A SECURITY SPECIALIST ………… 275
CHAPTER 18: INTELLECTUAL PROPERTY RIGHTS …….. 283

PART 3: SELL YOUR COMPANY ………………… 295

ABOUT THE AUTHORS ……………………………………… 307
THINK LIKE THE UNCONVENTIONAL STRATEGIST ………. 323
APPENDIX A: KEY TERMINOLOGY ……………………………. 327
APPENDIX B: ACRONYMS …………………………………….. 363

INTRODUCTION

What You Can Expect

If you are reading this book, we assume you have already decided to start a government contracting business or have already started one, and you really want someone to tell you what to do next in simple terms and without a lot of fluff. This book is a primer—a general how-to book. We focus on the essentials and explain the steps you need to take, why you need to take those steps, and the order in which you should take them. Where applicable, we cite resource references and websites that provide more detail for people who want to dig deeper.

What You Will Not See

There are no sections asking if you have done market research, if you have assessed whether or not you are an entrepreneur or a risk taker, and so on. There are plenty of books available that ask those questions. If you are reading this book, we assume you have already asked yourself these questions, and you are serious about getting down to business.

Why We Wrote This Book

We started, own and co-own several businesses. Some are government contracting businesses, and we wish this book had existed when we started our first one. Such a book, with topics and sections specifically for government contractors, would have saved us a lot of time, energy and money. After talking to many new business owners, we recognized that they, too, wished for a book written by serial business starters, who could offer step-by-step procedures to follow and would share their lessons learned. We wanted to document our experiences and create a reference to use when we mentor business owners. At the same time, we wanted to offer the book to our customers, so they could understand the process we go through with each new startup.

We Love What We Do!

We love the business world, but mostly, we love helping others start their own business, achieve their business and life goals, and eventually, write their own success stories. We hope that as you follow the steps in this book, you will be on the way to achieving your business and life goals, too.

STRATEGIC PLANNING or PLANNING STRATEGICALLY

While many people starting a new government contracting business will focus primarily (if not solely) on getting that first contract to bring revenue into the company, we encourage you, from day one, to be strategic (think big picture) in your thinking and not just tactical (focusing only on the first contract). To fully market and grow your company, you need to be (or become) a strategic thinker.

Strategic planning is about making choices. It is a process designed to support leaders in being intentional about their goals and objectives to achieve their vision. At the highest level, strategic planning involves envisioning and documenting where you want the company to be in three to five years; putting specific, measureable goals and objectives in place to meet your vision; and then working towards that vision by knocking off the outlined goals and objectives.

When first starting a business, many people may not take time to draft a strategic plan. In fact, for most small, government contracting new-starts, a *formal* strategic plan is not necessary or required to get started. But even knowing that, we put this chapter up front, because we want you to be strategic — to think strategically — in everything you do.

As you start your company there is so much to consider, for example:

- What products will we offer?
- Will we be a services company?
- Will we be a vendor?
- Do we need a business plan? Why do we need a business plan? What goes into a business plan?

- How do we develop our budget? Track our financials? Fund our work? Get paid for our work?
- What about technology? What tools do we need in our "back office"?
- Will we need a facility?
- Will we do classified work? Will we need classified workspace? How do we go about getting classified space?
- Will we start off by becoming a subcontractor? How do we get a subcontract?
- When will it make sense to try to get our first prime? How do we get that first prime?
- What insurance do we need?
- Do we need a Board of Advisors? Board of Directors? Both?
- Do we need a marketing plan? What is a marketing plan, and how do we go about creating one?
- How do we network effectively, and where do we go to network?
- What are the different kinds of government contracts? Which type of contract makes sense for our company? How do we go about getting that first contract?
- What is a Request for Proposal **(RFP)**?
- How do we write a proposal in response to an RFP?
- What if we have a business idea that we want to propose to the government that is *not* in response to an RFP? Or, just what is an unsolicited proposal? A "white paper"?
- Okay, now that we have our first contract, what exactly are our contract responsibilities?
- How do we keep track of our employees' time? Why is that important?

Strategic Planning or Planning Strategically

- How do we go about hiring employees? How do we pay those employees? Keep them motivated? Reward them? Provide them benefits?
- Should we hire a security specialist? What would a security specialist do for us?
- What do we need to know about taxes?
- What do we need think about in terms of emergency preparedness?
- Where do we find the right mentors?
- How do business partners protect themselves with the appropriate legal documents?
- Do we know where to go to get the support we need? A lawyer? A government contracts expert? An accountant? A government contracting financial expert? A security specialist?

> **Have we got you thinking? Do you understand *why* you need to think strategically?**
>
> There really is a lot to do and to learn if you plan to start your own company! *Read through that list again and write down your own list of questions.* This list was not meant to be comprehensive, so we know you will think of additional items. Next, spend some time thinking through whether or not you can answer those questions or if you need help in answering them.
>
> Ask yourself if you can or will or even should try to tackle all of this on your own, or if you will outsource specific tasks or hire people in-house to do aspects of the work.

Often new company owners try to do too many of these functions themselves, even if they do not have the true experience or knowledge to do the functions. Sadly, we have worked with too many people who signed legal contracts without ever having a legal review to help them understand what they were really signing. They were so happy to get the contract that they signed it just to get the revenue stream.

As company owners and strategic thinkers, we highly recommend that you narrow your marketing, networking and new-business development efforts towards opportunities that closely match your company core competencies and overall long range plans. When you focus your time and resources, your probability of growing and probability of winning (**Pwin**) contracts will be higher. You will also reduce overall business development costs because you will not spend money on developing proposals against opportunities that your company does not have qualifications for—proposals you most likely will lose to a more qualified company.

An oft-repeated adage says if you hear about an opportunity only when an RFP comes out, you are already behind the power curve. We can tell you from years of experience that it's true because there are companies that have been doing strategic planning and capture planning on a regular basis. They meet often with their customers and have a strong understanding of the customer's mission, requirements, strategic plans and acquisition strategy. They know in advance that an RFP will be coming out, and they are prepared to make a bid or no-bid decision, in many cases before the draft RFP is released. Often, those contractors helped the government shape the draft or final RFP before it was ever released to the public, which only improves their chances of winning the bid. As you grow in knowledge of your customers, get to know the key decision makers and perform well for them, you, too, may be in a position to help shape future acquisitions, either formally or informally.

Strategic Planning or Planning Strategically

At some point, you need to move beyond informal strategic planning and draft a strategic plan to guide you through the next several years. When we consult with for-profit and not-for-profit organizations, we usually ask customers to do their strategic planning away from the office where they can focus solely on planning and not be sidetracked by phone calls, emails or people walking into their office.

You can find plenty of books and websites to guide you through the development of a strategic plan. Many sources include templates that make the process easy to follow. A strategic plan can be a well-crafted one-page document, but plans often run 10 to 20 pages.

> **A strategic plan can include several sections, for example:**
> - Cover Page
> - Introductions
> - Mission Statement
> - Vision Statement
> - Organizational History and Profile
> - Core Business Strategies
> - Program Goals and Objectives
> - Financial, Administrative, and Governance Goals and Objectives

You can do a web search to find templates and create your own strategic plan, or you can hire an expert to guide you through the planning process. You never want to completely outsource strategic planning because you need to "own" the plan, and ownership of a plan requires your input into it. Most new-start companies need someone who can facilitate the planning process. An experienced facilitator, who has gone through the process numerous times, can help you think outside the box and bring to mind issues that you may not have considered addressing. The plan needs to capture where *you are today* and *where you want to be* in about five *years* (or longer). Most importantly, it should address how you will get there.

> This chapter is less about creating a formal strategic plan and more about thinking strategically. There are many issues to think through before you can put together an effective business plan, grow your company, market, network, get a contract, write a proposal, hire employees, prepare for emergencies and so much more. The rest of this book will help you answer the kinds of questions asked in this chapter.
>
> **What Follows** is a chapter-by-chapter, topic-by-topic summary of what you can expect as you read the book.

WHAT FOLLOWS

We have divided the remainder of the book into three parts and two appendices.

Part 1: Start Your Company breaks into four chapters:

Chapter 1: Basics for How to Start Up Your Company walks you through the first steps of starting your company with sections on choosing an entity type, ordering business entity materials from your state, choosing a business name, coordinating marketing basics, preparing and filing articles (of organization or of incorporation), choosing a management structure, preparing company records book, preparing legal documents, registering with your state's department of taxation, applying for business licenses and permits, and holding your first board meetings.

Chapter 2: Startup Preparation for Government Contracting focuses on those unique startup activities a company needs to do to prepare to operate as a government contractor. These activities include, applying for a Universal Numbering System **(DUNS)** number, registering with the government's System for Award Management **(SAM)** and applying for small business certifications.

Chapter 3: Taxes are a part of everyday life in the business world. It is important to be aware of what your tax obligations are, as well as how to legally reduce your tax burden wherever possible.

While whole books are written on just this topic, we address these three key topics:

1. **Legal Structure and Tax Implication**
2. **Taxes 101: The Basics**
3. **Employment Taxes and Self-Employment**

Chapter 4: Business Planning. As you start your business, you need to plan, budget, pick the right business location and protect your business, so we address each of these key topics:

1. **Write a Business Plan**
2. **Budgeting and Financials**
3. **Choose a Business Location**
4. **Business Insurance Needs**

Part 2: Grow Your Company is the most comprehensive part of the book with 14 chapters. We assume you have read through Part 1 of this book, have stood up your company, done your business planning and are ready to go after your first contract. Chapters 5-12 walk through what you need to know as you target your first contract:

Chapter 5: Essential Steps to Ensure Long-Term Growth
Chapter 6: Networking
Chapter 7: Understanding Contracts
Chapter 8: What's All This about Request for Proposals?
Chapter 9: The Proposal Process
Chapter 10: GSA Schedules
Chapter 11: Writing White Papers
Chapter 12: Targeting Your First Contract

Once you have your first contract in place, you are ready for chapters 13-18, where we help you understand your contract responsibilities, the essentials of hiring and taking care of your employees, hiring a security specialist, and understanding and protecting your intellectual property:

Chapter 13: Contract Responsibilities
Chapter 14: Time and Labor Charging
Chapter 15: Defense Contract Audit Agency

What Follows

Chapter 16: Hiring
Chapter 17: Hiring a Security Specialist
Chapter 18: Intellectual Property Rights

Part 3: Sell Your Company summarizes our belief that you should plan your exit from your business even as you are standing up the company. We recommend you think through the possible scenarios and ensure you and your business partners get the proper contractual language and documents in place at the same time you are starting your company together. The chapter discusses reasons for selling, understanding the Buy-Sell Agreement, and protecting you, your family and your business.

Appendix A: Key Terminology summarizes key terminology used throughout the book and offers a brief description of each key term.

Appendix B: Acronyms lists each of the acronyms we used throughout the book.

As you read the rest of this book, we hope you will enjoy the journey as much as we enjoy it every time we start our next company!

PART 1: START YOUR COMPANY

> Get ready for step-by-step instructions on how to officially stand up your company and prepare to do business.
>
> **Chapter 1** guides you through the basic steps that a business (government contracting or otherwise) needs to go through, while **Chapter 2** guides you through the steps required for a company that specifically wishes to do business with the federal government.
>
> While we realize that there many different entity types to choose from, and we do touch on each of those entity types in **Chapter 1**, this book focuses most heavily on the LLC and S-Corp, by far the two most popular forms chosen by small businesses.

CHAPTER 1: BASICS FOR HOW TO START YOUR COMPANY

This chapter details some of the key decisions you need to make; explains how to register with all the proper authorities, whether federal, state or local; and teaches you how to prepare the proper internal documentation to help further legitimize your business. If you go step by step, you will see that start up is not difficult to accomplish. The process can be time consuming, but many steps can now be accomplished online.

You need to accomplish at least these *14 key steps*:

1. **Choose an Entity Type for Your Business**
2. **Order Materials from Your State**
3. **Choose a Name for Your Business**
4. **Establish a Logo and Website**
5. **Prepare and File Articles (Organization, Incorporation)**
6. **Choose a Management Structure**
7. **Prepare Company Records Book**
8. **Prepare Either Operating Agreement or Bylaws and Buy-Sell Agreement**
9. **Apply for Federal Employee Identification Number**
10. **Set Up Company Bank Account**
11. **Register with Your State Department of Taxation**
12. **Determine If Your Company Is Liable for Unemployment Tax**
13. **Apply for Business Licenses and Permits**
14. **Hold First Official Board Meeting**

Now, let us look at each of those *14 key steps* in detail:

1. CHOOSE AN ENTITY TYPE FOR YOUR BUSINESS

One of the first steps in starting your own business is to decide what type of business structure you would like to use, and that decision will be largely dictated by the type of business you are going to create. The two most popular and widely used options are the Limited Liability Corporation **(LLC)** and the S Corporation **(S-Corp)**, so most of our discussion focuses on these two entity types. There are, however, several other options, including Sole Proprietorship, General Partnership, Limited Partnership, Limited Liability Partnership, Professional Corporation and the C Corporation (regular corporation).

> We cannot overemphasize the importance of this decision, and we highly recommend you consult with a lawyer, accountant and/or tax advisor to help choose which business structure is right for you — before you file any paperwork with the state. You can also see *Chapter 3* of this book for an overview of each entity type.

2. ORDER MATERIALS FROM YOUR STATE

Once you decide on business structure, you should order the corresponding materials needed to stand up your business in the state that you decide to file in. In most cases, these materials can easily be found online. In Virginia, for example, the startup materials for an LLC can be found on the **Virginia State Corporation Commission website**.

www.scc.virginia.gov/clk/dom_llc.aspx

These materials include, but are not limited to, forms for filing your Articles of Organization, Reservation of LLC Name and Statement of Change of Registered Agent.

Chapter 1: Basics For How To Start Your Company

Similarly, the startup materials for a corporation can be found at (**www.scc.virginia.gov/clk/dom_corp.aspx**), and include forms such as Articles of Incorporation, Application for Reservation or for Renewal of Reservation of a Corporate Name, Guide for Articles of Merger, etc. A guide will accompany each of these forms with instructions on how to complete the form and where to send it.

To find your startup forms, simply do a web search for "*your state's name* state corporation commission." In most cases, you will be directly led to your state's site. There you typically can find a section called *Forms and Fees*, or even a *Start a Business* section that will have everything you need to get started.

3. CHOOSE A NAME FOR YOUR BUSINESS

When you decide on a business name, it cannot be a name that is already registered in your state. Although not absolutely necessary, it is also a good choice to avoid a name that is being used in any other state as well to avoid a potential conflict. You do not want your name to be even close to that of a national brand name, as these companies place a very high emphasis on protecting their names, trademarks and copyrights. You can quickly check a potential name by conducting a web search. . If you do not find any hits or close matches, you are probably on the right track.

You should try to think of several different options for a company name, just in case your first choice is already in use (and you would be surprised how often this is the case). When you have chosen a potential name (and potential just-in-case options), you should immediately reserve the name with the state, on the off chance that someone else may be considering the same name and beat you to getting it. We have found the Virginia State Corporation Commission very helpful in this regard. We simply give them a call, and they perform a search to tell us whether or not the name is already in use, or if there is even a very similar name already in use.

> As you choose a name for your business, make sure the name meets your state's naming requirements.

These requirements vary by state and can usually be found in the state's Articles paperwork. You need to be aware of three main rules. First, a designator of some sort is typically required in your official name such as *Limited Liability Company, Incorporated, Limited,* or some abbreviation of one of these *(LLC, Inc., Ltd.,* etc.) Second, words that allude to the formation of certain kinds of business, such as banking and insurance, are often prohibited from being used in a company name unless you have the proper permits to operate in those fields. Finally, if you plan to operate a professional LLC or professional corporation, be aware most states have special naming requirements for these businesses, which include, but are not limited to, state-licensed professions in the fields of law, accounting, engineering, architecture and medicine.

> *DBA or Doing Business As*
>
> Given the various naming requirements, many companies decide that they want to publicly use a name that is different from their official business name. For this purpose, they use what is called a Doing Business As **(DBA)** business name. You also commonly see this referred to as an assumed, fictitious or trade name. For example, a bakery wants to have their storefront business operate under a different name than their official business name. In this case, they would simply reserve their legal name, we will call it *Baking Sciences, LLC,* with the state, and use that name to file their Articles.

Chapter 1: Basics For How To Start Your Company

> Next they could file an Assumed or Fictitious Business Name form with their state with the name *The Cupcake Factory*. This would allow them to put *The Cupcake Factory* on their storefront and operate publicly under that name, while maintaining the less appealing *Baking Sciences, LLC* as their legal name for official purposes.
>
> Companies may opt to use a DBA simply for its ease of use. For example, the official name of one of Tom's companies is **Intelligence Consulting Enterprise Solutions, Inc.,** which is quite a mouthful. Instead, they use the DBA name **ICES**, which is a lot easier for people to remember and say. And besides, who wants to write all of that every time?

Legalities aside, once you pick a name for your company, you are going to use it for a long time. Your company name is often the first piece of information people learn about your business. For these reasons, you want to choose a name that is distinctive, appealing, and easy to remember. It's also a good idea to avoid specifics like your name, geographic location or the name of the goods/services you will provide. For example, names like Steve's Stereos or Southwest Bakery can be both forgettable and limiting. What if you decide to expand your stereo store to sell TVs and computers, or you want to expand your bakery to the northeast side of town? You might come to regret choosing such a limiting name down the road. These are not ironclad rules, but they are good guidelines to keep in mind.

4. ESTABLISH A LOGO AND WEBSITE

You don't need to address a lot of marketing issues early in the startup process, but you do need to acquire a logo and establish a web presence. Simply having a polished logo for use on business cards, letterheads, email signatures, etc., can go a long way to making you and your business look professional. For those of us who aren't particularly creative or artistic, it can be a great idea to team up with a graphic designer.

> *Designer and Motion Graphics Artist*
>
> We have a great relationship with **David Kay** (**www.davidkay.tv**), a Designer and Motion Graphics Artist exactly for this purpose. Whenever one of our business partners needs graphics, motion graphics or a logo, we pass along the name of the company and a description of the business to David Kay.
>
> After a brief discussion with the client, David puts together a few designs to choose from. If you have any color scheme preferences, be sure to share those preferences in initial discussions with your designer of choice. Otherwise, designers can give you direction with color choices as well.

Whether you design it yourself or outsource the work, a logo and a color scheme can also go a long way to getting started with designing a website. Even before you begin work on website design, you should reserve your domain name with Go-Daddy or another domain registration service. Registration is fairly inexpensive, and it can save you the headache that can come if somebody beats you to a domain name. We usually use the .com domain, but we like to also reserve .net and .org domains to block other companies from using them. Additionally, you can have the .net and .org domains redirect to your primary .com domain, so potential customers will find you no matter what they type.

If you neglect domain registration now and operate your business for a couple years without a website, you may find that someone else reserved or is even using the domain that you want. This situation can get sticky and even expensive if you have to buy the domain name from them at an inflated price.

5. PREPARE AND FILE ARTICLES (ORGANIZATION, INCORPORATION)

The next step in the process is to file your articles with the state in which you will operate. For an LLC, you file **Articles of Organization**. For a corporation, you file **Articles of Incorporation**. Both types of articles usually consist of a simple one-to-two page form that asks for basic information such as your official business name, primary business address, and the name and information of the initial **registered agent,** whose sole purpose is to receive or forward any process, notice or demand to the business entity. After the state reviews and accepts your articles, you will receive a certificate from the State Corporation Commission or similar governing agency certifying your existence as new business. Filing fees usually run around $100, and to maintain your status, you will pay annual registration fees of about the same amount.

6. CHOOSE A MANAGEMENT STRUCTURE

Companies that opt for an LLC structure must also choose a management structure for their business. The first and most common option is known as **member-managed**. For most small businesses, the owners, also known as **members**, are going to be directly involved in the day-to-day operations and management of the LLC. In this case, they will want to choose the member-managed format, which, in most states, is actually the default format. Smaller business can benefit from this structure because it eliminates an extra level of bureaucracy on overhead.

A second option, **manager-managed**, is for those companies that plan on bringing in outside investors who will be official members of the LLC, but who will not be involved in the day-to-day operations or management of the company. In this case, the company will want to designate one or more people as managers. These managers can be designated from within the pool of members, non-members hired specifically as managers, or a combination of both.

In some states, the initial members and managers are designated in the articles of organization and can be changed in the future by filing appropriate paperwork with your state. In other states, such as Virginia, one registered agent is named in the articles and members and managers are named later in an operating agreement. As the operating agreement is primarily an internal document (it is not filed with your state or any other governing body), it is easier to make changes among members or managers in the future.

7. PREPARE COMPANY RECORDS BOOK

Law does not require an official company records book, but it is a good idea to have one for organizational purposes. Typically a simple binder, or perhaps a designated place in a filing cabinet located in your primary business office, it contains a copy of all of your most important organizational documents. These documents should be available for quick reference for internal purposes, as well as for an outside party that could require access to the information. The binder will contain just about everything needed to show you are operating as a legitimate business in the eyes of the government, including, but not limited to:

- A copy of your Articles
- State Corporation Commission certificate
- Operating Agreement or Bylaws
- Buy/Sell Agreement
- Federal Employee Identification Number **(EIN)**

Chapter 1: Basics For How To Start Your Company

- Local and state business licenses
- Initial and ongoing Meeting Minutes
- Stock Certificates and stubs
- Corporate Seal

> If you do not want to assemble a company records book yourself, a quick web search will display a number of companies that sell sample company records books. These books are usually specific to an LLC, S-Corp, etc., and come prepared with section dividers, blank stock certificates, and even various forms that you might find useful in your business.

8. PREPARE EITHER OPERATING AGREEMENT OR BYLAWS AND BUY-SELL AGREEMENT

Once you complete filing Articles, you should put in place an operating agreement (if you are an LLC) or bylaws (if you are a corporation). These are both internal documents, put together and signed by the owners/members of a business, which lay out the rules and regulations for how the business will be run.

Here is a general overview of what goes into each kind of document so that you are aware of exactly what they are and what their purpose is. You can find fantastic books that walk you through preparing these documents, so we'll skip step-by-step instructions for what can be a lengthy process. After you prepare a draft, it is always a good idea to have a lawyer review it for what you might need to add or change. If you want to spend the money, you can have a lawyer prepare the entire document.

Operating agreements and bylaws cover similar topics but are different enough to warrant separate discussions. For an LLC, see 8a, *Preparing Your Operating Agreement*. For a corporation, move on to 8b, *Preparing your Bylaws and Buy/Sell Agreement*.

8a. Preparing Your Operating Agreement. An LLC Operating Agreement typically includes:

> **Preliminary Provisions.** This section includes much of the same information found in your articles of organization, such as the name, address and state of formation of the LLC; the effective date of the operating agreement; information about the registered agent and office; and statement of your business purposes. The statement of purpose should be brief and concise, so it gives a good general idea of what your business will do without limiting the scope too much in case you want to expand down the road.
>
> **Membership Provisions.** This section covers the basic rights and responsibilities of the members of the LLC. Information includes, but is not limited to: whether the LLC is member-managed; members' percentage interest and voting rights in the LLC; compensation of members; and members' meetings.
>
> **Manager Provisions (only necessary if manager-managed).** If you choose to be a manager-managed LLC, this section lays out the rules and regulations for managers. It includes, but is not limited to: naming of managers; authority and voting rights of managers; information about management terms; provisions for managers' meetings; and, of course, provisions for the compensation of the managers.
>
> **Tax and Financial Provisions.** This section establishes the tax classification for your LLC (partnership, sole proprietorship or corporation) and the accounting method used (either cash or accrual). It also details how you will handle income tax returns and reports, as well as setting up bank accounts in the name of your business.

Chapter 1: Basics For How To Start Your Company

While most LLC owners choose to be taxed as a partnership (or sole proprietorship, in the case of a single-member LLC), some choose to be taxed as an S-Corp or even a C-Corp. You should discuss this decision with your accountant, as there will be many tax implications to consider, and the decision should be documented appropriately in your official records.

Capital Provisions. This section discusses exactly how you will handle capital contributions, allocations and distributions to and from members and the LLC.

Buy/Sell Provisions. This portion of the operating agreement can be very detailed and as lengthy as the rest of the sections combined. It lays out exactly what will happen if you decide to sell your business in whole or in part. It includes procedures for when an individual member decides to sell their membership interest in the LLC. This might not seem terribly important when first starting up, but it can also make life a whole lot easier when you have the ground rules laid out in advance, so there will be no room for conflict or confusion.

8b. Preparing Your Corporate Bylaws and Buy/Sell Agreement. For a corporation, the buy/sell agreement typically is a separate document from the bylaws. Here is an overview of the different sections typically included in the bylaw, followed by a brief summary of what goes into the buy/sell agreement.

Bylaw Key Sections may include:

1. Offices. States the physical address of the corporation's principal office.

2. Shareholders' Meetings. This section lays out guidelines for holding shareholders' meetings. It includes, but is not limited to: the location where meetings will be held;

provisions for regular meetings, whether they be annual, quarterly, etc.; provisions for special meetings; information about how to give notice of meetings; voting procedures; and how to take action without holding a meeting.

3. Board of Directors. This section discusses everything pertaining to the Board of Directors **(BOD)** of the corporation, including but not limited to: powers of the BOD; the number, tenure and election of directors; provisions for BOD meetings; and compensation for the directors.

4. Officers. This section details the rights and responsibilities of the various officers of the corporation. The officers most often defined in the bylaws are the President, Secretary and Treasurer, but you may see other titles such as Vice President and Chairman of the Board. This section also lays out provisions for appointment, resignation, and removal of officers

5. Executive Committees. If included in the bylaws, this section allows the BOD to appoint committees that report directly to the board. These committees can be given the power to approve corporate decisions in various designated business areas on behalf of the board.

6. Shares. This section discusses topics relating to shares, such as issuing certificates and the issuance of shares.

Buy/Sell Agreement. As noted, this is typically a separate document from the bylaws, but it is similar to the buy/sell provisions found in an LLC operating agreement. The buy/sell agreement spells out all provisions for an owner to sell his/her interest in the company, as well as the rights of the company itself in this case. It also details provisions for the purchase of stock by the company in the case of a deceased owner.

Chapter 1: Basics For How To Start Your Company

9. APPLY FOR FEDERAL EMPLOYEE IDENTIFICATION NUMBER

After you file Articles and have your basic paperwork in place, you should apply for a Federal Employer Identification Number **(EIN or FEIN)**, also known as a federal tax identification number. A very important number, it is basically the business equivalent to your personal Social Security number. It will be used to identify your business when filing tax returns, applying for business licenses, and opening bank accounts. The process for obtaining this is straightforward and can be accomplished online at the **IRS website**.

www.irs.gov/Businesses/Small-Businesses-&-Self-Employed/Apply-for-an-Employer-Identification-Number-(EIN)-Online

After you finish the application process online, your EIN will typically be emailed in a matter of minutes. Once received, you should print out several copies. One copy (at a minimum) goes in your company records book, and you need physical copies when you open a company bank account.

10. SET UP COMPANY BANK ACCOUNT

When you have a federal EIN, you can set up your company bank account. Ideally, you will find a small-business friendly bank that charges minimal fees, or even better, no fees at all. You can usually find a bank that forgoes monthly fees as long as you maintain a minimum monthly balance. Another factor to consider is that at some point, your company will probably want to open a line of credit **(LOC)**, so be sure to do your research and talk to several banks. Before making a final decision, ask yourself if this bank is where you want to open your LOC.

> **Be prepared when you go to the bank to set up your business account!**
>
> When you are ready to set up your bank account, you need to bring several things, including personal identification, your SCC certificate and proof of your business EIN. You also need money for your initial deposit. Something to keep in mind is whether or not you want overdraft protection for your account. The two main types of overdraft protection are by attaching either a savings account or a credit card to your main checking account. If you decide to open a savings account, be sure to have extra cash on hand to deposit in it.

11. REGISTER WITH YOUR STATE DEPARTMENT OF TAXATION

No matter where your business will operate, you must know and comply with your state and local tax laws. For example, virtually all states levy income taxes. C corporations and LLC owners that elect the corporate tax treatment are taxed on their income separately from their owners.

S corporations, sole proprietors, partnerships and LLC owners that elect the sole proprietorship or partnership tax treatment are treated as pass-through entities, in which case, the owners list the business income on their personal taxes. You can go to the **SBA website** for a complete listing of the information you need to register for taxes by state.

www.sba.gov/content/learn-about-your-state-and-local-tax-obligations

Chapter 1: Basics For How To Start Your Company

12. DETERMINE IF YOUR COMPANY IS LIABLE FOR UNEMPLOYMENT TAX

If you do not plan to have employees, then you do not have to address unemployment tax liability immediately. Requirements vary by state, and you should read them, so you'll be prepared if you later decide to hire employees. To give you a general idea of whether or not you may need to register for state unemployment tax, here are the Virginia requirements.

Your business is subject to unemployment tax if it meets one or more of the following conditions:

- Has at least one employee (10 for agricultural business) for some portion of any day, in each of 20 different weeks in a calendar year.
- Has $1,500 in total gross quarterly payroll ($20,000 agricultural business or $1,000 for domestic labor) in any calendar quarter.
- Has acquired another business subject to the tax.
- Is a governmental operation or political subdivision.
- Is a non-profit organization and has four or more employees for some portion of a day during any 20 different weeks in a calendar year.

> You can find specific requirements on each state employment commission website, and in most cases you can register for the tax electronically.

13. APPLY FOR BUSINESS LICENSES AND PERMITS

There are a number of different federal, state and local licenses that you may be required to hold in order to operate your business legally. Agriculture, aviation, firearms, commercial fishing, and transportation are just a few industries that require special licenses to operate. Even if you only want to operate your business from a home office, you will likely need a permit to do so. A quick and easy way to figure out which licenses and permits may be required is to use the SBA's **Permit Me** tool (**www.sba.gov/licenses-and-permits**). You simply enter your city/state or zip code and your business type, and the site gives you all the information you need to obtain the proper licenses and permits.

14. HOLD FIRST OFFICIAL BOARD MEETING

Part of running your business will be holding board meetings and having the Board Secretary keep official minutes of those meetings. These meetings can be held on a regular basis, such as annually or quarterly, or you can hold meetings as the need arises. Additionally, meetings can be held in person, virtually, or purely on paper. The main purpose of board meetings is to document important decisions made on behalf of the company.

> **At a minimum, your first meeting minutes should account for the following decisions:**
> 1. Appoint a chairperson
> 2. Appoint officers
> 3. Establish a principle office
> 4. Discuss and approve the operating agreement
> 5. Approve the opening of a company bank account
> 6. Authorize payment for applicable startup costs

Chapter 1: Basics For How To Start Your Company

> **After you hold your first board meeting, a number of other situations would typically call for a documented board meeting to take place. These situations include, but are not limited to:**
>
> 1. Amending your operating agreement or bylaws
> 2. Amending your articles of organization/incorporation
> 3. Approving significant purchases, such as real estate
> 4. Selling of major LLC assets
> 5. Selling or expanding divisions of the company
> 6. Adding of a new member
> 7. Voting on any other matters that require approval by the members or shareholders, including important legal, business, financial or tax decisions

CHAPTER 2: STARTUP PREPARATION FOR GOVERNMENT CONTRACTING

Congratulations! If you followed all the steps in **Chapter 1**, you created a legal business entity and laid the foundation to begin conducting business. There are just a few more steps to take before you can start doing business with the federal government. This chapter guides you through obtaining a Data Universal Numbering System **(DUNS** or **D-U-N-S)** number and registering with the System for Award Management **(SAM)**, and it also introduces the various Small Business Administration **(SBA)** programs that you should be aware of.

1. APPLY FOR A DUNS NUMBER

The Data Universal Numbering System generates a unique nine-character identification number for business entities interested in contracting with the federal government. These numbers are issued by the private company **Dun & Bradstreet** and can be obtained for free online at their website (**www.dnb.com/get-a-duns-number.html**).

> **Will you need more than one DUNS number?**
>
> You need to obtain a different DUNS number for each physical address where your business is located, as well as each legally distinct division of your company that may be co-housed at the same location. You also need your DUNS number before you can register with the SAM.

2. REGISTER WITH SAM

Once you obtain your DUNS number, the next step is to register with the System for Award Management **(SAM)**.

www.sam.gov/portal/public/SAM

The General Services Administration **(GSA)** instituted SAM in 2012 to consolidate nine different systems. As of this writing, SAM is in Phase 1 and currently replaces the functionality of the following four systems:

- Central Contractor Registry **(CCR)**
- Federal Agency Registration **(Fedreg)**
- Online Representations and Certifications Application **(ORCA)**
- Excluded Parties List System **(EPLS)**

In the future, SAM will also replace:

- Federal Business Opportunities **(FBO)**
- Federal Procurement Data System-Next Generation **(FPDS-NG)**
- Electronic Subcontracting Reporting System/FFATA Subaward Reporting System **(eSRS/FSRS)**
- Wage Determinations Online **(WDOL)**
- Past Performance Information Retrieval System **(PPIRS/CPARS/FAPIIS)**
- Catalog of Federal Domestic Assistance **(CFDA)**

Chapter 2: Startup Preparation For Government Contracting

You must register with SAM if any of the following apply to you or your business:

- You would like to be eligible to be awarded contracts by the federal government.
- You are applying for assistance awards from the federal government.
- You are a federal government entity engaged in intra-governmental buying or selling.
- You have been otherwise directed to register by a government official.

There are two types of accounts within SAM, **Individual Accounts** and **System Accounts**. In the majority of cases, you will set up an individual account, as system accounts are used to represent a particular information technology system. Before you can register a business, you first must establish an individual account for which you must provide some minimal personal information. The benefit of an individual account is that you can maintain the account even if you move from one company to another.

Once an individual account is set up, you can register your business under the *Register New Entity* tab. To start the process, you need your DUNS number, your Employer Identification Number **(EIN),** the legal name of your business that you registered with the IRS and your company's bank account information.

During the SAM registration process, your business will be assigned a Commercial and Government Entity **(CAGE)** Code. The Defense Logistics Agency **(DLA)** Logistics Information Service, the Department of Defense's **(DOD)** largest logistics combat support agency, assigns this five-character identification number.

A CAGE code is used primarily when doing business with the DOD but is also used by other agencies, such as the Department of Transportation **(DOT)** and NASA. Primarily, a CAGE code streamlines the process of communicating and doing business with government agencies.

Registering with SAM also requires an **NAICS Code**. NAICS stands for North American Industry Classification System and is implemented by the U.S. Census Bureau. Federal statistical agencies use NAICS to classifying business establishments. You are not "assigned" a NAICS code, but rather, you can look up the classification code for your industry, or industries if your business operates in a variety of sectors, at the **Census Bureau website**:

www.census.gov/cgi-bin/sssd/naics/naicsrch?chart=2012

We usually select several NAICS codes for each of our companies, as the work performed by one company often spans multiple industry classifications. These codes will be very important for your business if you intend to go after any contracts that are set aside for any of the various small business designations, which are explained in the next section.

3. SMALL BUSINESS PROGRAMS

To ensure contracts are awarded to a diverse array of businesses, the government has in place a variety of different small business programs. To qualify for a program, a business must meet certain requirements ranging from size standards regarding total income and number of employees, to the socioeconomic background of the owner. Each year, the government sets aside a portion of all government contracts to be awarded to businesses that qualify for these programs. For some programs, businesses are able to "self-certify" when registering with SAM, while others entail a more rigorous application process. Here is an overview of each program.

Chapter 2: Startup Preparation For Government Contracting

Small Business

The small business designation is the most broad-sweeping of the designations, and you must be a small business to qualify for any of the following designations. To qualify as a small business, you must meet the SBA's definition of a **business concern,** and you must also meet the size standard qualifications for your specific NAICS code.

The SBA defines a business concern as a for-profit organization that: has a place of business in the United States or makes a significant contribution to the U.S. economy through payment of taxes or use of American products, materials or labor; is independently owned and operated; and is not dominant in its field on a national basis.

The size standards are limitations on total annual receipts of the business and the number of employees that the business may employ. These standards vary by industry and continue to change, so check with **SBA Small Business Size Standards website** to determine whether or not you meet the requirements.

www.sba.gov/category/navigation-structure/contracting/contracting-officials/eligibility-size-standards

There is no application process needed to qualify as a small business. As long as you meet the requirements for your industry, you are able to self-certify when you register with **SAM.**

Veteran-Owned Small Business (VOSB)

To qualify as veteran-owned, a business concern must be 51% owned and controlled by veterans of the U.S. military. This is a self-certified designation.

Service-Disabled Veteran Owned Small Business (SDVOSB)

To be eligible for the SDVOSB designation, you and your business must meet the following criteria:

- The Service Disabled Veteran **(SDV)** must have a service-connected disability that has been determined by the Department of Veterans Affairs **(VA)** or Department of Defense **(DOD)**.
- The business must be qualified as small under the NAICS code assigned to the procurement.
- The SDV must unconditionally own 51% of the business concern.
- The SDV must control the management and daily operations of the business, and must also hold the highest officer position in the company.

This is a self-certified designation, but service-disabled status of the owner must be established through the VA or DOD.

Women-Owned Small Business (WOSB)

To qualify as women-owned, a business concern must simply be at least 51% owned and controlled by a woman or women. For a WOSB and the next program, Economically Disadvantaged WOSB, there are two options for certification. You can either self-certify while registering with SAM with the supporting documents, or you can have one of several third-party organizations approved by the SBA certify your business.

Chapter 2: Startup Preparation For Government Contracting

Economically Disadvantaged Women-Owned Small Business (EDWOSB)

In order for a small business to qualify for this program, it must be a WOSB and the owners must be able to demonstrate an economic disadvantage. To show the disadvantage, the owner must meet the following requirements:

- Personal net worth is less than $750,000, excluding:
    - Ownership in business and primary personal residence
    - Income reinvested or used to pay taxes of business
    - Transferred assets within two years if to or on behalf of immediate family member for select purposes

- Adjusted gross income average over three years is $350,000 or less, excluding income reinvested or used to pay taxes of business

- Fair market value of assets is $6 million or less, excluding funds reinvested in IRA or other official retirement account

As with a WOSB, you can either self-certify for this program with the proper documentation, or you can be certified by a third-party organization that has been approved by the SBA.

HUBZone Small Business

HUBZone stands for Historically Underutilized Business Zones, and the HUBZone program is designed to encourage economic development within these designated areas. A business must apply and be accepted into the program by the SBA and meet all of the following criteria:

- It must be a small business by SBA standards.
- It must be owned and controlled at least 51% by U.S. citizens, or a Community Development Corporation, an agricultural cooperative, or an Indian tribe.
- Its principal office must be located within a "Historically Underutilized Business Zone," which includes lands considered "Indian Country" and military facilities closed by the **Base Realignment and Closure Act (www.brac.gov/)**.
- At least 35% of its employees must reside in a HUBZone.

8(a) Business Development Program

To qualify for this nine-year business development program, small business owners must be able to demonstrate that they are both socially and economically disadvantaged, and the business must demonstrate potential for success. Individuals who are members of the following groups are considered to be socially disadvantaged:

- Black Americans
- Hispanic Americans
- Native Americans (American Indians, Eskimos, Aleuts, and Native Hawaiians)
- Asian Pacific Americans (persons with origins from Japan, China, the Philippines, Vietnam, Korea, Samoa,

Chapter 2: Startup Preparation For Government Contracting

> Guam, U.S. Trust Territory of the Pacific Islands [Republic of Palau], Commonwealth of the Northern Mariana Islands, Laos, Cambodia [Kampuchea], Taiwan; Burma, Thailand, Malaysia, Indonesia, Singapore, Brunei, Republic of the Marshall Islands, Federated States of Micronesia, Macao, Hong Kong, Fiji, Tonga, Kiribati, Tuvalu, or Nauru; Subcontinent Asian Americans (persons with origins from India, Pakistan, Bangladesh, Sri Lanka, Bhutan, the Maldives Islands or Nepal)

- Members of other groups designated by the SBA

If you do not belong to one of these groups, you still may claim a social disadvantage if you are able to back up your claim with evidence. Some examples of other factors that can contribute to a social disadvantage include race, ethnic origin, gender, physical handicap or long-term residence in an isolated area.

To be considered economically disadvantaged, owners must meet the following qualifications:

- Personal net worth is less than $750,000, excluding:
    - Ownership in business and primary personal residence
    - Income reinvested or used to pay taxes of business
    - Transferred assets within two years if to or on behalf of immediate family member for select purposes
- Adjusted gross income average over three years is $350,000 or less, excluding income reinvested or used to pay taxes of business

- Fair market value of assets is $6 million or less, excluding funds reinvested in IRA or other official retirement account

Before applying for the 8(a) program, **a company must be in business for a minimum of two years** and be able to show a **balance** of commercial and government-contracting work. Finally, when reviewing applications, the SBA will consider the following criteria when evaluating the potential for success of the business:

- The technical and managerial experience of the applicant firm's managers
- The firm's operating history, ability of the firm to access credit and capital
- The firm's financial capacity
- The firm's record of performance
- Whether the applicant firm or individuals employed by the firm hold the requisite licenses if the firm is engaged in an industry requiring professional licensing

Once accepted into the 8(a) program, a business will participate in a four-year developmental stage followed by a five-year transitional stage. During this time they will undergo annual reviews to ensure they still meet all requirements and are headed in the right direction. While the requirements are stringent, participation in the 8(a) program can be highly beneficial. Aside from the ability to bid on contracts set aside specifically for business in the 8(a) program, participants can take advantage of a variety of resources provided by the SBA, such as specialized business training, counseling, marketing assistance and more.

Chapter 2: Startup Preparation For Government Contracting

Small Disadvantaged Business (SDB)

To qualify as an SDB, a business company must meet the following requirements:

- The firm must be 51% or more owned and control by one or more disadvantaged persons.
- The disadvantaged person or persons must be socially disadvantaged and economically disadvantaged as defined under the requirements for the 8(a) program.
- The firm must be small, according to SBA's size standards.

Again, congratulations!

You have now created a legal business entity and have laid the foundation for your company to begin doing business – including business with the federal government.

CHAPTER 3: TAXES

> **It is important to be aware of your tax obligations, as well as how to legally reduce your tax burden wherever possible.**

Unfortunately for all of us, taxes are a part of everyday life in the business world. While entire books are written solely on this topic, we will address these three key topics in this chapter:

1. **Legal Structure and Tax Implication**
2. **Taxes 101: The Basics**
3. **Employment Taxes and Self-Employment**

1. LEGAL STRUCTURE AND TAX IMPLICATIONS

As mentioned in **Chapter 1**, you must choose a legal entity type for your business. Each entity type has implications regarding the liability of the owners, as well as for how you will deal with taxes. Here's a look at the different business types and their impact on taxes.

A. Sole Proprietorship. A single person owns and maintains complete control of the business.

> **Liability.** The owner of the business is solely liable for the actions and debts of the business. The owner's assets are at risk when legal action is brought against the business, which is one of the biggest downsides of a sole proprietorship.

> **Taxes.** Income and expenses are reported on the personal tax return of the owner.

This model can be attractive because potential losses of the business can be used to offset income from other sources and reduce the owner's overall tax burden. Another upside is that the income from the business is taxed only once, as opposed to income from other entities that will be taxed twice (see Section D, Corporation). In addition to paying taxes on income, a sole proprietor must pay self-employment taxes, which are calculated using Schedule SE when filing a personal tax return.

B. General Partnership. Very similar to a sole proprietorship, a **general partnership** is also referred to simply as a **partnership** and is often used when two or more individuals own and control a business. In a general partnership, all partners take an active role in running the business.

> **Liability.** As with a sole proprietorship, each owner in a partnership is individually responsible for all debts of the business. Responsibility is not in proportion to ownership, which means one partner may be responsible for the entire debt if no other partners have the assets to help repay a debt. For this reason, partnerships can be viewed as too high risk and are not generally a preferred entity choice.
>
> **Taxes.** As with a sole proprietorship, a partnership is not taxed as a separate entity and the income or losses from the business "pass through" to the individual partners. The income or losses are filed using Form 1065, and each partner uses Schedule K-1 to report their share of the business income. One upside of a partnership is that, at the end of the year, partners are allowed to divide up the profits and losses as they see fit. This means that if the partnership operates at a loss, and one partner has an otherwise relatively high income, then most or all of the partnership's loss may be allocated to that partner to reduce their tax burden.
> This flexibility may be very appealing for owners with various situations as long as they balance the liability implications.

Chapter 3: Taxes

C. Limited Partnership. This is a specific type of partnership in which one or more of the partners are passive investors who do not take part in the day-to-day operation of the business. These investors are known as **limited partners**, while the controlling partners are known as **general partners**.

> **Liability.** General partners maintain personal liability for all debts of the business, while the liability of limited partners is limited to the amount of their investment in the business.
>
> **Taxes.** Taxes are handled very similarly to a general partnership, except that the amount of losses a limited partner may claim are limited. In reality, limited partnerships can be complicated and expensive to establish. For this reason they can be impractical, and businesses rarely opt for this legal designation.

D. Corporation. A regular corporation, or C Corporation **(C-Corp),** is one of the more complicated and expensive ways to run a business, but it does offer advantages. Once created (incorporated), a corporation becomes a separate entity from its owners that continues in perpetuity in the eyes of the law. Owners of the corporation, also known as shareholders, elect a board of directors that will effectively manage the day-to-day operations of the company. One of the main advantages of the corporate structure is the ability to raise funds by issuing new stock to sell to potential shareholders.

> **Liability.** Since a corporation is a separate entity in the eyes of the law, the shareholders in the company are not generally liable for the company's debts and obligations outside of the amount they invest in the company.
> This protection is part of what makes the corporation model appealing.
>
> **Taxes.** As a corporation is treated as its own legal entity, it is treated as such for tax purposes. This means that all income

is taxed on the corporate level, and then shareholders pay income tax again when they receive dividends. This "double-taxation" is one of the biggest downsides of the corporate structure. One way to lessen the amount of tax paid is to pay a reasonable salary to shareholders who take an active role in the company, therefore reducing the amount of total profit that the corporation actually makes. Also, the corporation has the choice to retain earnings for re-investment as opposed to distributing all earnings to the shareholders, which is another way to mitigate personal income taxes, even if it is a short-term solution.

Professional Corporation (PC). This is a special type of corporation that may be used in professions requiring a license to practice, such as attorneys, physicians, architects, etc. This type of corporation does not provide liability protection for its owner(s) against professional negligence/malpractice.

> **Seek legal advice before choosing an entity type!**
>
> If your profession requires a license to practice, we *strongly* recommend that you consult with a lawyer before choosing an entity type for your business.

E. Subchapter S Corporation. Also known as an S Corporation or **S-Corp**, a Subchapter S Corporation is very similar to a C-Corp, but it offers some very distinct advantages as well as some limitations. First, shareholders of S-Corps must be individuals, estates or certain kinds of trusts. This means that an S-Corp cannot be owned by another entity such as a C-Corp, LLC, etc. The one exception to this rule is that one S-Corp may own another qualified S-Corp as a Qualified Subchapter S Subsidiary **(QSSS)** as long as it owns 100% of the shares of the subsidiary as defined under Title 26, Section 1361 of the U.S.

Chapter 3: Taxes

Code. Additionally, S-Corps are limited to no more than 100 shareholders, making them better suited for small businesses. One downside is that S-Corps may only issue one class of stock, whereas C-Corps are able to customize and issue various different classes of stock, such as preferred or common stock.

>**Liability.** As with a C-Corp, shareholders' liability is generally limited to the amount they have invested in the company.

>**Taxes.** S-Corps offer many tax advantages over C-Corps, which make them a popular choice for small business owners. First and foremost, income from an S-Corp passes through to the individual shareholders' tax returns, therefore eliminating the double-taxation that occurs with the standard corporation. S-Corps can also take advantage of the **cash** method of accounting, whereas C-Corps must use the **accrual** method.

>>**Cash Accounting.** In cash accounting, money is recorded on the books at the time it is actually paid out or received. For example, if you sell a product in December 2013 but do not receive payment for said product until January 2014, the sale goes on the books in January and the income is counted for the 2014 year (assuming you use the calendar year as your fiscal year).

>>**Accrual Accounting.** In accrual accounting, money is recorded when it is actually *earned*. In the above example, since the product was sold in December, that is when the income is recorded for tax purposes even though payment has not actually been received.

F. Limited Liability Corporation (LLC). The LLC is a relatively new, yet highly popular, entity choice for new businesses that combines some of the best aspects of partnerships and corporations. In most ways, an LLC is very similar to an S-Corp except that there is no limitation on the number of owners or members in an LLC.

> **Liability.** Much like a corporation, an LLC is its own separate entity, which means that members' liability is limited to the amount of their investment.
>
> **Taxes**. Flexibility is a key benefit of an LLC. LLC owners can choose whether they wish to be taxed as a corporation or as a partnership. More and more, we see new LLC owners file to be taxed as an S-Corp.

Consider the tax implications of your entity type!

We recommend that you talk to your tax advisor and accountant about the tax implications for your specific situation.

Limited Liability Partnership (LLP). Similar to a professional corporation, this entity type is often used for professions that require a license to practice. The key difference between an LLP and an LLC is that the partners in an LLP may be held personally liable for their own negligence. An LLP does, however, protect partners from being held liable for the negligence of other partners in the company.

2. TAXES 101: THE BASICS

The fun truth about owning a business is that the taxman always comes to take his piece of the pie.

Knowing how to legally reduce your tax burden as much as possible is one of the most important parts of running a business.

Chapter 3: Taxes

Since most company owners cannot keep up with the tax laws, regular meetings with your tax advisor and accountant are integral to managing your tax responsibilities. To demonstrate how it works, here is a very simplified tax example:

You own a business selling pies. If you sell 10,000 pies in a year at $20 a pie, you will have a total (or gross) **income** of $200,000 for the year. Fortunately, a business's income tax is not based solely on gross income. Instead, it is based on net income after accounting for things like expenses and depreciation. One of the most basic expenses is Cost of Goods Sold **(COGS)**. This is the actual cost of the supplies used to produce the products that you are selling. In this example, COGS would include the eggs, flour, sugar, berries and other ingredients used to make the pies. If it takes $10 of supplies to produce each pie, your total COGS will be $100,000, and your total *taxable* income will be reduced to $100,000 for the year.

Sounds pretty simple, right? In reality, tax calculations become much more complicated. For example, how do you account for the employees that you pay or the salary that you might pay yourself (if you are baking the pies)? What about the industrial oven that you bought or the kitchen space that you rent? What if you own a catering van? What if you took a prospective buyer to lunch to tell them about your pies and the services that you provide?

Each of these kinds of expenses has its own special rules that you should be familiar with, so let's take a look at each of them in more detail.

A. Business Expenses vs. Capital Expenses

Business and capital expenses are two of the most basic concepts that all business owners should understand. Business expenses generally comprise the largest portion of total expenses and tend to be simpler to account for, so we will discuss those first.

1. Business Expenses. Essentially the costs associated with conducting your trade or business, business expenses include things like COGS, salaries for employees or the cost of renting a workspace or storefront. Most business expense items are consumable, such as the eggs that go into a pie crust, or are things that you rent, such as your workspace or your employees' time and expertise. In general, business expenses are tax-deductible and will count against your taxable income. While most business expenses are fairly straightforward, some options warrant further explanation.

> **Home Office Expense.** If you work from home and regularly use part of your house exclusively for conducting business, you may be able to deduct part of the costs associated with the living space, including mortgage interest, utilities and depreciation, as business expenses. One of the most common ways to do this is as a flat percent. For example, if you have a room that you use as an office that comprises 10% of the total square footage of the house, you may be able to deduct 10% of your utilities or insurance costs as a business expense. The rules regarding home office expense deductions are very specific, so if you operate out of a home office, as many start-up small businesses do, be sure to *consult your tax advisor or accountant* about the options available to you.

> **Travel.** In general, travel expenses may be deducted as business expenses only if they are directly related to your business and if you travel outside of your **tax home**. Your tax home is considered the entire city or general area in which your business or work is located. For example, if you live in Chicago and travel to New York for two days of meetings, you are allowed to deduct the cost of transportation to and from New York, along with the cost of the hotel room while staying there. If you decided that you want to stay an extra couple of days to sightsee while you are there, the costs of the hotel for the extra two days are not considered business expenses and are not deductible. Similarly, if you decided to

Chapter 3: Taxes

bring your spouse along with you, and the cost for double-occupancy is $50 higher than the cost of a single-occupant room, that $50 is also not deductible as a business expense. Finally, when on business-related travel, 50% of your meals are typically allowed to be deducted as well.

Entertainment (see also the next section on Gifts). If you entertain a client, customer or employee, you may be able to deduct some of the related costs as business expenses if they meet one of the two following tests:

> **Directly-Related Test.** To meet the directly-related test for entertainment expenses (including entertainment-related meals), you must meet these three criteria:
>
> - The main purpose of the combined business and entertainment was the active conduct of business.
> - You did engage in business with the person during the entertainment period.
> - You had more than a general expectation of getting income or some other specific business benefit at some future time.
>
> **Associated Test.** Even if your expenses do not meet the directly-related test, they may meet the associated test. To meet this test for entertainment expenses, you must show that the entertainment is:
>
> - Associated with the active conduct of your trade or business, and
> - Directly before or after a substantial business discussion

> Since "entertainment" can be treated as a "gift," it is important that you know the gifting rules between government contractors and federal employees.

Gifts. If you give gifts in the course of your business, you may be able to deduct all or part of the cost of the gift. While gifts are commonplace in the commercial world, the gifting rules change when your customer is a federal employee. In fact, when government contractors give gifts to federal employees, they often can be fined or even go to jail. In addition, you could lose the contracts you have in place with that agency and be prohibited from contracting with that agency.

In general, government employees may accept gifts if any of the following are true:

The gift is based upon a pre-existing personal or family relationship with the government employee, so long as the gift is motivated by the relationship (like a birthday present to your family member).

The gift is valued at $20 or less, so long as the gift is not cash, and the employee accepts no more than $50 in gifts, in the aggregate, from the same source in the calendar year.

The gift consists of modest refreshments, such as juice and bagels at a conference, and not as part of a meal. The gift consists of free attendance at broadly attended gatherings (note that some agency-by-agency restrictions may apply to this exception).

> Because violation of the gift rules can result in very significant penalties to your business, you should make all of your owners, officers and employees understand the rules and faithfully follow them. Most companies have annual ethics training sessions for employees, which is a great time to address the gifting rules (as the rules may change year to year). We include gift rules in our employee handbooks and annually reinforce the information with our employees during all-hands meetings.

Chapter 3: Taxes

> **We recommend you implement similar practices to ensure companywide compliance to these important guidelines.**

Transportation. These expenses relate to business transportation that occurs within your tax home, that is, the entire city or general area in which your business or work is located. These include the ordinary and necessary costs of:

- Getting from one workplace to another in the course of your business or profession
- Visiting clients or customers
- Going to a business meeting away from your regular workplace
- Getting from your home to a temporary workplace when you have one or more regular places of work. These temporary workplaces can be either within the area of your tax home or outside that area.

> Daily transportation expenses incurred while traveling from your home to your regular place of business are generally not deductible.

Car Expenses. If you use your car for business purposes, you can generally deduct some of the expenses related to using your car. In most cases, you can use one of the following methods to calculate your deductible expenses:

> **Standard Mileage Rate.** This is a standard amount that you may deduct per mile that you travel in your car for business purposes. If you want to use this method, you must use it in the first year that the car is available for business use. You may change to the actual car expense method in later years.

Actual Car Expenses. If you do not want to use the standard mileage rate, you are allowed to deduct actual expenses that you incur related to the business use of your car. Some examples of deductible expenses are:

- Depreciation
- Licenses
- Tolls
- Lease payments
- Parking fees
- Repairs
- Tires

If you use your car for both personal and business use, you must divide your expenses between the two uses. For example, if you drive 4,000 miles in a year for business purposes and 6,000 a year for personal use, you may deduct 40% of your actual car expenses.

> **We recommend keeping a detailed journal** in your vehicle or on your portable electronic device to record the purpose of trips, odometer start and stop readings, and actual miles traveled. If you get audited, you can provide journal entries that support your expense reports and reimbursements.
>
> Some government contracts allow you to charge against the contract for your contract-related mileage. Make sure you read your contract thoroughly to understand the requirements surrounding mileage expenses.

2. Capital Expenses. Capital expenses are the cost of purchasing assets that your company will own and use for at least a year. Expenses include things like computers, an oven for baking pies, or even an automobile that is used primarily for business

Chapter 3: Taxes

purposes. Accounting for capital expenses can be more complex than figuring business expenses, and the two methods that may be used to do so are depreciation and amortization.

Depreciation. When a business buys a fixed asset with a useful life of over a year, the total cost of the asset generally may not be deducted in the year that it is purchased. Instead, the cost is divided up by the total estimated life of the asset and a portion is deducted each year. For example, if you buy a $30,000 catering van with an expected useful life of 15 years, you can write off $2,000 every year for 15 years as depreciation.

The IRS website (**www.irs.gov/Businesses/Small-Businesses-&-Self-Employed/A-Brief-Overview-of-Depreciation**) offers clear guidelines regarding property depreciation. You can depreciate property if it meets *all* of the following requirements:

- It must be property you own.
- It must be used in business or held to produce income. You never can depreciate inventory because it is not held for use in your business.
- It must have a useful life that extends substantially beyond the year it is placed in service.
- It must have a determinable useful life, which means that it must be something that wears out, decays, gets used up, becomes obsolete, or loses its value from natural causes. You can never depreciate the cost of land.

Amortization. Similar to depreciation, amortization allows you to deduct certain capital expenses over a period of time. The IRS allows you to amortize the costs associated with:

- Starting a business, including the costs of researching a business idea and creating a legal entity

- Getting a lease on business property
- Intangible assets defined in section 197 of the IRS Code, including business licenses, permits, patents, trademarks, trade secrets, customer loyalty (goodwill), and intangible value of physical items such as client lists, and accounting and inventory records
- Oil and gas exploration
- Pollution control facilities
- Research and experimentation

3. EMPLOYMENT TAXES AND SELF-EMPLOYMENT

Whether you are self-employed in a single-person business or you own a business with 50+ employees, you are responsible for paying employment taxes of one kind or another. The early phase of starting your business is the perfect time to learn about your tax responsibilities.

> It is important that you become familiar with the ins and outs of employment taxes **before** you hire your first employee.

As an informed business owner, you can avoid the possible pitfalls of not paying a particular tax simply because you were unaware of your responsibility.

Taxpayer Identification Number (TIN). If you are a sole proprietor with employees, or your business is any type of partnership, LLC or corporation, you need to obtain a Taxpayer Identification Number **(TIN)**, also known as a Federal Employer Identification Number **(FEIN or EIN)**. A TIN is obtained by registering with the IRS and is used as your primary identification number for tax purposes. If you are a sole

Chapter 3: Taxes

proprietor and have no employees, your personal Social Security number will be used as your primary identification number for tax purposes.

A. Employment Taxes/Payroll Taxes

As an employer, you will be responsible for withholding and paying various taxes for each of your employees. As state requirements vary, we will discuss only federal payroll taxes, which break down into three different types:

Income Tax. You must withhold a portion of your employees' income for federal income taxes. To figure how much federal withholding is necessary, have each new employee complete Form W-4 and keep it updated annually.

Federal Insurance Contributions Act (FICA) Taxes. FICA taxes are comprised of Social Security and Medicare taxes. As the employer, you are responsible for withholding 6.2% of an employee's income (on annual earnings of up to $113,700) for Social Security, and you must also match that figure with an additional 6.2% yourself, for a total of 12.4%. For Medicare, you must withhold 1.45% from your employee's income and also pay an additional 1.45% as the employer, for a total of 2.9% regardless of total income. All figures are for the year 2013 and may be subject to change from year to year.

For example, you have an employee with a salary of $150,000. Out of that $150,000, you must withhold $7,049 (6.2% of the first $113,700) for Social Security and $2,175 (1.45% of $150,000) for Medicare for a total of $9,224 in withholding. You must also pay an additional $9,224 in "employer side" taxes to match the total withheld from the employee's income, for a grand total of $18,448 paid in FICA taxes.

Along with income taxes, FICA withholdings must generally be deposited in a specified bank monthly. If the total amount owed is less than $2,500, withholdings may be deposited quarterly.

Federal Unemployment Tax (FUTA). This tax goes to the unemployment insurance system that is paid entirely by the employer, and therefore no withholding from an employee's pay is required.

As of 2013, the unemployment tax is 6% of gross income. However, this amount can be reduced by as much as 90% (down to 0.6% of gross income) as a credit for paying state unemployment taxes.

B. Self-Employment

You are considered self-employed if you operate your business as a sole proprietor, are a member of a partnership, a shareholder in an S-Corp, or a member in an LLC that chooses the partnership tax treatment. The common thread among each of these is that income "passes through" and is reported on your individual tax return.

If this applies to you, you will be responsible not only for filing an annual tax return, but you must estimate and pay income taxes and self-employment taxes regularly. To figure out how much to pay each quarter, use Form 1040-ES, Estimated Tax for Individuals. You can usually make quarterly payments online using the Electronic Federal Tax Payment System **(EFTPS)**.

Self-Employment Tax (SE Tax). Self-employment tax refers specifically to Social Security and Medicare taxes and is basically the same as FICA taxes that are paid for employees. For Social Security, you must pay 12.4% of self-employed income (up to $106,800) to Social Security and 2.9% to Medicare (regardless of income level). You may deduct the employer portion of your SE Tax (6.2% of first $106,800 and 1.45% of total)

Chapter 3: Taxes

from your adjusted gross income when calculating your income tax. Use Schedule SE (Form 1040) to calculate your self-employment tax.

Fringe Benefits. Fringe benefits are defined as things of value that a business provides to owners and employees above and beyond wages and bonuses. As a business owner, you should be informed about these voluntary benefits as they are generally tax-deductible for the business that provides them, and they may be wholly or partially tax-free or tax-deferred to their recipients.

IRS Publication 15b offers a full list of tax-advantaged fringe benefits and the rules of each. Here are some the most popular options:

- Athletic facilities
- Dependent care assistance
- Educational assistance
- Employee stock options
- Employer-provided cell phones
- Group-term life insurance
- Health benefits
- Retirement benefits

For more information, see **Chapter 16** on hiring, in which we go into more detail about some of these benefits. In our companies, *we outsource payroll*, and the payroll company handles many of the functions discussed in this last section. We recommend you outsource payroll services as well!

> After reading this chapter, you should have a good introduction to what some of your tax obligations will be as a business owner, as well as some ways for you to reduce your tax burden.
>
> ***The most important point we want to stress is that you need an accountant/tax advisor on your team.*** The accountant/advisor should have other government contractors as current clients, should know Federal Acquisition Records **(FAR)** and should have experience working within the government contracting space. The last thing you need is an accountant who has to learn with you! It is extremely important that, from day one, your accountant is part of your planning process and that you regularly meet with your accountant to discuss key decisions that affect your tax basis. We meet with our accountant a few times a year — to look towards the end of the current year, to plan into the next year and to make sure we are considering the tax implications of all of our decisions before the business year ends. You should do the same!

CHAPTER 4: BUSINESS PLANNING

At the beginning of the book, we encouraged you to *think strategically* from day one. You will find a strategic mindset helpful as you engage in forward-looking business planning and as you actually prepare your business plan. Here we address business planning, budgeting, picking the right business location and protecting your business.

> *I don't believe you can do today's job with yesterday's methods and be in business tomorrow. (Nelson Jackson)*

1. WRITE A BUSINESS PLAN

This chapter focuses more on business planning in general than the business plan itself, but since we get so many questions from people about business plans, we will start by walking through an outline of a sample business plan. As you delve into the outline, you can see why you need to think "big picture" and long term as you pull together the data for your business plan.

We put this section close to the front of the book because if you plan to go for outside funding or a line of credit to cover startup costs, or if you are trying to obtain capital for expansion, then you will need a strong business plan. You can search online for "business plans," and you will find lots of resources, including templates, samples and companies that specialize in helping people create business plans.

The following material reflects a "typical" business plan. Your plan may include all or some the items as you tailor it to reflect your specific needs—from startup phase all the way to asking the bank for more money after you have established your business.

> **Typical parts of a business plan can include:**
> A. Executive Summary
> B. Company Description
> C. Industry Overview or Market Analysis and Trends
> D. Risk Assessment
> E. Target Market or Service Line
> F. Competition
> G. Marketing Plan and Sales Strategy
> H. Management Team or Organization
> I. Operations
> J. Startup Expenses and Capital
> K. Financials
> L. Personal Financial Statements
> M. Funding Request
> N. Appendices

Let us look briefly at each of these parts, starting with the Executive Summary.

A. Executive Summary. In the executive summary, you will summarize your business plan in two pages or less. Make it professional, complete and concise! Do not forget to include your business goals and objectives, and if applying for a loan, state the amount of the loan you are seeking.

Chapter 4: Business Planning

> Think of the executive summary this way: If you had to explain the *basics* of your company to an investor, what would you say? Say that here! Your pitch to an investor is exactly what needs to go in the executive summary.

Most people write this summary after drafting the rest of their business plan, so they can summarize key components of the plan. Keep in mind, however, that you need to hook the reader with these two (or fewer) pages, or they may not read the rest of the document.

B. Company Description. Start with a brief company history. Give an overview of what your company does. Describe your products and/or services. Talk about your strengths. List the owners and note the company structure (such as partnership, LLC, sole proprietorship, corporation, etc.).

C. Industry Overview or Market Analysis and Trends. Talk about your industry and how it is growing or changing. Describe how you fit into this industry and what you have to offer that is unique or different from other companies.

D. Risk Assessment. What are the characteristics of your industry? Is the industry growing, declining or changing? What is the risk to your plan? What is the size of the market and what is your share of it? Do you anticipate increasing your market share? What is the demand for your product? What are the barriers?

E. Target Market or Service Line. Describe your product or service from your customer's point of view. What do your customers like or dislike about your products, services and your company?

F. Competition. List your major competitors. Describe their size, location and reputations. Compare your goods and services with theirs. What are their major advantages? What are the advantages of your product or service?

G. Marketing Plan and Sales Strategy. Developing a marketing plan and sales strategy is one of the most important things you will do to ensure that your company will be profitable. Market planning and sales strategy sessions compel you to examine your entire business and business objectives, to focus on both short-term and long-term, and to think about your target market. This planning provides a way to measure your progress and gives clarity as to who will do what and when. Marketing touches every part of your business operations. In developing a marketing, planning and sales strategy, you will work through a series of activities that are designed to identify customer needs, wants and requirements.

> **If you are a new company (or already established and growing), try to at least work through these four basic steps to get intentional about your marketing. You cannot wait for work to come to you!**
>
> 1. Learn the acquisition strategy (often a five-year strategy) for your agency.
>
> 2. Discover what contracts are in place today and when (if) those contracts will come up for recompetition (or "recompete" for short).
>
> 3. Research the current prime contractors and subcontractors. Get to know what they each specialize in and determine what value you can add to the existing contracts or those to be recompeted.

Chapter 4: Business Planning

> 4. Talk to the agency's small business advocates and learn about new contracts coming up as a result of their out-year acquisition strategy. While a lot of contracts run through their base and option years and get recompeted, many new contracts are initiated every year that may require your services or products.

Gathering information takes time, but you need to be intentional about marketing and to make this process a routine practice. Moreover, you not only need to get to know other companies and their offerings, they need to get to know you and what your company offers. Your goal is to be so well known that when your agency—or another company—thinks of "X," they automatically think of your company and your service/product. You will find that marketing can take a lot of time, money and preparation, but preparing and then executing against a strong marketing plan (even a basic one or two page plan) will ensure you are spending marketing funds wisely and appropriately.

In the past several years, the internet and social media have drastically changed the world of marketing—even for government contractors. While marketing used to focus solely on things like print ads, brochures, glossy posters, tradeshows, white papers, in-person presentations, articles, or even TV commercials (for larger companies), it now includes new vehicles and modes of promotion.

Vendors still write white papers and attend tradeshows, but now they also have access to YouTube, webinars, Rich Site Summary **(RSS)**, GoToMeeting, WebEx and more. You can inexpensively host a very informative website (but make sure it doesn't look cheap—always make your company look bigger than it is). People and companies network through LinkedIn, Facebook and Twitter. They write blogs and send e-newsletters and mass e-mails.

Marketing, however, is still all about networking, networking, and yes, networking! Many aspects of traditional marketing remain crucial to success and companies still need to:

- Understand your customer and how your services or products will help them be successful, efficient and save money.
- Maintain open and constant communication with your customers, so you are not simply reacting to an RFP when it hits the street.
- Pay attention to news and happenings so you understand trends in your industry.
- Attend business luncheons with both clients and competitors to build relationships, swap stories and pick each other's brains.
- "Sell" your product or service.

In your marketing plan and sales strategy, avoid the fluff, and instead be specific!

- Use statistics and numbers and note your sources. Marketing research does not have to be expensive or complex. In fact, many small business and new starts do not have the resources for complex planning, but they can gather basic market research.
- Explain your pricing policy and how you developed it.
- Describe the ways you will promote your product or service.

Chapter 4: Business Planning

The larger the company, the more comprehensive the marketing plan can be, but new starts can keep it simple. If you do not have funds to hire in-house staff to draft a marketing plan, there are resources available to guide you through the process of writing a marketing plan and developing a budget. A quick web search will result in plenty of marketing plan templates and examples.

> *You should update your marketing plan annually.*
>
> When you launch a new product or service, revisit and revise your latest marketing plan or develop a separate plan for the new product or service that you can add as an addendum to your primary plan.

H. Management Team or Organization. Describe your management team and management structure and explain who has what responsibility. Include resumes of all key managers. List important advisors, board members, etc.

I. Operations. Tell about your business location or plans to get a building, your staff, inventory, and the legal environment (licensing, bonding, permits, insurance, patent, trademarks, etc.).

J. Startup Expenses and Capital. You need to carefully research your startup costs. Keep good records and organize your costs by categories, for example:

- Building/real estate/lease/improvements
- Capital equipment
- Advertising

69

- Working capital (money needed to operate and pay bills while you get the business going)
- Contingencies (unforeseen expenses)
- Other

You also need to show the sources of your capital. Did you and your partners loan money to the company? Do you have outside investors or did you borrow money from family, friends or a bank?

K. Financials. In the financials section, you may summarize the key data in the body of the document and put the detailed information in the appendices. Financials typically include:

> **Financial History.** If your company is established and has been operating for a while, include financial statements for at least the past three years (put these details an appendix). Do a detailed forecast of your market by month and by year (three to five year projections). Include aging of accounts receivable, showing the total amounts owed to you from customers, how much is current, 30 days past due, 60 days past due, 90 days past due, and over 90 days past due.
>
> **Projected Balance Sheet.** Include a projected balance sheet showing assets, liabilities and items like owners' equity.
>
> **Cash Flow and Profit Projections.** This critical section shows in detail how your company will make a profit. Project your month-by-month sales and show where you begin to make a profit and how much profit you anticipate at the end of the year and the next few years (three to five).

Chapter 4: Business Planning

L. Personal Financial Statements of the Owners. Include personal financial statements of the owners. You can include this information as a separate section, a part of the "Management Team" section or even as an appendix.

M. Funding Request. Summarize how much capital you are seeking. This needs to be supported by details of the plan explaining why you need the amount you are asking for.

> *We have seen a lot of companies that never complete a detailed business plan like the one outlined above, or they do not complete a detailed business plan until they go for outside finances or a line-of-credit. It takes time to complete a plan and keep it updated; so many small businesses do not take the time. We are not saying that practice is "right," but it is a reality. You will need a plan to get outside funding or a line of credit!*

The preceding paragraphs give you a good idea of a typical business plan and the information to collect and include in it. While there are numerous websites that provide templates to format your business plan, the data and the content must come from you and your team.

> The financial section is a critical component of your business plan—and your business operations. If you want to run a successful company, you must master the budget and financials. You cannot ignore these essential elements, and you cannot simply delegate them to someone else in the company.

The budgeting and financials of a government contractor are similar to those of a commercial business in some ways, but can be very different at the same time. Let's take a look at *Budgeting and Financials* in more detail.

2. BUDGETING AND FINANCIALS

Usually the startup phase can put a big strain on the company finances because it can take so long to get paid for your work — you perform the work, invoice your customer based upon the best terms you can get and then you finally get paid for your work (within 30 days, 45 days, 60 days, etc.). Meanwhile you are building up the expenses of running the day-to-day functions.

> *You will hear terms like **Net 30** or **Net 45** or **Net 60**. What that means, using Net 30 as an example, is that payment of the entire invoice is required within 30 days from the invoice date or receipt of service or goods, whichever is later.*

We have seen more than one person, who left a well-paid job, start a company and go under in the first year because they did not have the resources to sustain them through the startup phase. You need a budget; you need to understand and stay on top of your finances; and you need to understand the basic tax laws surrounding your business. Your accountant should become one of your best friends. Maintaining enough resources to carry you through an extended startup phase is very important and very wise.

Chapter 4: Business Planning

A. Understanding Financial Statements

Financial statements are structured reports that provide detailed information about the finances of a company. These reports are used both internally and externally. Internally, owners and employees alike may use the information contained in various financial statements to make important business decisions or to get an overall feel on the financial health of the company. Externally, banks or investors may use the statements to help decide whether to loan funds to or invest in the company. Some of the most common financial statements are as follows:

> **Balance Sheet.** This is essentially a snapshot of the company's finances that shows the company's current assets, liabilities and equity at a given point in time.
>
> **Income Statements.** This provides a breakdown of a company's income, expenses and profits over a given period of time.
>
> **Statement of Cash Flows.** This is a report of the company's cash flow activities, including its operating, investing and financing activities.

> **Your ability to read and understand financial statements is essential to your success in business.**
>
> While there are a many books on the subject, sometimes it helps to get training from someone who has worked in the government-contracting arena for several years. The folks at **ConnekServ (www.ConnekServ.com)** can help you prepare your operating or annual financial statements/budgets and train you to read them.

B. Building Your Annual Budget

A budget is just an estimated financial plan, but the importance of building a realistic and comprehensive budget—and operating within it—cannot be overestimated. Your initial budget will include startup and capital costs in addition to ongoing operational costs. Your budget will serve as both a tracking tool and planning tool. We carefully track our actual figures against estimates to see how we are performing against the budget. While we measure our progress against our current year budget, we begin to make projections and prepare a detailed draft budget for the next year As we draw close to the end of each year, especially around October, we start refining our next year budget using "actuals-to-date" coupled with projections about company expenses and growth in the upcoming year.

In these budget meetings, we go line by line and discuss each expense, investment, contract, benefit offering, etc., to evaluate potential changes (good or bad) coming in the next year. We also look at actual expenses for several previous years to understand cost trends and to incorporate those actuals and trends as escalation factors in our next year budget, which increases confidence in our numbers.

Let's now look at some of the components of your annual budget. This is not an exhaustive list, but it is representative of what you will see in a government services contractor budget.

> For help in building your annual budget, contact our experts at **ConnekServ (www.ConnekServ.com)**.

Cost of Goods Sold (COGS). These are costs that can be directly attributed to the production of the goods or services sold. These include:

Chapter 4: Business Planning

- Direct salaries and wages
- Contract travel
- Contract Other Direct Costs **(ODCs)**

Fringe Accounts. Employment benefits given in addition to an employee's wage or salary are called "fringe benefits" (or "perks"). These include:

- Paid Time Off **(PTO)** leave expense
- Holiday leave expense
- Sick leave
- Group insurance

Overhead Accounts/Rates. Overhead Rate is a cost added directly to the production of the services or goods sold. It can include building costs, administrative salaries, commissions, etc. Overhead costs are also called "burden" or "indirect costs" that benefit multiple programs or contracts and are therefore not feasible to charge to just one program or contract. Overhead costs are generally pooled into related categories such as engineering or manufacturing. These include:

- Indirect labor—overhead
- Office supplies
- Communications—telephone and internet
- Dues and subscriptions
- Recruiting services

General Services Administration (G&A) Accounts. G&A expenses represent the cost of activities related to the operation of the business as a whole. Like overhead expenses, these are not directly attributable to any single program or contract. These include:

- Business development expense

- State and town income tax expense
- Licenses, permits and fees (e.g., annual business license)
- Security consultant services
- Outside services (CPA, legal, etc.)
- Website development and maintenance
- Business insurance

Unallowables. Unallowables are certain costs that the federal government will not reimburse for contracts that include costs as a portion of the price. For example:

- Advertising
- Life and Long Term Disability **(LTD)** insurance
- Entertainment
- Alcohol
- Non-business related travel

C. Key Budget Terms

Forward Pricing Rates are written agreements negotiated between a contractor and the government to make certain rates available during a specified period for use in pricing contracts and/or modifications.

These rates represent reasonable projections of specific costs that are not easily estimated for, identified with, or generated by a specific contract, contract end item or task. Projections may include rates for things such as labor, indirect costs, material obsolescence and usage, spare-parts provisioning and material handling.

Wrap Rate generally refers to labor rates that are calculated to include all costs—such as salary, fringe benefits, overhead, G&A and profit. In some cases, they also include a pro rata share of ODCs and/or material costs.

Chapter 4: Business Planning

Often, a wrap rate can be calculated by dividing (a) total price, or (b) total labor costs through G&A and profit, by the number of labor hours (or hours by category, in some cases).

Direct Labor is defined as work expenses attributable to the actual manufacture of a good. For service industry businesses, direct labor cost refers to the cost of labor required to provide the service. Direct labor cost includes all expenditures, not just wages. Examples include employer-paid Social Security, Medicare and unemployment taxes; workmen's compensation insurance; expenditures for health insurance; and contributions to pension plans.

Other Direct Costs (ODCs) are the cost of supplies, facilities and services provided by the contractor in support of contract performance. In other words, an ODC is a cost which by its nature may be considered indirect but which, under some circumstances, can be identified specifically with a particular cost objective (i.e., a product, service, program, function or project). ODCs may properly include, in varying degrees, the three basic elements of cost: labor, material and indirect cost.

D. Technology and Infrastructure

As a business owner, it is vital that you understand and use advanced technologies to increase your business efficiency and help you expand your operations.

> **Accounting Software.** Even if you have an accountant or a bookkeeper, accounting software is important. It allows you to see your profits and losses at a glance. It can also help you design and maintain a budget for your business.

Time Tracking Software. A time-tracking device will help you determine which tasks result in profit and which tasks do not. This knowledge will help you determine what tasks can be eliminated, outsourced or improved. If you are considering software that requires a fee, ask for a free trial to make sure it is the right software for you.

Some tools our clients use include:

QuickBooks. Accounting software, expense reporting and much more.

Deltek. Enterprise Resource Planning **(ERP)** software and information solutions for project-based organizations, which helps monitor and analyze critical company information. Accounting software, web-based timesheet software, expense reporting and much more.

Procas. Accounting software, web-based timesheet software, expense reporting and much more.

3. CHOOSE A BUSINESS LOCATION

The Small Business Administration **(SBA)** does a very good job of walking you through key things to consider in choosing a business location. Here is some additional guidance, but we recommend you start by reading "Tips for Choosing Your Business Location" at the following website:

www.sba.gov/content/tips-choosing-business-location

> The ideal location for your business depends on a number of factors. The most important consideration is the kind of business you are running. Before you begin scouting a location, consider the following factors that can help you select the right location for your business.

Chapter 4: Business Planning

A. Determine Your Business Activity. Your business activity is an important determining factor of where your business should be located. Answering the following questions can quickly narrow your location choices.

- Do customers come to you?
- Do you have to go to your customers?
- Do you have employees?
- Do you manufacture products for distribution?

For example, if your business depends heavily on pedestrian or drive-by traffic, you want to seek locations where there are minimal restrictions on signs that can help attract passing customers.

B. Ease of Access. You should evaluate the ease of access to you and your team and your facility. Are there plenty of parking spaces? Is the space handicap accessible? What other access issues affect your business?

C. Proximity to Your Customers. Will you make frequent trips to your customer? Or will your customer often visit your office? If so, you may want to locate your business near your main customer base.

D. Home-Based Business. Many new government contractors work from their homes and delay paying for office space until they really need it. You can keep your rates down quite a bit—and thus be competitive—if you can limit office space and the staff and infrastructure associated with getting an office up and running.

Sometimes companies operate out of their homes for years since their employees all work at a customer or prime contractor site. In those cases, there is no need to set up an office that basically sits empty most of the time.

In cases where your team is located away from the company headquarters, there are a lot of ways to conduct business with your team while operating virtually. We use teleconferences, GoToMeeting, Skype and other similar tools to communicate with our team. We also use mailing lists, company websites and regular all-hands meetings to spread key information to and get feedback from our team.

Additionally, almost every city includes shared office space companies. You can rent-share equipment and space—including conference rooms—until you need and can afford your own space. A great example of this in the Northern Virginia area is the Mason Enterprise Center **(MEC)**. The MEC is a university-based economic development enterprise that offers guidance to small business through the start-up phase and as they continue to grow.

They have numerous locations throughout the region where small businesses can rent office space, either virtual or physical. They also provide free counseling to small businesses and offer classes covering a variety of different topics, which allows them to provide value above and beyond the standard shared-office-space companies. The classes offered by the MEC cover a wide variety of topics, including: Financing a Business, How to Build a Business Website, Successful Teaming Agreements, Cyber-Security, and more. For more information visit their website at:

www.masonenterprisecenter.org

E. SCIF Space. If you plan to do classified work in your facility, you eventually will need space with a Sensitive Compartmented Information Facility **(SCIF)**. A SCIF is a U.S. Department of Defense term for a secure room. A SCIF guards against electronic surveillance and suppresses data leakage of sensitive security and military information. SCIFs are used to deny unauthorized personnel, such as

Chapter 4: Business Planning

foreign intelligence services or corporate spies, the opportunity for undetected entry into facilities for the exploitation of sensitive activities.

> **Will you need classified workspace?**
>
> Some companies rent office space with a SCIF, and others decide to build out the SCIF rather than move to a new location. It is not inexpensive to build out a SCIF, and we recommend you outsource the SCIF construction to experts in your area.

F. Facility Clearance (FCL). A Facility Clearance **(FCL)**, also known as a Facility Security Clearance, is essentially a determination by the federal government that it would be in the interest of national security for a particular company or organization to access classified information. Just as national security information is classified at one of three levels (Confidential, Secret, or Top Secret), facility clearances are granted at one of those three levels. A company can apply for a facility security clearance only when it is necessary for them to access classified information to respond to a request or perform on a contract. (A company cannot apply for an FCL of its own accord.)

That contract may be awarded to the company by either a federal government agency or by another company that already has an FCL of its own. The agency or cleared company then sponsors the uncleared company for the FCL at the appropriate level of classification (Confidential, Secret, or Top Secret).

> You can learn more about obtaining an FCL at **www.dss.mil**.
>
> We can also refer you to companies that specialize in helping companies obtain an FCL, just contact us at *info@TheUnconventionalStrategist.com*.

4. BUSINESS INSURANCE NEEDS

You will need business insurance to protect you and your business assets!

We prefer to partner with an independent agency that works with us and provides advice for the best coverage at the lowest price.

> An independent agency does not try to push their own products, but instead, looks across the various vendors and conducts plan comparisons to help tailor a solution to meet your needs.

Your independent agent will have the expertise to offer advice on which plans will best serve your company and employees. The agent will educate you on the seemingly endless set of acronyms and terms such as PPO, HMO, POS, HSA, HRA, Self-Funded and Fully-Funded plans, and explain the benefits of each, so you can make a well informed decision. From plan design to administrative assistance to expedited underwriting, your agent will guide you through the maze of employee benefits packages.

Allowing your agent to research and recommend plans makes the process easier and frees you to concentrate on business.

Chapter 4: Business Planning

> If you need help finding and independent agent, contact us at *info@TheUnconventionalStrategist.com*. Or check with your mentor and find out if they are pleased with their agent (you do have a mentor, don't you?).

Before we review a sampling of the kinds of insurance you may need, we want to point you to the SBA section on insurance at the following website:

www.sba.gov/category/navigation-structure/starting-managing-business/managing-business/running-business/insurance

As the SBA site says, insurance for your business will protect you from unforeseen dangers, and adequate insurance could make the difference between having to close your business after a disaster or continuing to operate. Do not short-change your business when it comes to insurance coverage.

A. Five Tips for Buying Business Insurance

Before we review insurance types, check out these **"Five Tips for Buying Business Insurance,"** from the SBA website (**www.sba.gov/content/buying-insurance**). You can use these steps to assess what types of insurance are best for your business and how to secure coverage to provide adequate protection and minimize risks.

> **1. Assess Your Risks.** Insurance companies determine the level of risk they will accept when issuing policies. This process is called underwriting. The insurance company reviews your application and determines whether it will provide all or a portion of the coverage being requested. Each underwritten policy carries a premium and a deductible. A premium is the price you pay for insurance.

Premiums vary widely among insurance companies, and depend on a number of risk factors, including your business location, building type, local fire protection services, and the amount of insurance you purchase.

A deductible is the amount of money you agree to pay when making a claim. Generally, the higher deductible you agree to pay, the lower your premium will be. However, when you agree to take on a high deductible you are taking on some financial risk. So, it is important to assess your own risks before you go shopping.

2. Shop Around. The National Federation of Independent Businesses provides information for choosing insurance to help you assess your risks and to make sure you have insured every aspect of your business. The extent and costs of coverage vary from company to company. Some brokers specialize in insuring specific types of business, while others can connect you with policies specific to your business activities.

For example, if you operate a tow truck service, you will want to find an agent that can help find policies that specifically cover automotive service businesses. Often specialist brokers can get you the best coverage and the best rates.

3. Consider a Business Owner's Policy. Insurance can be purchased separately or in a package called a business owners' policy (**BOP**). Purchasing separate policies from different insurers can result in higher total premiums. A BOP combines typical coverage options into a standard package and is offered at a premium that is less than if each type of coverage was purchased separately. Typically, BOPs consist of covering property, general liability, vehicles, business interruption and other types of coverage common to most types of businesses. BOPs simplify the insurance buying process and can save you money. However, make sure you understand the extent of coverage in any BOP you are considering. Not every type of insurance is included in a BOP. If your business has unique risks, you may require additional coverage.

4. Find a Reputable, Licensed Agent. Commercial insurance brokers can help you find policies that match your business needs. Brokers receive commissions from insurance companies when they sell policies, so it is important you find a broker that is reputable and is interested in your needs as much as his own. Make sure your broker understands all the risks associated with your business.

Finding a good insurance agent is as important as finding a good lawyer or accountant. You should always look for one that has a license. State governments regulate the insurance industry and license insurance brokers. Many states provide a directory of licensed agents.

5. Assess Your Insurance Coverage on an Annual Basis. As your business grows, so do your liabilities. You do not want to be caught underinsured should disaster strike. If you have purchased or replaced equipment or expanded operations, you should contact your insurance broker to discuss changes in your business and how they affect your coverage.

B. Insurance You May Need

Here are some types of insurance you may need to consider. The list is not exhaustive (nor is it in any priority order), but it introduces common insurance products and options. The SBA does a great job of explaining insurance products and where noted, the information here comes from its website, **www.sba.gov/content/types-business-insurance**. You will need some products as you start your company, and you will acquire others as your company grows.

> We recommend you meet annually with your agent to ensure you maintain adequate insurance as you grow. You will find that your contracts include insurance requirement limits that you must maintain in order to receive the final contract. You will, at a minimum, need to maintain those insurances and limits. Do not just focus only on the insurance required in your contract, but instead, talk to your insurance agent and make sure you are covered for the type of work you do.

1. Commercial Automobile Insurance. Any vehicle owned by your business should be insured for liability and possibly replacement purposes. Your independent agent will shop, compare and explain plans and rates for you.

2. Commercial Property Insurance. From SBA.gov: "Property insurance covers everything related to the loss and damage of company property due to a wide-variety of events such as fire, smoke, wind and hail storms, civil disobedience and vandalism. The definition of 'property' is broad and includes lost income, business interruption, buildings, computers, company papers and money.

Property insurance policies come in two basic forms: (1) **all-risk policies** covering a wide-range of incidents and perils except those noted in the policy; (2) **peril-specific policies** that cover losses from only those perils listed in the policy. Examples of peril-specific policies include fire, flood, crime and **business interruption insurance**.
All-risk policies generally cover risks faced by the average small business, while peril-specific policies are usually purchased when there is high risk of peril in a certain area. Consult your insurance agent or broker about the type of business property insurance best suited for your small business."

Chapter 4: Business Planning

3. Directors and Officers (D&O) Insurance. Directors and Officers **(D&O)** insurance covers claims arising from the actual or alleged wrongful acts of individual directors or officers. Coverage protects the executives as well as the company.

D&O insurance also helps the company attract and retain outside directors and corporate officers, minimizing their exposure to the risks of doing business in today's complex marketplace. With claims against private companies on the rise, D&O insurance is becoming a more routine purchase as companies grow.

4. Errors and Omissions Insurance (Professional Liability Insurance). From SBA.gov:

"Business owners providing services should consider having professional liability insurance (also known as **errors and omissions insurance**). This type of liability coverage protects your business against malpractice, errors, and negligence in provision of services to your customers. Depending on your profession, you may be required by your state government to carry such a policy. For example, physicians are required to purchase malpractice insurance as a condition of practicing in certain states."

> In an increasingly litigious environment, business owners cannot afford to leave themselves open to lawsuits arising from the inevitable and potentially costly human error. Should that error create defects in the product or service you deliver to a customer, you could be held liable for fines or other monetary damages your customer may incur as a result. Your independent agent can help you mitigate those risks with Errors and Omissions insurance.

5. Home-Based Business Insurance. From SBA.gov:

"Contrary to popular belief, homeowners' insurance policies do not generally cover home-based business losses. Depending on risks to your business, you may add riders to your homeowners' policy to cover normal business risks such as property damage. However, homeowners' policies only go so far in covering home-based businesses and you may need to purchase additional policies to cover other risks, such as general and professional liability."

6. General Liability Insurance. From SBA.gov:

"Liability insurance (also known as Commercial General Business Liability) protects a company's assets and pays for obligations—medical costs, for example—incurred if someone gets hurt on your property or when there are property damages or injuries caused by you or your employees. Liability insurance also covers the cost of your legal defense and any settlement or award should you be successfully sued. Typically these include compensatory damages, non-monetary losses suffered by the injured party, and punitive damages.

General liability insurance can also protect you against any liability as a tenant if you cause damage to a property that you rent, such as by fire or other covered loss. Finally, it can also cover claims of false or misleading advertising, including libel, slander, and copyright infringement." **(http://sba.gov**, "General Liability Insurance—How It Works and What Coverage Is Right for You," by Caron Beesley, January 2012)

The right general liability coverage will protect your interests and give you the peace of mind of knowing you are covered should a liability issue arise. Your independent agent can help you find the coverage that meets your company's needs, while saving you the time and hassle of shopping for it yourself.

7. Product Liability Insurance. From SBA.gov:

"Companies that manufacture, wholesale, distribute, and retail a product may be liable for its safety. Product liability insurance protects against financial loss as a result of a defect product that causes injury or bodily harm.
The amount of insurance you should purchase depends on the products you sell or manufacture. A clothing store would have far less risk than a small appliance store, for example."

8. Workers' Compensation Insurance. From SBA.gov:

"Workers' compensation insurance provides coverage for an employee who has suffered an injury or illness resulting from job-related duties. Coverage includes medical and rehabilitation costs and lost wages for employees injured on the job. This insurance can be obtained from a licensed insurance company. The law in most states requires some form of workers' compensation insurance. Refer to the workers' compensation authority in your particular state."

Check out your unique state requirements for workers' compensation, but know that businesses with employees usually are required to carry workers' compensation insurance coverage through a commercial carrier, on a self-insured basis or through the state workers' compensation insurance program. Workers' compensation insurance pays for employees' medical expenses and missed wages.

> There is no room for guesswork when it comes to your company's compliance with workers' compensation requirements. You need an insurance agent who will ensure that you have a clear understanding of the regulations, help determine the level of coverage required, and secure the best rates possible. Your agent can also guide you through the application and enrollment process and provide claims assistance.

PART 2: GROW YOUR COMPANY

If you read Part 1 of the book and followed the steps we outlined, then you have filed all the necessary paperwork and stood up your company.

Congratulations!

Now you are ready to think about the *day-to-day tasks of growing your company.* How do you manage and operate your company? Remember, we started by saying the purpose of this book was to summarize and document key things we wish we had known when we started in the government contracting business. The book is not meant to capture every detail about every possible type of company or every business scenario, but it does strive to address the key elements every government contractor should be thinking of and planning for as they set out to grow their company.

This is the most comprehensive part of the book with 14 chapters. In Chapters 5-12, we help you prepare for your first contract by addressing those steps that you need to take from your earliest business planning up until you get your first contract. Then, in Chapters 13-18, we guide you through the steps to take once you have your first contract in place (or are about to have your first contract in place).

CHAPTER 5: ESSENTIAL STEPS TO ENSURE LONG-TERM GROWTH

Now that you have successfully started your company, you may be wondering what you need to do next to grow your business. There are actually several, repeatable, essential steps you can take to ensure steady growth for the long term. Focusing on and preparing for growth early is important, but choosing the right approach to growing your company will depend on the type of business you own, your available resources and the connections you establish, in addition to how much time, money and overall resources you are willing to invest.

> **We obviously cannot cover every possible step to grow your business in one chapter. Instead, our main goal is to introduce you to 16 of the most common and repeatable essential steps that we use and see others use most often.**
>
> Feel free to contact us at *info@TheUnconventionalStrategist.com* to discuss these and other steps in more detail.

The following steps are not sequential and do not build upon one another. In other words, you do not have to follow this order to successfully grow. Instead, this is a list of proven steps to consider as you go about growing your business.

1. GET A SUBCONTRACT AND THEN GET A PRIME CONTRACT

> *Get a subcontract in place and grow through basic organic growth—an approach that many new government-contracting companies follow.*

Many government contractors get their first contract as a subcontractor to a larger prime contractor and then follow the standard path that progresses along these lines (or a variation of this development track):

- Expand their first subcontract by adding more employees to that contract and/or selling more products through that contract.

- Get added as a subcontractor to a second contract in the same general customer space.

- Continue to get added as a subcontractor to various contracts in the same market space.

- **Get enough past performance established in your primary customer space and grow enough that you can consider going after a prime contract.**

- Once you get your first *prime contract*, use it to leverage quid pro quo opportunities with other companies. In other words, if you are in a strong position to prime or already have a prime contract, other companies will clamor to get on your team. This is a great time to negotiate quid pro quo opportunities with one or more companies. You agree to add them to your team if they add your company to a contract(s) they have.

- Continue to add more subcontracts.

- Continue to go after more prime contracts and to leverage these new quid pro quo opportunities to grow.

Chapter 5: Essential Steps To Ensure Long-Term Growth

- Add new **core competencies** to your company portfolio.
- Expand that new core competency into your other markets using the same approaches above.
- While you are doing the above steps, you should be diversifying into your current market and diversifying into **other customer spaces.** This reduces your risk substantially, especially if you do as we do and go after government contracts and commercial contracts.
- The key is to diversify onto multiple contracts and into multiple agencies over time to reduce risk. Customers can face budget cuts, and you do not want all your employees on one contract in one agency. More on this throughout this chapter and the book.
- And on and on and on.

> *The key to real growth is through prime contracting.*
>
> Only when you have prime contracts are you in real control (if there is any such thing as "real control" in government contracting!). As long as you are a subcontractor, you have much less leverage with other companies in terms of quid pro quo opportunities.

Prime contractors like small businesses as subcontractors for several reasons, including:

- Large prime contractors must meet small business targets on specific contracts in order to satisfy government requirements.
- They have small business targets to meet within their own company.
- You can help round out a prime bid on an upcoming acquisition (RFP) with core competencies the large prime contractor does not have or is in short supply of.

- Your rate structure is lower than theirs, and they can make money off of your rates by adding a multiplier to your rates and selling that rate to their customer.

- You can go after small business set-aside contracts that they cannot pursue (that is a good opportunity for a quid pro quo deal, so you can get added to one or more of their other contracts).

- Once you have established a mutually satisfying relationship with large companies, they will often come back to you and ask you to "front" (prime) a small business effort that they would not otherwise be able to bid on.

Some downsides of subcontracting: We mention these downsides because if you want to grow, you need to consider both the benefits and drawbacks of subcontracting.

- It can be hard to get on team as a subcontractor because there is so much competition. It is not impossible, but the old days of larger company primes rounding up and signing every small business they could find to get them off the market is gone. Primes are more selective, and they have to be in this budget-constrained market. You need to offer an essential product or service that makes business sense for you to be seriously considered for their team.

- You are at the mercy of the prime contractor, usually their program manager or business manager or staffing manager, in terms of growth opportunities on the contract. In order for your company to grow, those managers must know your name and know your company, and you must have a solid relationship with them.

- If there are budget cuts, subcontractors are often the first to get cut.

- Rates are being driven further and further down, and the primes use subcontractors to make their budgets work for them.

Chapter 5: Essential Steps To Ensure Long-Term Growth

- Prime contractors will sometimes sign a subcontract with you and then try to force rate changes, or other changes, upon you. In this case you may have no choice but to live with consequences that may include little or no growth, or even worse, being cut from the contract altogether over time. This does happen!
- Recently, larger primes have been reducing their overhead by eliminating small businesses that have only one or two or a few employees. The fewer subcontractors they have to manage, the less overhead staff that is needed to manage the contract and subcontracts.
- The list goes on and on and on.

2. DIVERSIFY

Diversification is not only an excellent strategy for growth; it also enables you to reduce your risk. Diversify your contracts, diversify your customer base (go into other markets), diversify your core competencies, and diversify the contractors you team with, prime with, or subcontract to. Diversify by selling complementary services and/or products or by becoming an expert in your field and then training others, blogging and selling your expertise. This list is as big as your imagination.

3. OPEN ANOTHER BUSINESS LOCATION (GEOGRAPHIC EXPANSION)

In this model, companies grow to a point in their current market space where they may have saturated their growth opportunities. To renew growth, they open a new office in a neighboring area or state, or they expand work to a neighboring agency. You will find it easier to stay on top of things in multiple office locations if you keep the business offices within driving distance of each other. On the other hand, with today's technology, staying in touch virtually through various online meeting packages makes even daily conversation very easy and reduces travel and associated overhead costs.

So whether your new office is in the next city or the next state, or across the country, virtual meetings definitely make it easier to expand, manage and grow your business while reducing some costs.

4. MAKE SURE YOU HAVE AN INTERNET PRESENCE

Your business needs a strong online presence in order to maximize your exposure. Your website should highlight your *core competencies*, your *customers*, and your *prime and subcontracts*. Additionally your site should highlight the benefits you provide to your employees, so you can recruit other outstanding employees—who often bring their own connections, which can help you recruit even more employees and connect your company to their network—resulting in even more contracts or business ideas. We cannot tell you how many times we have tried to research a company and found no website or only a very limited placeholder website. In today's market, you want to advertise on your website and make it easy for your customers and potential business partners to easily find you (your website) and to clearly understand what products and services you have to offer and what core competencies you specialize in.

5. HIRE A GOVERNMENT EMPLOYEE

Some government employees can go right back to work in the agency they just left, but other government employees, who control budgets or are in control of certain programs and agency acquisition strategies, are limited in the positions they can accept in the government and commercial markets. Even when government employees have a "waiting period" before they can market to or work in the last agency where they worked as a government employee, they still can legally bring a wealth of connections and insight into the future of that agency. If you hire government employees, make sure you know their restrictions and how those restrictions affect your business and their work placement and options.

Chapter 5: Essential Steps To Ensure Long-Term Growth

6. JOIN A MENTOR PROTÉGÉ PROGRAM

Many larger companies have established mentor protégé programs in which they agree to partner with you and help you grow. There are pros and cons to mentor protégé programs, so you should weigh those benefits and drawbacks to decide what works best for you. Agreeing to be a mentor means that the larger company is committed to helping you grow, and they have set aside resources to be able to serve as a mentor to you. They will meet with you regularly and offer advice and help in your business and strategic planning. These mentors often offer office space, proposal support and introductions to new customers that will make it worth your while to join with them as a protégé.

7. LICENSE YOUR PRODUCTS

Licensing can be an effective, low-cost growth approach, particularly if you have a service product or product others want or need. We discuss this topic in more detail later on in our chapter devoted to Intellectual Property.

8. FORM AN ALLIANCE

Aligning yourself with one or more businesses can be a powerful way to grow your company. In an alliance, you work together and augment each company's core competencies as you pursue new opportunities. You can effectively be a well-rounded team, and you can split the costs of marketing. An alliance also helps you appear bigger than you actually are.

9. JOINT VENTURES

A joint venture (**JV**) is a formal business arrangement in which two or more parties agree to pool their resources for the purpose of accomplishing a specific business activity. Each participant is responsible for the profits, losses and costs associated with the

JV; however, the venture maintains its own entity, separate and apart from the participants' other business interests. There are downsides and risks to joint ventures, so do your research and work with a lawyer who can advise you as you consider this option.

10. INVESTORS

Sometimes an infusion of cash is just what a company needs to take it to the next level, but you should seek outside counsel and legal advice before taking on investors. Investors want to make money, so you must perform. They also tend to want to tell you how to run your business, which for entrepreneurs can sometimes cause more difficulty than the investment is worth.

11. GENERAL SERVICES ADMINISTRATION SCHEDULES (GSA SCHEDULES)

Sometimes GSA schedules open the door to new sales and new customers. Simply being on a GSA schedule does not guarantee you will make money; you need to have someone who knows how to market your services and the schedule. If you do not have the time to allocate to getting on GSA schedules, there are companies that specialize in helping other companies through this process. Their services will cost several thousand dollars, but it is an option for you to consider, and if necessary, to factor into budget planning. We will talk in depth about GSA schedules in **Chapter 10**.

12. CONSIDER A BOARD OF DIRECTORS AND/OR ADVISORS

The right directors and advisors can help you grow through their advice and connections. They can often open doors that you would otherwise never have access to. There are many ways to incentivize these directors and advisors that will make it worth your while if you choose this option.

Chapter 5: Essential Steps To Ensure Long-Term Growth

> We can help you consider your options on this matter. Contact us at *info@TheUnconventionalStrategist.com*, and we will talk you through some options. We may even be available to advise you and your company if we both see a benefit and business match.

One of the main differences between advisors and directors is that advisors have no fiduciary responsibility to the shareholders. Some potential board members actually prefer the role of advisor to director to completely avoid fiduciary responsibility. We use both, advisors and directors, and we have found that three to five members is about right for most small businesses.

The decision about who to bring in as part of your board-of-advisor or board-of-director team ultimately comes down to who will work with you and in the best interests of your company to add value—to help you manage and grow your company.

To maximize the support of your advisors and directors, you should hold board meetings quarterly or semi-annually and capture their recommendations and discussions.

13. MAXIMIZE YOUR SMALL BUSINESS STATUS

Whether you are a small business with no other certifications, or you have certifications such as VOSB, SDVOSB, WOSB, 8(a) or others, make sure to advertise and maximize your exposure and business potential as much as possible. Be sure that you do not rely solely on your small business status or certifications, but maximize where you can.

14. ONCE YOU HAVE BEEN IN BUSINESS TWO YEARS, PURSUE 8(A) CERTIFICATIONS

If you meet the requirements for the 8(a) program you can go after 8(a) set-aside contracts and even acquire a contract or a set of contracts from other companies that are graduating from their 8(a) status. Do not wait until the two-year point to plan for and go after 8(a) status, as it can be a long and involved application process. We discuss 8(a) contracts in detail in **Chapter 2**, but make sure that you are in a position to pursue 8(a) status as soon as you are eligible.

(Briefly, an 8(a) business is one that is owned and operated by a socially or economically disadvantaged individual(s) and is eligible to receive government contracts under the Small Business Administration's Business Development Program.)

15. GET ON QUALIFIED VENDORS LISTS (QVL)

A Qualified Vendor (also known as a responsible vendor) is a vendor that is determined by a buying organization (agency) to meet minimum set standards of business competence, reputation, financial ability, and product quality for placement on the vendors list. Agencies often make Qualified Vendors Lists **(QVL)** for certain categories of work. Know your agency and know whether or not they have QVLs. Often the agency will send out notices of vendors' conferences, Request For Information **(RFI)** notices and other advertisements that you need to know about to stay abreast of the acquisitions and strategies of that agency.

16. GROW THROUGH MERGERS AND ACQUISITION (M&A)

As you grow, you may want to consider growing your company through M&A. One of the main reasons companies acquire or merge is to achieve greater growth than they could through

Chapter 5: Essential Steps To Ensure Long-Term Growth

internal or organic growth. We will briefly discuss M&A here since this could be a separate book in itself.

It is often difficult for companies to grow at more than a modest pace through organic efforts. Your market space may be saturated; your contacts or brand recognition in other customer spaces may be limited or non-existent making it hard to enter that new space.

M&A offers several ways to grow; and we will look at just a few:

- **Diversification**
- **Geographic**
- **Full Service**
- **Product Supplementation**
- **Synergy**
- **Vertical Integration**

Diversification. Companies often diversify through M&A when they want to avoid risk inherent in their primary customer space. Too often, we see company owners focus on one core customer space and grow their company by growing on only one contract. We know a company that has three contracts with 45 employees on one contract, 1 employee on second contract and 2 employees on their third contract. We know several small businesses that have grown on only one contract — yes, you read it right, all of their work, even after several years in business, is on ONE contract. These companies are at high risk should their key customers take a budget cut.

To reduce risk, these companies — and your company — need to get on multiple contracts in their current customer space and on contracts in other customer spaces. One of our former co-workers started a company and in three years grew to 22 employees — all on one contract. When budget cut after budget cut caused her company to lose employee after employee, the owner continued to believe the customer loved her company and employees so much that is was only a matter of time before she would grow again and recoup her losses. Today she is a three-person company because she did not diversify. While these are small companies, and they may not be in a position to consider M&A, we think these examples make the point well that diversification is critical in reducing risk to your company. M&A is one option for your strategic planning kit to reduce risk — and diversify your company.

Geographic. Sometimes a company may have grown solely within a certain geographic area and wants to expand its business concepts into a new region. Rather than taking the time and expense to set up shop in a new place — where you not be familiar with the region and the customer space — you may round out or expand your company through M&A. Merging with or acquiring a company that already does business in that new geographic location can be the start to becoming a nationally recognized company in your core products or services field.

Full Service. Perhaps you offer a relatively limited product line or service but want to expand to become a full-service provider. You can look for a company or companies and use M&A to round out your products and services to be a full-service provider to your customers.

Product Supplementation. Perhaps a company wants to supplement its product line with products similar or supplemental to their current offerings. The company may be able to fill a hole in their service or product line more effectively through M&A rather than organic growth.

Synergy. As cost reduction and price reduction become more and more important in competitive bidding, the synergy M&A strategy may be an effective way to grow while reducing the cost of doing business. If you can use M&A for synergy, you can

Chapter 5: Essential Steps To Ensure Long-Term Growth

potentially increase your revenue and reduce your aggregate costs by identifying and eliminating overlapping functional areas within the new business.

Vertical Integration. You may find that over time you want to have complete control over every aspect of the supply chain. If so, you may consider M&A to acquire your key suppliers to ensure you have control over the entire vertical supply chain.

> In the last several paragraphs we have described, however briefly, a number of M&A strategies that you may want to pursue to grow your company. While we presented only a high-level summary of a few of the M&A strategies, they are legitimate approaches to growth for every company to add to their strategic planning process.

CHAPTER 6: NETWORKING

> *"It's not about who you know, but who wants to know you." (J.D. Kathuria)*

It is really very simple, to grow your company: You need to network . . . network . . . and network some more! You want people to know you and know about your company. When others have a need, you want them to instantly think about you and how your company can do that job better than any other company.

Networking is such an integral part of government contracting that the topic appears in multiple chapters throughout this entire book. For that reason, and the fact that **there are a lot of books available on the topic of networking, we have decided to use this chapter to focus on creating a *list of lessons that we have learned throughout our years working as government contractors.*** We will expand on some of these ideas after the bullet points, but to avoid repetition, we will not go into too much detail.

1. NETWORKING LESSONS LEARNED

- First, if you are a company owner or an executive in a company, it is *your job to network*, so you need to understand *how* to network!

- You will never grow your network or your company if you sit in your office and just push paper all day. If you are not plugged in, then you have only your own resources to draw from, and you will be left behind by your competition.

- People will not invite you into their networks or to be a part of a bid because you and your company are not known well enough in your market space. You will find that you have missed opportunity after opportunity because you did not even know it existed.

- Focus on developing and growing relationships over growing the number of connections you have. Remember to think of "quality" over "quantity."

- You have to create and foster relationships before they become necessary. When you need a relationship, it is too late to try to build it.

- Relationships are about give and take. Too often people "take" and do not give back. Ask yourself, "What do I have to offer this person?"

- Relationships are tangible assets that should be nurtured and invested in.

- Be intentional and strategic about growing your network.

- Develop a diverse network of relationships.

- Schedule networking activity into your daily routine.

- Create strategic relationships.

- Networking involves follow-up. Send handwritten notes and say "Thank You!" Yes! Even today, handwritten thank-you notes are a smart idea and greatly appreciated.

- Expect a quid pro quo relationship—that is how it works in most cases. But we do not recommend you go in with quid pro quo in mind. Figure out what the others need and help them out in some way. People will remember.

- Your network needs to have confidence in you and your ability to deliver.

- Networking involves adding value to the relationship.

- Know your competition and know your peers.

- You will find that the networks you establish will help you in life and not just in work—but you have to get to know those connections, and they need to know and trust you.

- People need to trust you and feel comfortable with you.

Chapter 6: Networking

- It is true what they say: Achieving success is not just about how smart or talented you are, it is about the people you know.

- It is not enough to be outstanding in your field; you have to be known.

- As you go higher into the corporate structure, it really is about who you know and who knows you. You may bump into "old boy networks," that is, people who have long-time work relationships and friendships and rarely invite newcomers into their work space. Your best bet in these situations is to be as competitive and competent as possible—and to recognize the situation for what it is.

- Have mentors who will help you build your network.

- Expect some rejection—perhaps a lot of rejection.

- Your "reach" expands exponentially as you grow your diverse and strategic network.

- Use technology to connect and grow your network and stay in touch, but do not let technology take the place of face-to-face networking.

- Consider which of your current contacts might have a connection you need to get to know and ask your contact to make an introduction.

- Understand that you do not have to market yourself or your company every time you have a networking opportunity. It can be more important just to show your interest in the other person and build the relationship.

- Plan to network for the rest of your life.

2. ERRORS PEOPLE MAKE IN NETWORKING

Here are some mistakes people make all the time. This list could be many pages long, but we will keep it short and say that they do not do the things we listed above and instead they do the following:

- They never offer to help others.
- They only come around when they need something.
- They keep going back to the same dry well in their networking.
- They are not strategic about networking. Some people spend too much of their time just attending meetings and never get their real job done.
- They do not start with the end in mind; they just randomly network to grow numbers.
- They send out resumes of people and say, "Let me know if you know of an opening we could help you fill with this person"—yet they barely know the people who they are contacting. They have contacts, not relationships.
- They assume that because they worked with or for someone in the past that person will automatically be anxious to add them to a contract.
- They market themselves and their company rather than focus on building the relationship.

3. HOW WE HELP NEW CLIENTS TARGET STRATEGIC NETWORKING OPPORTUNITIES

Our clients often ask us, "How do you target strategic networking opportunities?" and "Where do we start?"

You start by identifying *where* (what agency, what customer space, etc.) and *with whom* you need to network and then you invest your time in those "targets." You focus your efforts on the *people*, *places* and *groups* where you can network within your target space. That sounds simple, but it takes some time to think through and to map out a good networking plan.

When we sit down with the new (or even existing) business owners, we like to have them tell us about their networking plan

Chapter 6: Networking

and their approach to networking. Then we ask them a lot of questions to help us help them round out their networking plan.

We ask the questions like:

- What are your core competencies, services and products?
- What agency (agencies) do you plan to focus on first?
- Who do you know in that agency (government and contractor)? What influence do they have? What role do they play? Are they decision makers, in control of the purse strings?
- Who are the key decision makers that you do not know but that you need to get to know?
- Who are the key prime contract holders in that agency and in the space you want to operate in?
- Make a list of who you know in those companies.
- Make a list of the key primes where you do not know anyone.
- Make a list of who you do know that might be able to introduce you to the primes where you are an unknown.
- Can those people also introduce you to the key government decision makers you will need to get to know?
- What are the key meetings, forums and events that regularly happen in that agency space?
- Who do you know that can introduce you to the organizer and hopefully get you an invitation to the event?
- Start your own networking group—start small and keep it intimate. Grow the group if things work, but remember that too large a group tends to become bureaucratic and burdensome.
- Who runs the Small Business Program Office in the agency you are targeting? Plan to get to know them. Other names you may hear include: OSBP (Office of Small Business Programs), OSDBU (Office of Small and Disadvantaged

Business Utilization), SADBU (Small and Disadvantaged Business Utilization).

- What business development **(BD)** groups exist that you can join? If you go, plan to share information and contribute. Do not be one of those members who shows up just to gather information and does not share with the others. BD meetings are sometimes called, "*liars clubs*" because BD folks tend to want only to gather "intelligence" about upcoming RFPs. They will either not share any intelligence they have or they tend to only give a little bit of the information for fear they will give up some advantage they have (or believe they have).

4. HOW WE HELP CLIENTS BUILD A NETWORKING PLAN FOR ONE AGENCY

We could go on and on with general examples. Instead, let us give you some specific and practical examples that have worked for us in one specific agency. You can follow a similar approach in your market space.

We helped several companies build a networking plan for the National Geospatial-Intelligence Agency **(NGA),** and each time, we follow the same process to develop a very intentional networking plan.

> *We use this agency as an example because we have been involved with the agency since it became a separate government agency back in 1996 (NGA was originally known as the National Imagery and Mapping Agency, or NIMA).*

Using the positive and negative points previously mentioned, here is an example of our conversations with a new client:

Chapter 6: Networking

- First, we get to know the client's core competencies, services and products.

- We walk the client through the NGA organizational chart and explain how the agency is structured and who the key decision makers are.

- We share how they can find the strategic planning documents for the NGA, so they can understand where the agency is headed and start to map out where they can plug in.

- We walk them through the acquisition plan for the NGA—what contracts are currently in place and what contracts are ending or coming up for re-compete. A lot of agencies have their high-level acquisition plans in the form of "fishbone charts" or "waterfall charts." Always try to get your hands on these types of acquisition plans because they usually are full of information about when contracts start and end and what contracts will be competed next.

- We tell them who the key large primes are for each contract at NGA.

- We tell them who the key small business primes are for each contract at NGA.

- We tell them which contracts are small business set-asides and the type of set-aside (e.g., service disabled veteran owned small business **(SDVOSB),** woman owned small business **(WOSB),** etc.).

- We tell them about the various business development groups they may want to look into where BD folks meet to discuss upcoming RFPs and key meetings.

- We tell them who the small business advocate is at the NGA and how to contact that individual/office. For instance, at NGA they have the Small Business Program Office and a "Small Business Interaction" page on their website you should investigate.

- We explain where they can get access to unclassified and classified RFP information. Some information is too sensitive to post on unclassified websites. The government posts sensitive information on internal sites, which you can access if you have terminals in your secure facilities, or, if you have the appropriate clearances, you can go to "reading rooms" at the agency to review the RFIs/RFPs, etc. Reading rooms are really helpful to small businesses that do not yet have secure facilities but have the clearances and want to stay on top of upcoming acquisitions. These locations also have "Announcements" sections, where they post important information about the RFIs/RFPs or upcoming meetings/conferences. They often post bidder lists, briefing slides from bidders' conferences, etc. Again, this is really helpful for new companies trying to grow on a limited budget and with limited business development staff.

5. MORE PRACTICAL AND SPECIFIC NGA NETWORKING EXAMPLES

What follows are some specific topics that we share with our NGA clients. *We share these, but once again, you should tailor this approach and these examples to your agency and build your own networking plans.*

Get to know the NGA (or your target agency) Small Business Advocate Office

Most agencies have a small business program office **(SBPO)** that is committed to supporting small businesses. These offices usually understand the current contracts and the upcoming acquisitions, so they are useful for people to get to know. The SBPO will regularly collaborate with the acquisition contracts office of the agency and will be aware of the agency acquisition strategy and the upcoming small business set-aside contracts for 8(a), HUBZone, Woman-Owned, Service-Disabled Veteran-Owned, etc.

Chapter 6: Networking

> The SBPO advises the agency leaders on all matters related to small business and usually is committed to maximizing the contributions of small business in agency acquisitions. The SBPO provides leadership and governance to the agency to help meet the small business requirements of the agency.

Terms you may hear:

- OSBP: Office of Small Business Programs
- OSDBU: Office of Small and Disadvantaged Business Utilization
- SADBU: Small and Disadvantaged Business Utilization

You can work with the SBPO to get registered on the agency Qualified Vendor List **(QVL)** (to be able to do business with that agency). Typically, you can go to their website and register by email or online. The information needed to register will include things like:

- Vendor name and address
- Business type (e.g. small woman owned)
- NAICS code(s) with title description
- CAGE code
- Highest clearance level (facility clearance/personnel clearance)
- Point of contact with telephone number, email and business website address
- GSA number
- DUNS number

SBPO Presentations. The SBPO regularly schedules helpful presentations to keep contractors informed of agency happenings and upcoming acquisitions. We especially look

115

for presentations where the agency lays out their five- or multi-year acquisition strategy and describes the RFIs and RFPs that will be released over the next several years. Make sure you get on the QVL, so you can be notified of these presentations. Often, the SBPO will bring in other large businesses to talk about their companies and their mentor-protégé programs.

Key Meetings, Forums, Conferences, Symposiums

There are meetings, forums, conferences and symposiums of all sizes. Some meet every month, so you have to find the right balance and be strategic in allocating your time.

Here are some examples. First, two large forums that are not just for NGA players, but also for all who are interested in NGA and the geospatial arena.

GEOINT Symposium

The United States Geospatial Intelligence Foundation (**USGIF**) (**www.usgif.org**) holds this symposium, and it is truly a must attend for networking in the geospatial arena. The GEOINT Symposium has become the preeminent and largest networking event for the defense, intelligence and homeland security communities, hosting thousands of contractors and government employees. Each year since 2003, GEOINT Symposia have brought together an exciting agenda of keynote speakers, panel discussions and breakout sessions to provide attendees a unique opportunity to learn from leading experts, share best practices, and uncover the latest developments and upcoming programs from government, military and private-sector leaders.

USGIF Small Business Advisory Working Group (SBAWG)

The SBAWG was created to guide **USGIF** in its representation of the sustaining members of the foundation. The primary

Chapter 6: Networking

objective of the SBAWG is to assist small business members seeking to gain traction in the GEOINT market by facilitating access and opportunities to build relationships between the Intelligence Community, Department of Defense, and Civil agencies, prime contractors, and other small businesses. The SBAWG conducts monthly meetings, and it also hosts quarterly luncheons featuring key decision makers, acquisition officials, and SBPO representatives from government and military agencies.

> ***On a personal note:*** *Our company,* ***ICES****, not only participates in the SBAWG monthly meetings, but I (Tom) was also offered an opportunity to serve on the **inaugural SBAWG Steering Committee** to help provide strategic direction to the SBAWG. This is quite an honor and also provides a tremendous opportunity to get my name and the names of my companies in front of hundreds of others conducting business in this field.*

Here are examples of **smaller** business developer's forums for NGA:

Virginia Intelligence Meeting (VIM). The monthly VIM focuses on contractors that have a presence in the NGA and National Reconnaissance Office **(NRO)** who want to network together and discuss teaming opportunities on upcoming acquisitions. They usually discuss upcoming RFIs/RFPs, key meetings like bidders' conferences, etc. It is an invitation-only meeting, but if you are interested, send an email with your contact information to *info@TheUnconventionalStrategist.com*, and we will connect you with the VIM leader.

Small Business Development Consortium (SBDC). Operating much like the VIM, this meeting has a larger number of small businesses that meet monthly to discuss opportunities and learn about each other's capabilities. They focus on various agencies, not just the NGA or NRO market. This **SBDC** is easier to join.

You can always start your own small business development forum like we did a few years back. We called it *The RFP Forum*.

Why did we start our own forum? We attended several BD networking and marketing forums over the years and decided to start our own so that we could control the agenda and limit attendance to people and companies that were serious about participating, serious about sharing, and serious about growing not only in their current agency but in other agencies as well.

We wanted a forum where small businesses that were thriving and specializing in one agency but wanted to diversify their business and expand into other agencies could spend quality time every month sharing information about what was going on in their agency and learning about what was going on in the other agencies.

In the forum, each person attending shared the latest news on upcoming acquisitions, RFIs/RFPs, bidders' conferences, solicitation conferences, and key personnel changes in their companies and in their government customer space. Each member would stay abreast of the acquisition strategy of their primary agency and then share that information with the other members, so we could all leverage off of each other's "intel." We used that information to target our upcoming capture and business development energy.

> We set our forum up to help each other grow and to help each other work through problems they were facing. While government contracting is a very competitive market space, you still can learn from each other and share and grow together.

Chapter 6: Networking

Networking wrap-up!

After reading this chapter on networking, you may be—you probably are—overwhelmed because there is so much you can do to network and get your name and the name of your company out there. However, take a deep breath and remember what we said up front, networking is a process that should become a routine part of what you do from now on. It is not something that you need to try to tackle all at once up front!

> **Be intentional and be strategic in your networking. Do not become one of those people that only network and never accomplish anything because you spend all of your time in meetings and never increase your revenue.**
>
> The goal is to build relationships over time and constantly grow your network *and* your business through those relationships. Networking truly is a marathon!
>
> Need some help focusing or prioritizing? Shoot an email to *info@TheUnconventionalStrategist.com*, and we will be happy to spend time outlining a good plan of attack with you!

CHAPTER 7: UNDERSTANDING CONTRACTS

You have stood up your company. Now you need a contract, so you can start bringing in revenue! But what kind of contract will work best for you to sell your products or services? As with everything related to government contracting, that answer depends on several factors and is different for every company. There are many types of contracts, and it takes a while to learn the various kinds of contracts and their inner workings. On top of that, the government will, in most cases, dictate the type of contract to be used to meet their needs.

> In this chapter, our primary goal is to offer an overview of the types of government contracts that you may encounter over the next several years and to introduce you to some key contract terminology.

Frankly, reading a government contract, much like reading a request for proposal **(RFP),** can be difficult and boring. In fact, you may find this chapter a little difficult to read, so grab a cup of coffee and jump in! This overview focuses on a concise summary of key information you need to know to get started in government contracting, without going into *too* much detail. Once you read through the material and gain a basic understanding of government contract types, this chapter can serve as a good reference guide as contract needs arise in the future.

> You will do yourself a big favor if you get some expert help as you start in government contracting and as you grow and encounter different kinds of contracts. A mentor, if you can find one, would be helpful, or you can reach out to our contracts experts at **ConnekServ (www.ConnekServ.com)** to help you with your contract needs.

To begin, the Federal Acquisition Regulations **(FAR)** covers "everything" government contractors need to know about contracts—sort of. It takes years of experience and a lot of patience to wade through the FAR, but all of the rules are there for your examination. The FAR makes for nice bedtime reading since it goes into excruciating detail about government contracting and the various kinds of contracts.

The government employs a wide selection of contract types in order to provide the flexibility necessary to acquire the very large variety and volume of supplies and services they require.

1. CONTRACT TYPES ARE GROUPED INTO TWO BROAD CATEGORIES:

   A. **Fixed-price contracts**

   B. **Cost-reimbursement contracts**

Specific contract types range from *fixed price*, in which the contractor has full responsibility for the performance costs and resulting profit (or loss), to *cost-reimbursement*, in which the contractor has minimal responsibility for the performance costs and the negotiated fee (profit) is fixed. In between are the various *incentive contracts,* in which the contractor's responsibility for the performance costs and the profit or fee incentives offered are tailored to the uncertainties and risks involved in the contract performance.

Chapter 7: Understanding Contracts

A. Fixed-Price Contracts

Fixed-price types of contracts provide for a *firm price*, or, where appropriate, an *adjustable price*. Fixed-price contracts providing for an adjustable price may include a ceiling price, a target price (including target cost) or both. Unless otherwise specified in the contract, the ceiling price or target price is subject to adjustment or the revision of the contract price under circumstances provided by the government. The government uses firm-fixed-price or fixed-price with economic price adjustment contracts when acquiring commercial items.

Firm-fixed-priced contracts provide for a price that is not subject to any adjustment on the basis of the contractor's cost experience in performing the contract. This contract type places upon the contractor maximum risk and full responsibility for all costs and the resulting profit or loss. It provides maximum incentive for the contractor to control costs and perform effectively and imposes a minimum administrative burden upon contracting parties. Let's look at some examples of fixed-price contracts.

> **Firm-Fixed-Price (FFP) Contract.** The contract price is the price bid, with no incentives or fees added. The cost responsibility is placed wholly on the contractor. This is the government's preferred type of contract when cost risk is minimal or can be predicted with an acceptable degree of certainty.
>
> **Firm-Fixed-Price (FFP), Level-of-Effort Term Contract.** The contractor is required to devote a specified level of effort over a stated period of time for a fixed dollar amount. This type of contract is usually found in the contracts for investigation or study in a specific research and development area.

Firm-Fixed-Price (FFP) Materials Reimbursement Type Contract. This type of contract is used for the purchase of repair and overhaul services to provide a firm fixed-price for services with reimbursement for cost of materials used.

Fixed-Price Contract with Economic Price Adjustment. These contracts are used as appropriate to protect both the government and the contractor when there is serious doubt about the stability of labor or material prices during the life of the contract. Price adjustment provisions are incorporated into the contract and can provide for both upward and downward adjustments as required and justified.

Fixed-Price Incentive Contracts. A fixed-price incentive contract is a fixed-price type contract with provisions incorporated into the contract for adjustment of profit. The final contract price is based on a comparison between the final negotiated total costs and the total target costs.

Fixed-Price Redetermination. These contracts provide for a firm fixed-price for an initial period of contract performance and for prospective redetermination (as decided by the government), upward or downward, at stated times during the performance of the contract.

If you have stuck with us so far in this chapter, you have a basic understanding of *fixed-price contracts,* and you are ready for a second cup of coffee and the following overview of *cost reimbursement contracts.*

B. Cost Reimbursement Contracts

Cost-reimbursement type contracts provide for contractors to get payment for allowable incurred costs, to the extent prescribed in the contract. The key words there are "incurred costs" and "prescribed in the contract."

Chapter 7: Understanding Contracts

The contract establishes an estimate of total cost for the purpose of obligating funds and establishing a ceiling that the contractor may not exceed (except at their own risk) without the approval of the contracting officer.

Cost-reimbursement contracts are suitable for use **only** when uncertainties involved in contract performance do not permit costs to be estimated with sufficient accuracy to use any type of fixed price contract. Let's briefly look at some different kinds of cost contracts:

> **Cost Contracts.** The contractor receives no fee aside from reimbursed costs. This type of contract may be appropriate for research and development work, particularly with non-profit educational institutions or other non-profit organizations.
>
> **Cost-Sharing Contracts.** The contractor receives no fee and is reimbursed only for an agreed-upon portion of its allowable costs. This type of contract may be used when the contractor agrees to absorb a portion of the costs, in the expectation of substantial compensating benefits.
>
> **Cost-Plus Incentive Fee Contracts.** Also known as CPIF, this contract type provides for an initial negotiated fee to be adjusted later by a formula based on the relationship of total allowable costs to total target costs.
>
> **Cost-Plus-Award-Fee Contracts.** Also known as CPAF, this contract type provides for a fee consisting of (a) a base amount (which may be zero) fixed at inception of the contract and (b) an award amount, based upon a judgmental evaluation by the government, sufficient to provide motivation for excellence in contract performance.
>
> **Cost-Plus-Fixed-Fee.** Also known as CPFF, this contract type provides for payment to the contractor of a negotiated fee that is fixed at the beginning of the contract. The fixed

fee does not vary with actual cost, but may be adjusted as a result of changes in the work to be performed under the terms of the contract. This contract type permits contracting for efforts that might otherwise present too great a risk to contractors, but it provides the contractor only a minimum incentive to control costs while the government's cost responsibility is maximized.

2. KEY CONTRACT TERMINOLOGY

Now that you have an understanding of the two broad categories of contracts, fixed-price and cost reimbursement, we want to spend time on key contract terminology that you need to understand as you go about selling your services and products.

> **Delivery-order contract** means a contract for supplies that does not procure or specify a firm quantity of supplies (other than a minimum or maximum quantity) and that provides for the issuance of orders for the delivery of supplies during the period of the contract.
>
> **Task-order contract** means a contract for services that does not procure or specify a firm quantity of services (other than potentially a minimum and/or a maximum quantity) and that provides for the issuance of orders for the performance of tasks during the period of the contract.
>
> **Indefinite-Delivery Contracts** include three types: **definite-quantity contracts, requirements contracts**, and **indefinite-quantity contracts**. The appropriate type of indefinite-delivery contract may be used to acquire supplies and/or services when the exact times and/or exact quantities of future deliveries are not known at the time of contract award. Requirements contracts and indefinite-quantity contracts are also known as delivery-order contracts or task-order contracts.

Chapter 7: Understanding Contracts

Definite-Quantity Contracts provide for delivery of a definite quantity of specific supplies or services for a fixed period, with deliveries or performance to be scheduled at designated locations upon order.

Requirements Contracts provide for filling all actual purchase requirements of designated government activities for supplies or services during a specified contract period (from one contractor), with deliveries or performance to be scheduled by placing orders with the contractor.

Indefinite-Quantity Contracts provide for an indefinite quantity, within stated limits, of supplies or services during a fixed period. The government places orders for individual requirements. Quantity limits may be stated as number of units or as dollar values. Indefinite-Delivery Indefinite Quantity Contracts require some extra attention, so they will be discussed more in-depth in the next section.

Indefinite-Delivery Indefinite-Quantity (IDIQ) Contracts provide for an indefinite quantity of services for a fixed time. They are used when the government cannot determine, above a specified minimum, the precise quantities of supplies or services that it will require during the contract period.

Often the government awards more than one winner for an IDIQ prime contract. The "winners" essentially gain the right to compete for Delivery Orders (for supplies) or Task Orders (for services). Each company awarded a prime contract must prepare a proposal response for each competitive Delivery Order/Task Order **(DO/TO)** that comes out.

The government believes the IDIQ type contracts help streamline the contract process, reduce costs through competition and speed up service delivery. The government places Delivery Orders (for supplies) or Task Orders (for services) against the basic contract for individual requirements. Minimum and maximum quantity limits are specified in the basic contract as either number of units (for supplies) or as dollar values (for services).

IDIQ contracts are most often used for service contracts and architect-engineering services. Awards are usually for several (two to four) base years and one or more option years. Sometimes they are for only one base year and multiple option years. We have seen everything from one option year to eight option years. As always, the government decides and will specify the contract periods (base and option years) in the solicitation.

IDIQs have *some* downsides for contractors. For example, every time the government releases a DO/TO, each prime (if they choose to bid) goes through the proposal process to prepare a response to the DO/TO. The government will then review the proposals and select a winner for that particular DO/TO. A lot of work goes into preparing proposals, and a lot of bid and proposal **(B&P)** dollars are spent by each team as they prepare their response to each DO/TO.

The government regularly requires a response to the DO/TO within 5-10 days. This results in a lot of hours, energy and B&P dollars spent on preparing DO/TO responses in a very short period of time.

Some companies tire of the quick turnaround process of recruiting people to do the work, preparing the proposal and waiting for a decision that may not go their way. Other companies believe the IDIQ contract is just an empty bucket and the chance of ever winning any work is too slim compared to the time and energy they invest in it.

Chapter 7: Understanding Contracts

Granted, some companies are *very* successful with IDIQ contracts, but that is because they spend a lot of time and resources on their responses. Additionally, these companies are often larger, more mature businesses, and they typically can afford to put a lot of time and energy into creating templates and quick-turn responses that can be tailored and rewritten into each new DO/TO. We are not big fans of IDIQ type contracts because small businesses rarely have the resources (people or dollars) to actively compete in IDIQ-type contracts.

Time and Materials (T&M) Contract. In plain English, T&M is an arrangement under which the contractor is paid on the basis of (1) actual cost of direct labor, usually at specified hourly rates, (2) actual cost of materials and equipment usage, and (3) an agreed upon fixed add-on to cover the contractor's overheads and profit.

> *Or, straight from the FAR itself (and this will help you appreciate the "plain English" version):*

Subpart 16.6 — Time-and-Materials (FAR Subpart 16.6), Labor-Hour, and Letter Contracts
16.600 Scope.
  Time-and-materials contracts and labor-hour contracts are not fixed-price contracts.

16.601 Time-and-materials contracts.
  (a) Definitions for the purposes of Time-and-Materials Contracts.
  "Direct materials" means those materials that enter directly into the end product, or that are used or consumed directly in connection with the furnishing of the end product or service.

"*Hourly rate*" means the rate(s) prescribed in the contract for payment for labor that meets the labor category qualifications of a labor category specified in the contract that are—

(1) Performed by the contractor;

(2) Performed by the subcontractors; or

(3) Transferred between divisions, subsidiaries, or affiliates of the contractor under a common control.

"Materials" means—

(1) Direct materials, including supplies transferred between divisions, subsidiaries, or affiliates of the contractor under a common control;

(2) Subcontracts for supplies and incidental services for which there is not a labor category specified in the contract;

(3) Other direct costs (*e.g.*, incidental services for which there is not a labor category specified in the contract, travel, computer usage charges, etc.); and

(4) Applicable indirect costs.

(b) *Description*. A time-and-materials contract provides for acquiring supplies or services on the basis of—

(1) Direct labor hours at specified fixed hourly rates that include wages, overhead, general and administrative expenses, and profit; and

(2) Actual cost for materials

Application. A time-and-materials contract may be used only when it is not possible at the time of placing the contract to estimate accurately the extent or duration of the work or to anticipate costs with any reasonable degree of confidence.

> Okay, we hope you see what we mean about trying to read and understand the FAR. Every time we read anything from the FAR, we walk away with a new appreciation for contracts experts. It takes truly special people to want to work contracts for a living.

Chapter 7: Understanding Contracts

Agreements. Different from contracts but important to understand, agreements come in several types. Here is an overview of basic agreements and basic ordering agreements.

> **A. Basic Agreements.** A written instrument of understanding, negotiated between an agency or contracting activity and a contractor, that (1) contains contract clauses applying to future contracts between the parties during its term and (2) contemplates separate future contracts that will incorporate by reference or attachment the required and applicable clauses agreed upon in the basic agreement. A basic agreement is not a contract.
>
> **B. Basic Ordering Agreements.** A written instrument of understanding, negotiated between an agency, contracting activity, or contracting office and a contractor, that contains (1) terms and clauses applying to future contracts (orders) between the parties during its term, (2) a description, as specific as practicable, of supplies or services to be provided, and (3) methods for pricing, issuing, and delivering future orders under the basic ordering agreement. A basic ordering agreement is not a contract.

By now you should have a high-level understanding of the various types of government contracts, as well as some key terminology associated with government contracting. You also should know where to look to dig deeper into these topics on your own (that is, the Federal Acquisition Regulations or FAR).

Also, do not forget that you can always reach out to our experts at **ConnekServ (www.ConnekServ.com)** for help with all of your contracts needs.

CHAPTER 8: WHAT'S ALL THIS ABOUT REQUESTS FOR PROPOSALS

The Request for Proposal **(RFP)** is one of the primary methods the government uses to communicate their needs and requirements. Additionally, an RFP outlines the manner in which the contractor must fulfill those needs and requirements. Companies invest a lot of time, energy and money in preparing and responding to RFPs, and it's a process that all government contractors should be familiar with. In this chapter we will focus on the following RFP-related topics:

1. **Overview of the Government Request For Proposal (RFP)**
2. **Making Bid/No-Bid Decisions**
3. **Estimating Your Probability of Win (Pwin)**
4. **The Business Case for Your Bid**
5. **Wired RFPs**
6. **The Typical RFP Lifecycle in Government Contracting**
7. **Prime to Subcontractor RFPs**
8. **Influencing RFPs to Your Favor**

Let's take a look at each of these in detail:

1. OVERVIEW OF THE GOVERNMENT REQUEST FOR PROPOSAL (RFP)

The Federal Acquisition Regulation **(FAR)** mandates the format of federal government RFPs, which usually include the following sections:

Section A. Information to Offerors
Section B. Supplies or Services and Price/Costs

Section C. Statement of Work **(SOW)**

Section D. Packages and Marking

Section E. Inspection and Acceptance

Section F. Deliveries or Performance

Section G. Contract Administrative Data

Section H. Special Contract Requirements

Section I. Contract Clauses/General Provisions

Section J. Attachments, Exhibits

Section K. Representations/Certifications and Statements of Offerors

Section L. Proposal Preparation Instructions and Other Directions

Section M. Evaluation Criteria

Let's look at each of these RFP Sections in more detail:

Section A. Information to Offerors. This section includes the title of the procurement, procurement number, agency point of contact **(POC),** and instructions for how to acknowledge amendments. This is often a single-page form.

Section B. Supplies or Services and Price/Costs. Section B provides your requested pricing information. It defines the type of contract, identifies Contract Line Items **(CLINs),** Subcontract Line Items **(SLINs)** and all other billable items. This section may include the number of hours needed per year, per person, as well as level of resources needed. This section also identifies all billable items, describes the period of performance, and discusses potential option periods (if any).

Section C. Statement of Work (SOW). The Statement of Work **(SOW)** essentially describes what the government agency wants you to do or supply. The SOW is a formal document that captures and defines the work activities, deliverables, services, tasks and timeline that a vendor must execute. The SOW,

Chapter 8: What's All This About Requests For Proposals

typically provided with the government RFP, usually includes detailed requirements, with standard regulatory and governance terms and conditions. The SOW is usually incorporated into the winning team's contract, indirectly or by reference.

Section D. Packages and Marking. This section defines how all contract deliverables, such as reports and materials will be packaged and shipped. It includes specific instructions regarding timing, location and delivery details for your response to the RFP. Along with the preparation of a responsive proposal, the timing and delivery are the most important items to focus on. When and if you mail your proposal, allow plenty of days for the proposal to arrive on or before the due date.

> We recommend you deliver the proposal in person and get a signed receipt to show the RFP package(s) was delivered on time.

Section E. Inspection and Acceptance. This section describes the process by which the government officially accepts deliverables and what will happen if the work is not accepted. Typically, the government can inspect and test the goods and services at any time and place during the term of the award.

Section F. Deliveries or Performance. This section defines how the contracting officer will control the work performed and how you will deliver certain contract items. For example, this section:

- Addresses clauses incorporated by reference including the place of delivery or performance.

- Defines specific deliverables stated in the contract and expected by the government within a certain time period (the deliverables delivery schedule).

- Lists the period of performance for each phase of the contract (phases are often broken into a base year and one or more options years).

Section G. Contract Administrative Data. This section describes how the contracting officer and your company will communicate to ensure both performance and prompt payment. This section typically incorporates other clauses by reference, and you will be required to perform services, or provide goods, according to all terms and conditions set forth.

Section H. Special Contract Requirements. This section contains a range of special contract requirements which can include: Key Personnel, Emergency Preparedness, Protecting Sensitive Information, Background Investigations, Risk Level Designation for the contract, and standard Post-Government Employment Certifications. Specific areas under the Special Contract Requirements section may include:

- **Key Personnel.** You may need to make key personnel available for performance under the contract for the defined period provided on the RFP (typically one year) or as long as they are employed by your business. The contracting officer must authorize key personnel changes in writing before any new key personnel begin work on a project.

- **Emergency Preparedness.** Contract requirements for emergency preparedness cover services that are essential or critical to the federal government mission.

- **Protecting Sensitive Information.** The government must protect sensitive information during the course of project work and has special requirements about confidentiality and data protection.

- **Background Investigations.** You may need to undergo a background investigation if you:

Chapter 8: What's All This About Requests For Proposals

- Work on-site and have unescorted access to government offices or facilities
- Have access to government networks/systems
- Work on contracts and other awards for services with a value greater than a defined dollar amount, or on any contract or award at the discretion of the federal government

- **Risk Level Designation for the Contract.** Every federal government position, including those of contractors, must be designated with a sensitivity level. As a contractor, you must meet personnel security/suitability standards commensurate with your position's sensitivity level, and you will be subject to personnel investigation requirements. There usually is a reinvestigation requirement for individuals in high-risk positions and for people who have security clearances (if they continue to have a need for access to classified information).

- **Post-Government Employment Certifications.** If you plan to use a former federal government employee on your contract, then you typically need to complete and submit a post-government employment certification before that employee can work on the contract. Former government employees may be required to provide additional information about their responsibilities while employed at the agency and about their post-government work on the agency's contract or subcontract.

Section I. Contract Clauses/General Provisions. This section identifies the contract clauses incorporated by reference in the RFP. These clauses have the same force and effect as if they were given in full text and are incorporated into the contract. While this section does not require a separate response, its terms will be binding. Specific areas under the Contract Clauses/General Provisions section include:

- **Governing Law.** The contract is governed by federal law and will be construed accordingly. To the extent state law may apply, in the case where there is no applicable federal law, the state law that applies is the law of the state in which the federal government office executing the contract is located, and it serves as the governing law.

- **Independent Contractors.** The federal government retains independent contractors for the sole purpose of performing the services or providing the goods described in a contract. If subcontracting is permitted, then the term "Contractor" refers to both the contractor and all subcontractors at all levels. You must ensure that all subcontractors adhere to all the terms and conditions of the contracts that have flow-down requirements.

- **Subcontracting Reporting.** If subcontracting is approved under an award, you will usually be required to submit a Subcontracting Report, on a semiannual basis, addressing the following for each subcontractor:

    o Subcontractor's name, address and DUNS number

    o Subcontractor's type of business concern Minority or Women Owned Business **(MWOB),** Small Disadvantaged Business **(SDB),** Veteran–owned Business, etc.

    o North American Industry Classification System **(NAICS)** Code and corresponding geographic location of the subcontractor's place of performance

    o Period covered by report

    o Description of work performed by subcontractor during the report period

    o Percentage completion toward subcontracting plan goals

Chapter 8: What's All This About Requests For Proposals

- **Audit of Records.** The federal government, through its contracting officer or designated representative(s), has the right to audit and examine your records and inspect your facilities in the following ways:

    - **Examination of Costs.** The federal government agency can audit and examine your books and records, and your accounting procedures and practices, regardless of their form (e.g., machine readable media) or type (e.g., data bases, applications software, data base management software).

    - **Facilities Used for the Contract.** The federal government agency can inspect, at reasonable times, the facilities you use during performance of the contract.

    - **Reports of the Contractor.** The federal government agency can audit and examine your books, records, other documents and supporting materials.

    - **Computer Data.** The federal government agency can audit your computer data. Your computer data retention and transfer procedures must maintain the integrity, reliability and security of the original data.

- **Public Release of Contract Award and Advertising and Publicity Information.** You (as contractor), your affiliates, agents or subcontractors, and their respective employees:

    - Cannot issue press releases or provide other information to the public regarding any federal government contract award without written government approval.

    - Are typically restricted from statements to the media or from issuing press releases regarding your or their services under the contract.

    - Cannot issue or sponsor advertising or publicity that states or implies that the federal government agency endorses, recommends or prefers the contractor's services.

- Cannot use the agency's logo or other material without the government's written permission.

Section J. Attachments, Exhibits. This section lists all appendices to the RFP. These attachments and exhibits can cover a wide range of subjects ranging from technical specifications through statement of work items and labor categories required by the federal government. You should reference *Section J. Attachments, Exhibits* in your proposal by first reviewing and accepting stipulated contract clauses in the solicitation response, and then ensuring all appropriate signatures, including notarizations, are included in the solicitation response.

Section K. Representations/Certifications and Statements of Offerors. This section includes the elements that you must certify to bid on the contract, such as: you have acted according to procurement integrity regulations; your taxpayer identification number; the status of personnel; ownership of your firm; type of business organization; authorized negotiators; that your facilities are not segregated; that you comply with affirmative action guidelines; and whether you qualify as a small business, disadvantaged business, and/or women-owned business, etc. An official authorized to bind the contractor must complete the representations and certifications set out in federal government solicitations, and the documents must be returned with the proposal. They are legally binding.

You may see or hear the expression *"reps and certs"* (or *"reps & certs"*), which is shorthand for representations and certifications.

Section L. Proposal Preparation Instructions and Other Directions. This section provides instructions for preparing your proposal, including how to: format the documents, organize/outline material and submit questions regarding the RFP or procurement. It will also include directions on how the

Chapter 8: What's All This About Requests For Proposals

proposal is to be delivered and may have notices, conditions or other instructions.

Section M. Evaluation Criteria. This section outlines how the agency will assess and evaluate the incoming proposals. This process usually includes:

- Reviewing and assessing the "mission capability" of each written proposal against the stated evaluation sub-factors set forth in the solicitation. Mission capability ratings typically focus on strengths and weaknesses of the proposal and the extent to which proposed technical and management solutions fulfill the functional requirements.

- Reviewing and assessing the proposal according to responsiveness and compliance with submission requirements.

> Make sure you pay attention to and follow all instructions in the RFP. If you do not, it could affect costs, raise logistics issues and even result in a non-responsive proposal.

Best Value Evaluation Process. The government also uses a Best Value Evaluation Process (or source selection approach) for some solicitations. Best Value is, at some level, a subjective judgment, and it is not necessarily represented by the lowest price offered.

Lowest Price Technically Acceptable (LPTA). LPTA is another source selection approach that has been on the rise in the government-contracting arena. According to FAR 15.101-2, the LPTA approach is appropriate when "best value is expected to result from selection of the technically acceptable proposal with the lowest evaluated price." Essentially this means that the customer is not looking for the *best* proposal or the *best* person for the job. Instead, they are looking for the proposal that meets all of the minimum requirements at the lowest possible cost.

For practical purposes, in an LPTA competition all non-price factors are considered on a pass-fail basis. Either your proposal meets each individual requirement or it does not. Any value you feel your proposal might add above the minimum requirements will not, in theory, come into consideration at all. These factors vary with each solicitation but will be detailed in the RFP.

Some factors that *may* be considered include the technical capabilities of the offeror, the proposed performance approach, the management plan, subcontracting plan, key personnel and staffing, etc.

An interesting topic that comes up with the LPTA approach is that of past performance. If specific past performance requirements are not laid out in the RFP, then this factor may not be used in considering proposals. The company with no past performance at all will be considered on equal ground with the most experienced company, as long as all other minimum requirements are met.

When comparing non-price factors of a proposal, the customer may decide to open discussions with an offeror about the requirements that they do not appear to meet. This will give the offeror a chance to explain their capabilities better and enable the customer to make a more informed decision. If the customer enters into discussions with one respondent, however, they are required to do it for all bidders that are in the competitive range. For this reason, the government is often reluctant to take this approach.

Chapter 8: What's All This About Requests For Proposals

2. MAKING BID/NO-BID DECISIONS

Some companies would be better off bidding *fewer* proposals and putting their energy into winning more significant opportunities in which they have the strongest qualifications and past performance.

Going through the entire capture phase and then preparing compliant proposals requires (in most cases) a significant investment for your company. With the many opportunities available, you are always faced with the decision of where to allocate your bid and proposal **(B&P)** resources. You need to invest those limited resources where they will do the most good. Multiple bid/no-bid meetings are typically held with your key management staff to allow appropriate managers to review and speak into the bid decision process.

Since there may be changes in scope during the capture phase or the draft or final RFP phases, you may make several "decisions" to bid or not to bid. You will make the decision of whether or not to invest resources during the pre-RFP stage, and you will make another bid decision before you authorize the expenditure of resources on the actual proposal effort.

There are several things to consider in your bid/no-bid decision:

- Do you know the customer?
- What will it cost you to make the bid and can you make money if you win?
- Do you understand the technical requirements?
- What is your probability of winning **(Pwin)**?
- Were you aware of this RFP well before it came out or are you just hearing about and reacting to the RFP as it comes out?
- Do you have the overall capability to perform? Do you have

the resources to develop the proposal?

- Do you have the tools and facilities needed to perform the work?
- Do you have the "in-house" team to perform the work?
- Do you need teaming partners to round out your team and increase your Pwin, so you can bid a competitive proposal? Can you get those teammates?
- Do you have the ability to prepare the winning proposal?
- Can you compete on price?
- Do you have relevant past performance credentials to demonstrate that you can do this work?
- Do you have a business case for winning?

How you go about your bid decision process can be the difference between success and failure. For you to win, it helps if:

- You have a strong, positive relationship with the customer well before the RFP comes out.
- You understand the customer's needs and preferences.
- You have a cost-effective solution.
- You have strong past performance.
- You understand the customer's procurement, evaluation and selection methods.
- You have detailed knowledge of the competitive environment.

Chapter 8: What's All This About Requests For Proposals

3. ESTIMATING YOUR PROBABILITY OF WIN (Pwin)

Many companies try to determine their probability of winning **(Pwin)** the RFP. As they make projections of their Pwin, they ask themselves these types of questions:

- Regarding Your Competitors:
    - Who are the likely competitors?
    - How well do they know the customer—and, does the customer know them?
    - How well do your competitors understand the work to be performed?
    - How aggressively can they price their work?
    - What are their strengths and weaknesses?

- You and Your Team
    - How do you compare to the competition?
    - What is your "Best Value" offering and how does that compare to what you know about the customers?
    - Can you put together a strong technical, management and cost proposal with relevant past performance?
    - Do you know if the winner must have the "lowest price" to win? (The RFP will usually tell you the criteria and whether or not lowest price is the highest weighted factor, but sometimes you can determine this through conversations with the customer before the RFP comes out.)
    - Do you know who the incumbents are and whether the customer wants them back?

> Once you have honestly answered these questions, you should be able to arrive at a Pwin with some degree of accuracy and know whether or not you should spend your valuable time bidding this RFP. Some companies have formulas that weight these questions and input their weighted answers into a spreadsheet or program to provide them an actual Pwin value. Management then factors in this Pwin value as they consider their final bid/no-bid decision.

4. THE BUSINESS CASE FOR YOUR BID

Examine your business case as you decide whether or not to bid. Answer these questions:

- How well does the opportunity fit your company and your current growth goals, profit goals, etc.?
- Can you afford not to bid?
- Can you afford to lose?
- Can you afford to win (that is, can you afford to execute)?
- Will you be able to deliver the resources required to bid?
- Will you be able to deliver the resources required to perform?

5. WIRED RFPS

Every now and then you will find RFPs that are "wired" for a company (or an individual). Essentially that means the RFP requirements have been written in such a way that only one company could possibly meet the qualifications. When that happens, the odds are against you, and you really have to go through your own bid/no-bid process to decide if the RFP is worth bidding on.

Chapter 8: What's All This About Requests For Proposals

You should consider these items to be "red flags" in the bid/no-bid decision process:

- Emphasis on evaluation criteria which only an incumbent will be able to get high marks
- Short, inflexible deadlines
- Emphasis on criteria that is easy to bias to the company/individual/incumbent
- Evaluation practices that are outside the norm for that agency
- Prohibitions against rehiring incumbent staff
- Unusual labeling of key staff
- Use of multiple evaluation criteria to address the same technical or programmatic element.
- Processes specified in the RFP that cannot be mapped or flow charted so that only someone who has experience with them can figure out how they work
- Ambiguity that favors an incumbent
- Statements of Work that require you to know the customer's undocumented standard operating procedures (**SOPs**)
- Page limitations that make it impossible to respond to all of the requirements, so that only the preferred bidder will know what to focus on and what can be skipped without causing the proposal to be labeled "non-compliant."
- Fixed price proposals where you do not have enough information to know how long tasks will take to complete

Once you have considered these factors, you can make a decision if the RFP has been wired for another company and if it is worth pursuing.

6. THE TYPICAL RFP LIFECYCLE IN GOVERNMENT CONTRACTING

While there can be, and often are, other steps in the RFP cycle, here are the typical steps or phases:

- Pre-solicitation phase, Capture phase, Pre-RFP phase (These are several names all referring to the same timeframe, but each with its own unique meaning.)
- Solicitation phase
    - Request for Information **(RFI)** issued
        - Question and answer phase occurs between the government and contractors
    - Draft Request for Proposal **(DRFP)**
        - Question and answer phase on the draft RFP
    - Request for Proposal **(RFP)** [sometimes "final RFP"]
        - Question and answer phase on the final RFP
- Proposals are prepared (usually consisting of several volumes, for example: *Management, Technical, Security, Past Performance, Cost and Security* volumes)
- Government team evaluates the proposals
- Oral Presentations (if required) are made by bidding contractors to government evaluators
- Government Source Selection Committee **(SSC)** makes the award decision and briefs government senior management on the decision and rationale
- The government award decision is announced to the bidders—the winner(s) and the losing bidders

Chapter 8: What's All This About Requests For Proposals

Let's examine some of these phases in more detail:

Pre-solicitation Phase *or* Capture Phase *or* Pre-RFP Phase. In this phase, the government is shaping or refining their acquisition strategy and preparing to release the RFIs or RFPs. During this phase, a government contractor should be marketing to the government and even trying to help shape the acquisition strategy. In fact, the government often welcomes and even asks for input from industry as they prepare and execute their strategy.

Request for Information (RFI). A Request for Information **(RFI)** is essentially a tool (a document) used by the government to request information about your products, services or additional information about your business. The RFI, when used, is released prior to the RFP as part of the overall proposal process and is very important to the outcome of the proposal process because it allows the contractors a chance to provide input to the government prior to the release of the RFP. The government uses the input contractors provide to help make decisions on the final form of the RFP.

Contractors can also use the RFI response to state concerns or raise issues and to seek clarification on topics in the RFI before the RFP is released. Contractors can also ask questions or provide input strategically to try to influence the upcoming RFP in their favor (more on this at the end of the chapter).

Here is a sample RFI "cover letter," so you can see a sample format and the possible information included in a typical RFI.

RFI for Widget X
Solicitation Number: HM1234-12-T-1234
Office: Government Widget Agency

Notice Type:

Sources Sought

Synopsis:

This announcement is for information purposes only. The suggested North American Industry Classification System NAICS) code is 54321. If another NAICS code is more appropriate include that in your response. The Government seeks to identify interested bidders for this potential procurement action and to gather information that may influence the shape of any future Request for Proposal (RFP). This announcement does not constitute an RFP, and it does not restrict the Government to any ultimate acquisition approach or strategy. This announcement does not represent a commitment by the Government in any form. The Government will not pay for any information that is submitted by respondents to this announcement. This is not a request for proposals, quotations or bids.

Attachments:

(Here the Government may list the files they want your input on.)

Chapter 8: What's All This About Requests For Proposals

FedBizOps Posting Date:

Month Day, 2014

Widget X RFI and associated attachments can also be found on FBO.gov

Description:

RFI for Widget X (here the Government may provide more detail on their thoughts on Widget X, but the more detailed information is usually in the attachments).

Contracting Office Address:

Attn: Government Widget X Office

Reston, Virginia 20191

Place of Performance:

McLean, Virginia (See Attachment #1 for details)

Primary Point of Contact (POC):

Name of Primary POC,

Contract Specialist

Email address for POC

Phone Number for POC

Fax Number for POC

Set Aside:

Veteran-Owned, Small Business (VOSB)

Once the RFI stage closes, the government typically releases a draft RFP, hopefully using the input gathered from the various contractors like you.

Notice in the sample cover letter that the RFI mentions the plan to have a Veteran-Owned Small Business **(VOSB)** set-aside. If the input from the contractors' response shows that the government may be better served to have another type of set-aside (e.g., woman owned, service disabled, etc.), the RFP may come out with a different set-aside than stated in the RFI. When the government stated VOSB in the RFI, they expected enough response from VOSBs to warrant releasing the RFP with the VOSB requirement. However, if no VOSBs respond, or if the input to the government does not show that the responders could do the work, then the government may change their plans.

This is just a small example of the impact a contractor can make by responding to the RFIs. Remember, the government really wants to hear from you when they issue RFIs.

The next phase could be the draft RFP, if the government decides to release a draft, or the government could move straight to the final RFP stage. Let's take a look at the draft stage first.

Draft Request for Proposal (DRFP). This phase begins with customer release of the draft RFP and continues until the final RFP is issued. The government commonly issues a draft RFP for most major procurements. Potential bidders often are invited to comment on draft elements, and occasionally multiple drafts of some components are published electronically before release of the final RFP.

Soon before or after the procuring agency releases the draft RFP, the contractor's proposal manager must publish a proposal plan that lays out roles and responsibilities, resource requirements, and a schedule for proposal development. Work on critical

Chapter 8: What's All This About Requests For Proposals

components of the proposal should begin immediately after receipt of the draft RFP. Long lead-time activities include gathering draft RFP-specific information for proposal writers, developing solutions for key issues, and gathering cost data.

Request for Proposal (RFP) or Final RFP. We covered this material in the previous section of this chapter, so please refer back to "Overview of Government Request for Proposals (RFPs)."

Proposals Are Prepared and Delivered. When the RFP is released, there are some *basic steps* you need to go through to make a **final** bid/no-bid decision, and if you choose to bid, to determine your next steps in the proposal process.

> There are a lot of good books about proposals available, so we are not trying to delve into every detail of proposal writing. We want to offer you a general understanding of the basic steps you will go through in developing a proposal. **Chapter 9**, "The Proposal Process," offers more details, and here is a quick overview of the steps in that chapter.

Assess the Bid. Truly, you already should have assessed the bid in the pre-RFI stage, the RFI stage and the draft RFP stage as part of your strategic planning—do not wait until the final RFP is released. In this step you will determine if you have the technical capability to do the work. You will define the resources you need to complete the proposal volumes.

Assess whether you have the required past performance to demonstrate that you can do the job. Reassess your Pwin and brief it through to the appropriate management channels to get their approval to pursue. Make another bid/no-bid decision.

Analyze the Requirements. In this step you analyze the RFP requirements in great detail, you refine or develop your discriminators and win themes, prepare a draft outline of your proposal response, establish page limits and budget, assign writers, and plan for appropriate reviews by corporate leadership.

Design Your Draft Response. In this step you define your technical and management approaches, prepare cost estimates, pull together past performance data, and refine your outline while applying your win themes and discriminators. You then pull together the draft response components and hold a review by senior management, so they can provide input on whether or not your draft is on track or is weak in certain areas. At each stage it is important to hold these reviews, so management can redirect efforts if they see weakness in the proposal components. Usually the timelines are tight, and you want input from management as you go—not at the end when you have a final product, and you do not have time to regroup.

Develop Your Draft Response. Once management has reviewed and provided input on your draft approach, it is time to prepare your draft response. Here you will develop draft text, graphics, past performance summaries, resumes, cost estimates, a cost volume and staffing plan. Once again, hold a senior management review to get their valuable feedback on your draft RFP components.

We say *valuable* feedback, and we truly mean that. Sometimes the feedback is painful to hear if you are not on target, but management is there to help you see missteps and to offer input to guide you to a better response.

Develop Your Final Response. You are almost done! At this point, you will incorporate input from the senior management review and finalize all of the RFP volumes. You will conduct a final "QA" or white-glove of the proposal and deliver it to the customer per the instructions in the RFP.

Chapter 8: What's All This About Requests For Proposals

Orals. In some instances, the RFP may require you to present an oral proposal as part of your submission. The RFP will define exactly what material you are (and in some cases are not) to present. It will even define how many people can attend the presentation and who specifically can be presenters (usually the "key personnel" [like the program manager, the chief engineer, etc.] will be the presenters).

Evaluation of Proposals and Award(s) Decision and Announcement. The government goes through a very formal evaluation process that can take weeks or even months to complete. They must be very particular to evaluate based on the criteria outlined in the RFP, and they must document thoroughly the findings and rationale for their decision. More and more companies are protesting award decisions, so the government will protect itself by taking time to make sure they have made an award decision that can stand up to scrutiny and legal review.

Then . . .

You Win!! You have a "win party" and you invite us to attend and celebrate with you!

7. PRIME TO SUBCONTRACTOR RFPS

What about the scenario where you join a prime in a subcontracting opportunity? How does that work? The prime will send you, the subcontractor, an RFP, and you have to propose back to the prime by meeting all of their requirements, usually outlined in detail in a "cover letter." The prime's cover letter will list many items, but in particular, it will include the RFP number, the specific requirements documents you are required to complete (often the cover letter will include a long list of attachments that either are provided as information or are forms you need to complete and include in your proposal back to the prime), and the timeline your products are due back to the prime. Sometimes your proposal products are all due at the same time and sometimes the products are due on different dates.

Here is an example cover letter:

Date: December 12, 2014

To: Your company Name
             Your Company Address

Subject: Request for Proposal, RFP# XX-XXXXXXXX

Reference: RFP Name and Date

Dear (Your Contracts Officers Name):

Prime hereby solicits a proposal for services in support of the Prime Solicitation # HMXXXX-XX-R-XXXX with the Government Agency by way of a Subcontract Agreement.

No solicitation on Prime's behalf shall be construed in any manner to be an obligation on Prime's part to enter into a subcontract with your company or to result in any claim whatsoever against the United States Government for reimbursement of costs for any efforts expended by your company, regardless of whether or not Prime is successful in receiving a contract as a result of this proposal.

Special Proposal Instructions and Information
Type of Subcontract.
Period of Performance.
Subcontract Provisions.
Pricing.
Travel.
Other Direct Costs.

Subcontractor Information Due Dates
Pricing Table due:
Cover Letter due:

Certification G: Completed and executed.

Vendor Master Data Form: Completed and executed.

Chapter 8: What's All This About Requests For Proposals

DUNS Number: Please provide your company DUNS number for verification of Reps and Certs on SAM (**www.sam.gov).** If your company is not registered, it is requested that you go to the website and register.

DCAA Approval Status: In accordance with the instructions contained in Section 3.1 of Attachment 2.

DD254: Completed and executed.

Proprietary Package.

By responding to this quotation, the bidder hereby certifies that no gratuities were offered either directly or indirectly. Any situation where a gratuity is solicited should be reported immediately to

Ms. XXXX, Chief Procurement Officer at XXX-XXX-XXXX.

Questions of a contractual nature should be addressed to the undersigned at the aforementioned numbers.

Sincerely,
Prime
Name
Senior Subcontracts Manager

Attachments:
1. RFP General Provisions
2. RFP Preparation and Pricing Instructions
3. Statements of Work
4. Schedule A, Subcontract Agreement
5. Schedule B, Part I, FAR Clauses
6. Schedule B, Part II, DFAR Clauses
7. Subcontract Special Terms and Conditions
8. Representations and Certifications, Part C
9. Representations and Certifications, Part D
10. Representations and Certifications, Part G
11. Vendor Master Data Form and Instructions
12. DD Form 254 and Addendum
13. Agency Non-Disclosure Agreement (to be executed during subcontract performance)
14. OCI Disclosure and Analysis Form
15. Government Property Questionnaire
16. KPML (Key Personnel Management List)
17. Rate Template

8. INFLUENCING RFPS TO YOUR FAVOR

Early on, most new government contracting companies are concerned just with getting off the ground, getting a subcontract and getting some revenue coming into pay the bills. That said, keep this section in mind as you grow your company and as you plan for upcoming RFPs/acquisitions.

> You can and you should influence RFPs to work to your advantage and to your competitors' DISADVANTAGE.

To be in the best position to influence an RFP, you need to have already established a relationship with your customer. You need to know your customer—their mission, what drives them, what can make their lives better—so you can discuss their needs and make recommendations regarding how to get those needs fulfilled.

Here are some things you might consider as you plan to try to influence an RFP—all with the goal of making the final RFP in your favor and to your competition's disadvantage:

Award Process. You could advise the customer on the steps they should go through 1) in issuing the RFP, and/or 2) making a decision/selection.

Budget. You could offer the customer guidance on how to set their budget.

Conflict of Interest. You could offer your thoughts on what companies should be considered in a conflict of interest position and not able to bid on the new work.

Demonstrations. You could offer your opinion on whether or not demonstrations should be a part of the RFP.

Chapter 8: What's All This About Requests For Proposals

Evaluation Criteria. You could offer your thoughts on what evaluation criteria should be included in the RFP.

Intellectual Property. You could offer your thoughts on how the RFP should address intellectual property.

Locations. You could offer your thoughts on where the work should be performed.

Minimum Qualifications To Bid. You could offer your thoughts on what the minimum qualifications should be for contractors who want to bid on the RFP.

Number of Awards. You could offer your thoughts on the number of awards that should be given.

Pricing Structure. You could offer your thoughts on what the pricing structure should be for the contract. Fixed price? Award fee? Other types?

Quantities. You could offer your thoughts on the appropriate quantities of goods in the contract.

Requirements. You could offer your thoughts on specific requirements of the contract. This could be technical, format, cost, etc.

Resumes. You could offer your thoughts on whether or not resumes should be bid for some or all of the positions.

Risks. You could offer your thoughts on the potential risks associated with the RFP.

Schedule. You could offer your thoughts on the RFP schedule, the work performance schedule, etc.

Scope/Specifications. You could offer your thoughts on scope/specification topics.

Should There Even Be an RFP? You could offer your thoughts on whether there should even be an RFP.

Site Visits. You could offer your thoughts on whether or not site visits should be required to bid on the RFP.

Transition. You could offer your thoughts on any project start-up, phase-in, or transition requirements that could work to your advantage.

> One more thought on the subject of influencing the customer. Sometimes you have the opportunity to influence the RFP by your response to the RFI that precedes the RFP. Other times you will see one or more draft RFPs released before the final RFP and you can influence the RFP that way. Always keep in mind, however, that having an intimate knowledge of your customer provides you an opportunity to influence the RFP even before the RFI stage.

The government issues RFPs to procure goods and services; an RFP establishes how the contractor must perform to satisfy the government's needs and requirements. Each RFP is unique, reflecting specific requirements, and yet most RFPs have similar formats and sections, and most RFPs follow a typical cycle. As a contractor, you should evaluate each RFP's opportunities and drawbacks and invest your resources in winning the contracts that advance your business goals.

Now, that you have some understanding of RFPs, let us look at a typical *proposal process* you may go through to respond to an RFP.

CHAPTER 9: THE PROPOSAL PROCESS

The proposal process is so complex and rigorous that entire books are written on the subject, and many companies provide training on every aspect of it. This chapter takes a high-level view and focuses on key steps and terminology that you will encounter in responding to requests for proposals **(RFPs)**.

The proposal process begins long before the RFP is issued and consists of three main phases. First is the *Capture Management Phase*, followed by the *Proposal Management Phase* and finally the *Execution Phase* (if you win the contract).

1. CAPTURE MANAGEMENT PHASE

You have important work to do even before the RFP is issued. In this pre-release time, you should:

- Make sure you understand the upcoming opportunity.
- Assess your competitive advantage.
- Assess the viability of winning as a subcontractor and as a prime.
- Develop a capture plan based on what you know. You will continually revise and add to this "living document" as you learn more about the opportunity.
- Conduct a business assessment. (What are your risks? What is the return on investment? Do you have the skills and resources required?)
- Determine if the upcoming RFP meets your strategic objectives.
- Make sure you are prioritizing your valuable resources against the opportunities that you are most likely to win.

- Make a preliminary assessment of the resources required in terms of cost, people, infrastructure, etc.
- Spend time with the customer to try to position your company to be in the best position to win.

2. PROPOSAL MANAGEMENT PHASE

Some lessons we have learned about the proposal management phase:

- Commit the resources to win or do not bid! Responding to an RFP demands a lot of resources and time and requires commitment from everyone involved.
- Make sure you have allocated not only resources, but also bid and proposal **(B&P)** dollars.
- Engage your key staff early and make sure they are available for the duration of the proposal—i.e., this is not the time for vacation.
- Put someone in charge who will be involved every day throughout the entire process. It really helps if they have experience in government proposals.
- Resist the urge to start writing too soon! When the turnaround time is short, many companies find they want to jump into writing their response before they have a well thought-out proposal plan.
- Take the time to **plan** how you will respond.

After the RFP is issued, you will work through these key proposal activities:

- **Analyze the RFP Requirements**
    - Go through the RFP line by line and make sure you understand all the requirements. Develop a matrix

that you will use to verify that every RFP requirement is met.
- Evaluate (again) whether or not to bid on this effort.
- Assign writers.
- Government RFPs follow a standard format. The following is usually true:
  - Cost and contractual requirements are in Sections B through K.
  - Instructions to the offeror are in Section L.
  - Evaluation criteria are in Section M.
  - Technical performance requirements are in Section C and include a Statement of Work **(SOW)** or Statement of Objectives.
  - Management requirements are in the SOW, and the general management and special contract provisions are in Sections G and H.

- **Design Your Response**
  - Determine your themes and discriminators.
    - Develop an explicit statement of why the customer should select your proposal over other proposals.
    - The result of that statement will become your "win themes" that should drive all of the writing assignments.
    - Make sure you can substantiate your win themes—assertions without proof will not fly.
    - Your themes should parallel the evaluation criteria the government will use to evaluate your response.
    - Review your bid/no-bid material. This analysis is an excellent source for identifying potential

discriminators to set you apart from competing proposals.
- Build "feature-benefit" tables, which describe a "feature" and its resulting benefit to the customer.

o Design management volume response.

o Design technical volume response.

o Design cost volume response.

o From the volume designs, create the proposal outline for each volume.

o Prepare past performance volume response.
- In government contracting, "past performance" is the government's assessment of how well your company performed. It focuses not on a history of past contracts or experience but rather on the government's satisfaction with your work and its relevance to the potential work described in the RFP.
- Your past performance exemplars must show how you have satisfied similar customers in terms of responsiveness, cost, schedule, quality, etc.
- Your past performance exemplars must demonstrate to the evaluators that the previous work is directly relevant to the work that is to be performed.
- Select only exemplars that clearly show the customer was satisfied.
- Relevant exemplars are a must!

> Some of these volumes may be combined, e.g., often the management and technical volumes are combined.

Chapter 9: The Proposal Process

- **Develop and Integrate Your Response**

    o Write the first draft of each volume.

    o Have experts—other than the draft writers—conduct a complete formal review of the draft volumes.

    o Debrief the results of the review to the writing team.

    o Implement the guidance from the reviewers.

    o Update the proposal for a final review.

    > You may need more than one review cycle to get your response ready to deliver to your government customer. Make sure you allow time in your schedule for adequate review(s) and updates.

- **Finalize the Proposal Response and Deliver the Proposal Sets**

    o Produce a final copy and do a thorough assessment of the product to be delivered.

    - Production should be thought out well in advance; it should not be an afterthought.

        - A well-thought-out and executed production phase may make the difference between winning and losing.

        - Know how many copies are to be delivered and in what format. Some RFPs require only hardcopy files; some require softcopy files; and some require both hardcopy and softcopy files.

    o Produce the required number of sets of proposals and deliver them as directed in the RFP.

    - Plan for delivery from the beginning.

- Confirm that you know when and how the proposal is required to be delivered.
  - Know the drop-dead delivery time and allow plenty of margin for error in your schedule.
  - The condition of the proposal packaging and delivery is the first evidence the evaluators will see of your commitment to follow instructions and provide quality results.

Avoid These Common Mistakes

- Ignoring some RFP requirements.
- Not following all the RFP instructions.
- Not allowing enough planning time up front to make sure you have time to address all of the RFP.
- Not allowing time to **write**!
- Too many changes in the written material.
- No configuration baseline control.
- Not engaging the experts necessary to write their sections, technical or otherwise.
- Lack of an overall win theme or a win theme that does not demonstrate "why your company should win."
- Lack of discriminators that demonstrate why your company is better than the competition.
- Assertions without enough substantiation or back-up evidence.
- A focus on what you have to offer rather than how you will solve your customer's requirements/problems.
- Not lining up the appropriate experts to review your proposal drafts/iterations.
- Not incorporating your reviewers' relevant comments.

Chapter 9: The Proposal Process

> - Not allowing time for production and delivery.
> - Not performing a quality check on your entire delivery before turning it in.

3. EXECUTION PHASE

You have won, now it is time to execute. *That is what the rest of the book is all about*!

Several companies specialize in training other companies on capture management, proposal management and proposal writing. There are also companies that you can hire to do your capture management, proposal management and even your proposal writing. **Shipley Associates** is well known and a good source for such training. Check out: **www.shipleywins.com**

We can refer you to companies, both large and small, that provide on-site consultants to help you with capture planning, proposal management, proposal development and writing and much more. These experts live and breathe proposal work, and they can save you time, money and aggravation.

> While you need to provide technical and subject-matter experts to write against the RFP technical requirements, we cannot overemphasize the importance of a disciplined team and a well-defined, proven process in developing a winning proposal to respond to an RFP. If you do not have that expertise in-house, you should consider outsourcing some or most of your proposal functions.

Now that you have a basic understanding of traditional RFPs and the traditional proposal process, we want to introduce you to another way the government buys products and services — through the General Services Administration **(GSA)** Schedules. This topic is important enough to warrant its own chapter.

CHAPTER 10: GENERAL SERVICES ADMINISTRATION (GSA) SCHEDULES

As you grow your company, you may decide to get on one or more General Services Administration **(GSA)** Schedules. Here is an overview of the GSA and its mission plus information about GSA Schedules and their value to contractors.

An independent agency of the U.S. government, the GSA is divided into two primary divisions to serve two main purposes. The first division, the Public Building Service **(PBS)**, exists to acquire and manage real estate on behalf of the federal government. In fact, the very first act of the GSA was the complete renovation of the White House from 1949 to 1952, and today the PBS manages roughly 8,300 owned and leased buildings. The second division, on which we will focus, is the Federal Acquisition Service **(FAS)**. According to their website (**www.gsa.gov/portal/content/105080**), the FAS provides a wide variety of solutions to the federal government and its employees at the best possible value. These solutions include:

- Products and Services
- Technology
- Motor Vehicle Management
- Transportation
- Travel
- Procurement and Online Acquisition Tools

The GSA is best known for its Federal Supply Schedules, also known as GSA Schedule Contracts or Multiple Award Schedule **(MAS)**. The GSA primarily uses these vehicles to provide products and services to government agencies. Using MAS, the GSA negotiates long-term Indefinite Delivery Indefinite Quantity **(IDIQ)** contracts with vendors who wish to provide their services to the federal government. IDIQ contracts negotiate prices, delivery terms and other conditions up front, resulting in a streamlined procurement process when a government agency chooses to do business with a vendor on the schedule. See **Chapter 7** for more information about IDIQ contracts.

Why is this important? The government spends about $50 billion annually, that's 10% of all federal procurement spending, through GSA Schedules, and roughly 80% of MAS contractors are small businesses. Contracting with the GSA and getting on a Federal Supply Schedule can be a great way for small businesses to get a foot in the door and increase their revenues. Unfortunately, being on a GSA Schedule does not guarantee anything as only 40% of all MAS contracts actually generate sales per year. If you choose to go this route, you should not depend on GSA schedules as a primary source of revenue for your business.

1. THREE STEPS TO GETTING ON A GSA SCHEDULE

> The *good news* is that once you have a GSA Schedule Contract, it has the potential to last for 20 years. The contract will be for 5 years with three more potential 5-year extensions. The *bad news* is that getting on a GSA Schedule is not a very straightforward affair. The process involves many steps and can take several months to a year to complete.

The process can be very expensive as well. The GSA estimates that the most successful contractors invest between $80,000-$130,000 to find, manage and market their initial contract. Not all contractors invest this much, and in fact, there are companies that will assist you in landing your first contract for a fee of less than $20,000. However, as mentioned before, getting on the schedule doesn't guarantee actual sales. The reason that the most successful companies spend so much is that they employ

Chapter 10: General Services Administration (GSA) Schedules

full-time staff dedicated to managing and marketing their schedules. This staffing leads to a much higher investment but also allows them to maximize the revenue that they earn through the schedule.

Whichever way you decide to go, you must make sure that GSA Schedule Contracts fit into your long-term game plan before investing in the process. You may find it beneficial to have a long-term business plan in place and conduct market research on what comparable products and services are already being provided to the government.

> A great place to start exploring your options is the GSA **Vendor Toolbox**, a tool designed to help you decide whether or not GSA Schedules are the right decision for you. If you decide that GSA Schedule Contracts offer a good opportunity for you, then read on to learn about next steps in the process.

GSA Vendor Toolbox
https://interact.gsa.gov/blog/gsa-launches-new-vendor-toolbox

Step 1: Find the Right Solicitation

Once you have a plan, you need to search through the lists of Schedules to find one that matches your product or service. There are nine main offices that handle different types of solicitations (**GSA Schedule Solicitations**). Here is a brief description of each office, and you can find more information about each one at the following website:

GSA Schedule Solicitations
www.gsa.gov/portal/content/207509

Center for Innovative Acquisition Development

This office handles the Financial and Business Services **(FABS)** Schedule, which offers a wide variety of financial support services ranging from accounting and auditing to risk assessment and mitigation services.

Management Services Center

This office handles schedules offering a variety of different services. They are:

- Mission Oriented Business Integrated Services **(MOBIS)** Schedule, for consulting, facilitation, survey, training, and program and project management services

- Professional Engineering Services **(PES)** Schedule, for engineering support covering distinct phases of the project life cycle over the full range of disciplines

- Language Services Schedule, for translation, interpretation, comprehensive linguistics analytical support services, and services for the visually and hearing impaired

- Environmental Services Schedule, for a wide variety of environmental services

- Logistics Worldwide **(LOGWORLD)** Schedule, for logistics management and support services

- Consolidated Schedule, which includes supplies and services that may fall under more than one schedule. This schedule is often used by companies that offer a wide array of products and services, so they do not have to spend time and energy managing several different supply contracts.

Center for IT Schedule Programs

This office handles the General Purpose Commercial Information Technology Equipment, Software and Services

Chapter 10: General Services Administration (GSA) Schedules

Schedule. Also known quite simply as the IT Schedule, the name says it all.

Greater Southwest Acquisition Center

This office handles several different schedules offering a wide variety of products and services. Each schedule name is quite descriptive and self-explanatory.

- Buildings and Building Materials/Industrial Services and Supplies Schedule
- Food Service, Hospitality, Cleaning Equipment and Supplies, and Chemicals and Services Schedule
- Total Solutions for Law Enforcement, Security, Facility Management Systems, Fire, Rescue, Special Purpose Clothing, Marine Craft, and Emergency/Disaster Response Schedule
- Advertising & Integrated Marketing Solutions **(AIMS)** Schedule
- Temporary Administrative and Professional Staffing **(TAPS)** Schedule
- Scientific Equipment and Services Schedule

Center for Facilities Maintenance and Hardware

This office handles two different schedules:

- Hardware SuperStore Schedule, for a wide variety of appliances, tools and equipment
- Facilities Maintenance and Management Schedule, for all the government's facilities maintenance needs

National Administrative Services and Office Supplies Acquisition Center

This office handles several different schedules offering a wide variety of products and services. Each schedule name is quite descriptive and self-explanatory:

- Human Resources and EEO Services Schedule
- Office Products/Supplies and Services and New Products/Technology Schedule
- Photographic Equipment—Cameras, Photographic Printers, and Related Supplies and Services (Digital and Film-Based) Schedule
- Publication Media Schedule
- Shipping, Packaging and Packing Supplies Schedule

Integrated Workplace Acquisition Center

Formerly called the National Furniture Center, this office handles several different schedules primarily associated with furniture and office furnishings:

- Furniture Schedule
- Comprehensive Furniture Management Services Schedule
- Furniture and Floor Coverings Schedule
- Office, Imaging and Document Solutions Schedule, for copying and printing equipment
- Sports, Promotional, Outdoor, Recreational, Trophies, and Signs **(SPORTS)** Schedule

GSA Automotive

This office provides agencies with non-tactical vehicles and services at low prices. Schedules include:

Chapter 10: General Services Administration (GSA) Schedules

- Automotive Superstore Schedule
- Leasing of Automobiles and Light Trucks Schedule

Office of Travel and Transportation

This office handles two schedules:

- Transportation, Delivery and Relocation Solutions **(TDRS)** Schedule
- Travel Services Solutions Schedule

Step 2: Registration and Certifications

Registration and certification require a number of administrative steps. The first two are to obtain a Data Universal Numbering System **(DUNS)** number and register with the System for Award Management **(SAM)**. Luckily, if you followed all the steps in the first section of this book, then these items are already done. If not, you can refer back to **Chapter 2** to complete these steps.

Next, you need to obtain a Past Performance Evaluation through **Open Ratings (www.supplierriskmanager.com/ppe-order/login.seam)**. Operated by Dun & Bradstreet, the same company that provides DUNS numbers, they will provide an independent evaluation of your past performance, for a fee of around $200, by contacting 6-20 customer references. For each customer, you must provide the following contact information:

- First and last name
- Company name
- Telephone number
- Email address

Once contacted, the customers will be asked to answer a short 10-question survey about their experience working with you.

This process alone generally takes two to three weeks but can take up to 45 days depending on how long the references take to respond. According to the GSA, the most successful vendors generally have a successful track record of at least two years in federal contracting as either a prime or subcontractor. For these reasons, we again stress that GSA schedules should be only one part of your long-term business plan.

> Finally, it is important to note that the federal agencies that utilize GSA Schedule contracts often do so using funds that are appropriated for the various small business set-asides. If you believe your business qualifies for one of the small business designations, we recommend that you apply or self-certify as soon as possible to give yourself an advantage. Refer back to **Chapter 2** for more information about small business set-asides and how to certify.

Step 3: Prepare an Offer

Now that you have found a suitable solicitation that you intend to respond to and have taken all the preliminary administrative steps, you are ready to respond with an offer. All offers must be submitted electronically through a system called **eOffer/eMod (http://eoffer.gsa.gov/)**. Before you go online, you should read through the solicitation very thoroughly and make sure you are aware of all the requirements. If you omit any information or documentation while preparing your offer, it will likely be returned to you, delaying the entire process. The review process can take between one and four months, so you do not want to lengthen the time as a result of simple mistakes.

According to the **GSA (www.gsa.gov/portal/content/202577)**, your offer will be evaluated by a Procurement Contracting Officer **(PCO)** based on the following criteria:

Chapter 10: General Services Administration (GSA) Schedules

- **Responsibility.** You should be in a healthy financial state, i.e., financial resources to perform are available, accounting system and controls are in place and a good record of positive past performance is evidenced.

- **Responsiveness.** Follow all instructions and include necessary documentation.

- **Scope.** Ensure your offered products or services match the Schedule/Special Item Number **(SIN)** descriptions.

- **Subcontracting Plan.** To help agencies achieve their socioeconomic goals, large businesses must have a plan in place for subcontracting a percentage of their work to various types of small businesses. Contact the Small Business Administration **(SBA)** Commercial Marketing Representative **(CMR)** with questions about the subcontracting program and for help locating resources.

  www.sba.gov/content/commercial-market-representatives

- **Pricing Analysis and Review of Terms.** Prices should be fair and reasonable, with appropriate data supporting and explaining the pricing structure.

Once the review of your offer is complete, there typically will be a negotiation period. You and the PCO will meet to negotiate the price and the various terms of the contract. If your business meets all the criteria and you are able to agree on a fair price, then your offer will most likely be accepted. If an offer is rejected, you can always request a meeting with the PCO to find out what went wrong and alter your offer if necessary.

2. MANAGING YOUR GSA SCHEDULE CONTRACT

If you have made it this far and been awarded a GSA Schedule contract, congratulations! You have taken a big step towards doing business with the federal government and put yourself in a position to start generating revenue for your business. Unfortunately, as we have mentioned before, simply having a GSA Schedule contract is no guarantee of business, and you need to be proactive in order to stay on the GSA Schedule.

Just to maintain your contract, you must do $25,000 in sales within the first two years of the contract and an additional $25,000 each remaining year. You must report all sales within 30 days of the end of each quarter and pay an Industrial Funding Fee **(IFF)** equal to 0.75% of all sales for each quarter. Additionally, you will be required to participate in Contractor Assistance Visits **(CAVs)** twice during the five-year contract period. During these visits, an Administrative Contracting Officer **(ACO)** will meet with you and key personnel from your company to help you understand your requirements as a contractor, and the ACO will provide a report card with feedback on your compliance.

> If you have not done so already, one of the first things you should do as a vendor is to register with the **Vendor Support Center (https://vsc.gsa.gov/sipuser/startup_kit.cfm)**. This is the same support center that provides the Vendor Toolbox mentioned earlier in the chapter. Through the Vendor Support Center, you can securely manage your contract online. You will use this service for everything from uploading price lists to reporting your quarterly sales, so you want to become very familiar with it.

3. MARKETING YOUR GSA SCHEDULE CONTRACT

Once you have made sure you are aware of all of the administrative steps required to maintain your GSA Schedule Contract, you need to know how to market your contract in order to begin selling your products and services. At the very minimum, you want to list your website on your pricing list, so

Chapter 10: General Services Administration (GSA) Schedules

potential buyers can quickly and easily learn more about your company and offerings. Similarly, you should add the GSA logo to your website, along with information about your contract offerings, so that anyone who visits your website will be aware of your GSA Schedule contract. These are both fairly small, but important steps. Do not overlook them! Below is a list of other considerations when marketing your business to the federal government.

Know Your Customer

It is important to be familiar with the current landscape and to know not only what current contracts are in place but also what new contracts will be coming in the near future. Every agency's Small and Disadvantaged Business Utilization **(SDBU)** program operates a webpage that posts this information for the public. This is a great place to start looking for potential customers and to get familiar with which agencies need the products and services that you sell. Another good place to look is **FedBizOpps (www.fbo.gov/),** an online listing of all solicitations sorted by agency. GSA sales opportunities are not specifically listed on FedBizOpps, but it is still a great place to get a feel for what kinds of opportunities are available.

> As of the writing of this book, FedBizOpps is still fully functional. In the near future, however, the website will be taken down and the functionality of FedBizOpps will be moved under the SAM website.

Teaming

Teaming up with other companies can be a very viable way to sell to the government. Larger companies with GSA Schedule contracts are required to subcontract a certain percentage of their work to small businesses. If you have a good relationship with a prime contractor, why not take advantage of that relationship and team up to fulfill a contract? You help them fulfill a contract requirement, and you gain another foothold in world of government contracting. It's a win-win situation for everyone involved.

If you do not have an existing relationship with a prime contractor, getting a foothold as a subcontractor can be difficult but not impossible. Procurement Technical Assistance Centers **(PTACs)** and Small Business Development Centers **(SBDCs)** are great resources for small business looking for subcontracting opportunities. Many larger companies also have small business outreach offices dedicated to fulfilling their subcontracting requirements, so getting to know key personnel in those offices can be a great way to start.

Teaming up with other small businesses can be mutually beneficial as well. If you become aware of an agency need that your business can only partially fulfill, then it can be helpful to find another small business with complementary products or services. Together, your companies can offer the full package. Even other small businesses that offer the same products or services as you can provide a great teaming opportunity, especially if they have a different designation (such as Woman-Owned or Veteran-Owned) than your company has. In this situation, your teamed companies will help fulfill a contract need and help the agency meet their small business set-aside quotas. It's another win-win combination.

> If you decide to go this route, know that you do not need to walk this path alone. Many companies specialize in this area of business and will, for a fee, help you get on a GSA Schedule. The process demands a lot of time and work so give serious thought to outsourcing some of this effort.

Chapter 10: General Services Administration (GSA) Schedules

> **Resources**
>
> Luckily, there are many resources available to help businesses market themselves to the government. The GSA sponsors **Schedules Contractor Success-Marketing Matters!**, a group that offers blogs, webinars, discussions and training opportunities for contractors trying to navigate the waters of GSA Schedules. This is a great place not only to start learning about what you can do to succeed as a contractor, but also to have your voice heard as a vendor.
>
> https://interact.gsa.gov/groups/contractor-success

Now you have learned about the GSA and the different types of schedules. You know how to select the right schedule for your company, to get on those schedules, and to manage and market your schedule. Some companies choose to steer clear of GSA Schedules entirely while others do a large portion of their business through the GSA Schedules. The choice will be entirely up to you.

CHAPTER 11: WRITING WHITE PAPERS

1. WHAT IS A WHITE PAPER?

To ensure ongoing growth in your business, you must continually work to influence customers to choose your company and its products or services, and "white papers" are a sales and marketing technique that you may find useful. A white paper is an authoritative report or guide that helps readers to understand an issue, solve a problem or make a decision. White papers originated as tools used by governments. These "political" white papers are often used to inform the public about a topic before introducing legislation about that issue.

In recent years, the term "white paper" has taken on a somewhat broader meaning and more commonly refers to a tool used by companies to garner new business. Instead of government-issued white papers informing the public about subjects, businesses write white papers as authoritative reports about new ideas for potential customers, such as government agencies, in order to gain a new source of business.

We have used this method numerous times throughout the years to great success. Similar to an unsolicited proposal, a white paper is a method used to gain business when there is no RFP asking for proposals. Perhaps you have a business idea, product, tool or even process that will help your customer, or prospective customer, do their job faster or more efficiently. Since there is no RFP, you can put together a white paper to inform the customer of your business idea and hopefully get them to fund your company to perform that work. Or, perhaps you have business ideas that are outside the scope of a current contract. You can use a white paper to present your ideas to your existing customer and "convince" them to expand the scope of the contract to include the business idea.

A successful white paper not only informs and influences an existing customer or prospective customer, it reinforces the customer's decision to choose your company to do the work — and not just pass your idea to another contractor. To be successful with a white paper, you need to **know your customer** and get the white paper into the hands of a government official who either is a decision maker or who can work with you to influence the decision makers to read your white paper and then act on your business idea — i.e., fund it and choose your company to do the work.

Sometimes you may already be connected with the appropriate government manager, and other times you will need to research and learn about a new customer and perhaps be introduced to the government customer by someone in your network (yet another reason you need an expanded network!). White papers are most successful when you truly understand the customer and what keeps them up at night — and when you can demonstrate that your new business idea can help them sleep better.

You should treat a white paper as seriously as you treat any other proposal. Before you begin, you need to outline the primary business idea, define and understand your target audience, and pull together the essential data of your plan. After you have done all the prep work, you can then draft a white paper that engages the target audience, and hopefully, compels the customer to fund your idea.

2. PREPARE YOUR MESSAGE BEFORE YOU WRITE

Before you write the white paper, think through what you are trying to accomplish. What *message do* you want to communicate?

Do you want to:

- Create awareness of a new industry standard or trend?
- Provide information to help differentiate your company from the competition?
- Introduce a different technical approach?
- Sell your customer on a new product or service?

Think through what you want your customer to do after they read your white paper.

Do you want your customer to:

- Grant you a sole source contract?
- Fund further study to take your business idea to the next level?
- Integrate your business ideas into an RFP?
- Invite you to brief their boss, the **real** decision maker?

Define Your Target Audience.

You need to understand your target audience and the different levels of decision makers that comprise it. You may have to brief multiple decision makers — at multiple management levels — before your idea gains traction. If so, you should plan on writing multiple white papers as you tailor the information for specific decision makers at each level.

Decide what technical information is needed in the white paper.

Your goals, target audience and message content will help define the level of technical detail included in the white paper. Lower level or technical managers may want lots of technical detail, whereas higher-level managers may want only "executive summary" type of detail. In the latter case, technical specifications can be included in an appendix (in case the higher-level manager wants to dig deeper and read that level of detail). As with any other written product, you should begin by assembling all the relevant data before you even think about writing. And after you gather all the data, first outline your white paper — then you can begin writing.

3. HERE IS A SAMPLE FLOW FOR A WHITE PAPER:

> **You can easily tailor the following to your needs:**
>
> **Title Page—Cover Page**
>
> **Table of Contents**
>
> **List of Figures**
>
> **List of Tables**
>
> **Executive Summary**
>
> **Background**
>
> **Issues and Trends** (discuss the broad issues and trends in the federal government (or industry) that will introduce the reader to the topic)
>
> **Features** (discuss the specific features of your proposed solution)
>
> **Problem Statement** (provide a carefully crafted statement of the customer's problem or issue)

Chapter 11: Writing White Papers

> **Relevant Technologies** (describe the relevant technologies you are introducing)
>
> **Approach** (describe how your approach, services, technology or solution works)
>
> **Method of Solving or Solution** (incorporate a discussion of your method of solving the customer problem)
>
> **Task to Be Accomplished** (list the tasks to be completed)
>
> **Resources or Level of Effort** (list the resources required or level of effort)
>
> **Deliverables** (list the deliverables)
>
> **Travel** (list proposed travel)
>
> **Contract Vehicle** (identify the contract vehicle you propose. New sole source? Existing contract vehicle with new scope?)
>
> **Examples of Similar Work Performed** (include examples of other related work that has been performed recently)
>
> **List the Benefits** (provide a list of benefits to the customer)
>
> **Return on Investment (ROI)** (state the ROI))
>
> **Case Studies** (include some case studies)
>
> **Summary** (add a summary that wraps up your proposed solution and clearly proves your position as the best, and perhaps only, contractor to hire)

4. THINGS TO AVOID:

- Complex sentences, bad writing, unclear concepts, typos and spelling mistakes
- Technical acronyms and difficult terminology
- Technically complex explanations or details

- Writing that reads like a how-to manual or a book

5. HELPFUL TIPS ON WRITING YOUR WHITE PAPER:

- Put your "bottom line" in the introduction.
- Be factual and do not include unsubstantiated boasting or irrelevant information.
- Orient your audience by describing the general nature and working environment of your product or technology. Start with the basics and expand from there.
- Be specific and avoid generalities.
- Differentiate your business solution from others.
- Provide credible, objective third-party evidence.
- Illustrate objects with pictures, graphs or tables.
- Use plain, simple language.
- Consider white papers as a form of publicity.
- Remember, a white paper is a tool in your capture efforts and should be used to enhance other sales messages.
- Always give a white paper the attention and thoughtfulness that you'd give to an RFP response.

6. REMEMBER NOT TO GIVE AWAY THE FARM

In white papers, you must walk a fine line between providing the customer with enough information to convince them that you can solve their problems and not giving them so much detailed information that they do not need your company to perform the work.

Chapter 11: Writing White Papers

One last important thing to keep in mind: *White papers have a habit of finding their way into the hands of your competition.* You must imprint every page of a white paper with all the relevant "company private" or "company proprietary" markings to help protect your business ideas. Even with those markings, white papers can be "circulated" and even posted to the web without your permission. It happens!

You can use a white paper to inform and influence existing customers or prospective customers. A few reminders:

- Know your customer.

- Put your bottom line in the introduction.

- Prepare your message before you even begin writing. Think about what you want your customer to do after they read your white paper. Be very clear and provide actionable steps the customer can take.

- Keep it concise yet complete—keep it simple, not complex.

- Protect your company's private or proprietary information. Appropriately mark every page as white papers tend to get passed around and are often not protected once given to a customer.

CHAPTER 12: TARGETING YOUR FIRST CONTRACT

In this chapter we will tie many previous chapter topics together with some key takeaways that have helped us over the years and have helped our clients focus on targeting their first contract.

> Whatever you are selling—services or products or both—it helps to *understand the customer* and why your service or product will *help them advance their mission, increase efficiency, or provide a new capability—and more!* Unless you offer a truly unique product or service, you are entering an already crowded market place, filled with existing companies that you must compete with and distinguish yourself from. You must work very hard to stand out from the crowd.

We encourage you to be *intentional* and *focused* on your efforts. So many times we see people who attend every marketing and networking event—bidders' conferences, symposiums, etc.—so they can "press the flesh" and distribute business cards, all with the goal of getting their company noticed. These efforts, however, can be a huge time and financial drain on the company, and they yield few results in terms of landing new contracts.

In order to avoid wasted time and expense, we prefer to sit down, face to face, with our new clients to talk about getting *intentional* and *focusing* their time and resources on certain areas that will help them advance and get their first contract. We cover this material throughout the rest of the book, but we think it is important to summarize a few key points here.

1. MEETING OUR NEW CLIENTS

When we sit down with a new client, we try to understand:

- The product(s) or service(s) they offer
- Their core capabilities
- Where they have worked before (which government agencies)
- What government clients *they know*
- What government clients *know them*
- What sets them apart from their competition
- Who are the owners and key management and what their experience is

In most cases, *the first contract is the hardest contract to win*, again, unless you have something really special to offer that is in high demand.

Oftentimes a new government contracting company is started by a person (or people) who became known as a *subject matter expert* (**SME** is a government contracting term—it is pronounced with a *long "E"*) at an agency and decided to break out on their own. This situation can be ideal because the contractor already knows the:

- Government client space
- Contracts in place
- Key government leadership
- Major prime contractors

Additionally, the person (or people) is usually familiar with most of the players and may have good, working relationships with key government officials and other contractors.

Chapter 12: Targeting Your First Contract

Other times a new contractor is not well known in an agency but has a core capability that would be helpful to the agency. In this scenario, the contractor must begin to make connections and build relationships in order to gain access to key agency personnel. It's a longer process than the one faced by a contractor who has a history with the agency, but it's still all about winning that first contract.

2. TARGET ONE AGENCY

> We recommend that you begin by *targeting only one agency* to get your company established and recognized by government and by other contractors in your industry. Additionally, while you could target a prime contract, we find that *the easiest way to get your first contract is by joining in as a subcontractor to a larger, established prime contractor.* Once you are established and have credentials (that is, experience and past performance), you will find it easier to target prime contracts.

Typically every government agency has a multi-year strategic plan and/or an acquisition strategy that outlines the major contracts in place and many of the major contracts anticipated in the next five or so years. You need to get your hands on those documents and read them, so you can build a capture plan (your list of contracts to track so you stay ahead of future acquisitions) to help you stay intentional and focused on your marketing.

Here are steps that you may find useful as you pursue your first contract. This list is not exhaustive or chronological. Consider the following:

- **Target an agency where you already have experience** and where the government personnel and key prime contractors know you and your core capabilities. It helps if you are well connected and if you are a SME.

- Learn all you can about the **acquisition strategy of your target agency**.

- Ascertain **what contracts are in place today** and **who the prime contractors are**.

- Determine who the **major subcontractors** are on those contracts.

- Identify the **planned pipeline of contracts** and who the likely prime contractors are for each contract.

- Evaluate **where your core competencies will best fit** in existing contracts and/or pipeline contracts.

- Assess **who your competitors are** and build a strategy to make your company more competitive, cheaper, more efficient, or whatever it takes to set you apart.

- We encourage new clients to figure out what the **key marketing (networking) meetings** are and to attend those (or get invited, even if you have to find someone in the know to get an invitation). We addressed networking in detail in **Chapter 6**. The principles apply here as well, and you may want to reread that chapter.

    o At these marketing meetings, key business developers attend and discuss upcoming contracts and teaming opportunities often well in advance of an RFI or RFP.

    o You need to be in the know, and you can glean a lot of good intelligence in these meetings. Be prepared to share your knowledge as well; the people at these

Chapter 12: Targeting Your First Contract

meetings will welcome you if you provide information and do not attend just to see what information you can obtain.

- o Get to know the stronger business development players on a first-name basis and make sure they know your name and what your company has to offer.

- **Develop your own capture plan** (your list of contracts to track so you stay ahead of future acquisitions) and begin marketing your capabilities early in the lifecycle of the contract (even before the RFI, draft RFP, final RFP).

- Observe which **existing contracts you could be added to right now** based upon your core competencies. Contact those prime contractors about your core capabilities and how your company can help them be more successful. Leverage your network and connections (contractors and government employees) to find that first contract—one that you could be added to, one that could use your services or products. Remember that networking is an ongoing process. It's complex and multifaceted. We can list what seem like simple, easy steps, but it is really not always that easy. Keep at it!

- If you know a government client that wants you personally and knows that you can provide a service or product that is in strong demand, then consider whether you should pursue a new **sole-source contract** or if it would be better to be added as a **directed subcontractor** to an existing contract held by another prime contractor. Sometimes the quickest way to get on contract is the directed subcontractor route, but if you can manage it,, a sole-source contract is always the preferred option. You have much more control over your destiny and your finances when you are the prime contractor rather than a subcontractor.

3. GET YOUR COMPANY SOME VISIBILITY

The best way to become and stay visible is to add value to your market niche in as many ways as possible. Finding, developing and delivering content is one of the best ways to do this. The more visible you are, the more likely buyers will know you and your company. Also, the more good content you develop, find and share, the more your value rises within your industry.

Make yourself "visible" in your industry in as many positive ways as possible. When a prime contractor looks for a core competency or a product, you want them to automatically think of you and your company. . These days, there are many ways to raise your business profile and make others aware of your core capabilities. For example:

- Create a website displaying your service offerings and/or products
- Connect through a LinkedIn company page
- Connect through a Facebook company page
- Write a blog
- Attend and/or host webinars
- Speak at key forums
- Take leadership roles in key forums
- Excel on your current contracts and let others know about your successes
- Ask your references to make introductions to others in their company or with other companies
- And the list is limited only by your imagination

Chapter 12: Targeting Your First Contract

> Given everything we have just said, networking—and success—almost always comes down to *relationships.* If people know (and like) you, they are more likely to buy from you or partner with you. Stay visible with your network and continue to build strong relationships.

4. TARGETING SPECIFIC RFIs and RFPs

Here is more good-to-know information when you are looking at specific RFIs and RFPs to pursue *(this is another topic we could write an entire book on).*

We have always said that if you wait until an RFP comes out, you will be behind the power curve, and your competition will be way ahead of you in preparing to respond to—and win—the RFP.

Given that truth, we include the following information for several reasons. The primary reason is because we have, on more than one occasion, guided a future business partner through the legal process of standing up their new company on paper, while they remained employed in their current company. These concurrent activities allow them to remain employed with benefits (assuming there are no non-compete issues with their current company) while we work with them to market their capabilities through the RFP process (either to be added to an existing contract or an upcoming contract award).

At times, especially if the RFP process is a long and drawn-out, the person must wait patiently in their current company as the business owner awaits authorization to proceed **(ATP)** with the new company. As we said, this dual work process pays off because it ensures the person receives a paycheck (and valuable benefits) while simultaneously working to launch a company.

> Sadly, we have known more than one entrepreneur who saved money and left a well-paying job with benefits to launch a company only to find that getting their first contract was not as easy as they thought. Unprepared, they closed down their new company or put it on hold while they returned working as an employee at an existing company. Meanwhile, they drained their savings.

Whether you are sitting tight in your old job as you start a new company or you have already broken off and started a company, you should review your customer's history with other contractors and look ahead at upcoming RFPs. Just like you have favorite contractors to repair your house, government agencies tend to have favorite contractors that have performed well for them in the past. Learn which contractors have solid relationships (and past performance) with the customer leadership.

> It is well known that, even in full and open competitions, contractors who enjoy well established relationships and past performance will fair much better than contractors who are new to the agency, have little-to-no past performance or lack established relationships with key leadership. Agencies tend to award where they believe they have the least risk, so they more often award to known contractors (teams) rather than new, unknown companies.

To succeed, you must truly know and understand your agency's mission and values. As you assess every RFI and RFP, consider the mission of the issuing agency and your company's core competencies. Assess how well you can apply your core

Chapter 12: Targeting Your First Contract

competencies to solving the requirements of the RFP. For example, your company is well known as a provider of top-notch administrative support to the agency, which has just issued an RFP seeking systems engineers. Although you are well known and possess positive credentials, you would have a hard time convincing any agency evaluation team that you have the past performance to win that particular RFP.

Evaluate your competitors by determining who might bid on the work and what their chances are of winning over your chances of winning. What do you offer that they do not have—and what do they offer that you do not have? Consider whether it makes more sense to team with those potential competitors, and what the probability of win (**Pwin**) becomes if you team—either with you as prime or you as a subcontractor to your potential competition. You may find that your Pwin is actually much higher when you team with your competition.

Analyze the contract history and determine if this new contract is a re-compete of an existing contract. If the current contactor (team) is performing well and getting high marks or high award fees, then they are going to be hard to unseat.

Determine your need for partners. Decide if you can perform the work alone or if you need one or more partners to help you meet the requirements of the RFP. Agencies typically like to see a depth of capability, not only in terms of technical depth, but also in staff depth.

> The government typically likes to see "reach back," that is, do you and your team members have the ability to reach back into your companies to provide extra resources and skills as the contract requirements change.

5. TARGET SET-ASIDE CONTRACTS

Look for set-aside contracts. If you have read through this book from the beginning, we assume you know whether or not you meet the requirements for set-asides as a woman-owned, HUBZone, service disabled Veteran owned business or an 8(a), etc. The Small Business Administration website (**www.sba.gov**) also has a good overview if you need a quick reminder. Agencies often set aside RFPs and the resulting contracts to help small businesses, so keep your eyes and ears open for small business set-asides that your company core competencies align with.

We have subscribed to *Set-Aside Alert* (**www.setasidealert.com**), an information service focused on federal government contracts for small businesses, minority-owned and women-owned businesses, veteran- and SDV-owned businesses, SBA 8(a)-certified companies and HUBzone businesses. They provide subscribers with a monthly listing of set-asides nationwide. They also publish up-to-date intelligence on upcoming opportunities, including agency annual forecasts; a calendar of events for upcoming meetings/symposiums; and lists of teaming opportunities, recent small business contract awards and certified small businesses.

6. COMMERCIAL COMPANIES WANTING TO TARGET GOVERNMENT CONTRACTS

If you are an existing company operating in the commercial market and want to expand into the government contracting market, you should consider reaching out and talking to our experts at **Capital Connections** (**www.CapitalConnectionsLLC.com**).

Chapter 12: Targeting Your First Contract

Capital Connections, or **Capcon,** was founded to help commercial companies get into the government contracting market. **CapCon** experts can help you develop and organize a strategy to get the word out about your company. They also can help you develop a marketing and capture plan to move forward. Specializing in helping companies with a solid presence in the commercial market, **CapCon** understands how to break into government contracting and which agencies offer entry to the government market. Whether the task is creating your initial foray into the federal government, strategizing a marketing plan, or referring a client to trusted partners, the Capital Connections team of experienced, dedicated and committed professionals is prepared to work with you, regardless of your prior government contracting experience.

> Once you have targeted and won your first contract, there is still a lot to know and learn about managing your contract, people and resources. The next few chapters focus on helping you understand several key topics as you go about managing your contracts, hiring new employees or consultants, and protecting your company's intellectual property.

CHAPTER 13: CONTRACT RESPONSIBILITIES

Congratulations, your hard work paid off! You persevered to stand up your company, filed the appropriate small business certifications, developed marketing materials, networked your company core competencies, responded to a request for proposal **(RFP)** with a very detailed and time-consuming proposal, and you are about to be awarded a contract or subcontract.

Now what?

1. READ AND UNDERSTAND THE CONTRACT BEFORE YOU SIGN IT

This point is extremely important, so we will repeat it again: The very first thing you must do is *read* and *understand* the contract before you sign it. When you receive the contract, you may be surprised (perhaps even shocked) at the large size of the actual contract document. That is because government contracts are loaded with pages and pages of boilerplate terms and conditions **(T&C)** that, quite honestly, you probably will not initially understand unless you have done this kind of work before.

After you read and understand the contract, you will discover that many of the T&Cs appear in each and every contract, so the learning curve decreases a bit with each contract you read. Some of the terms and conditions change a little every now and then, but in general, the identical terms and conditions accompany every contract.

2. IF YOU ARE NEW TO GOVERNMENT CONTRACTING, GET HELP!

If you need help in understanding contract terms and conditions, you have many options. You can:

- Pay a lawyer who knows government contracting and the FAR and who has experience in the government-contracting arena to help you.

- Talk to your peers and mentors and ask them to help you. If they have worked in government contracting for years, then they can help you understand what you are committing to.

- Contact **ConnekServ** for help! Check out **www.ConnekServ.com** and get guidance from contract experts. Our experts can help you with end-to-end contract support, including:

    o **Contracts Formation.** Review and comment on contract T&Cs; negotiate contract provisions; define your contract risk mitigation strategies and explain contract obligations relative to the T&Cs.

    o **Policies and Procedures.** Help draft company policies and procedures to ensure compliance with U.S. law and the various statutes and regulations regarding doing business with state and federal government. Examples include timekeeping policies and procedures; organizational conflict of interest mitigation plans; and company confidentiality policies and the like.

    o **Pricing Support.** Pricing templates for all contract types including tailoring for specific procurements. Proposal pricing, strategy support and proposal volume and sealed package preparation.

Chapter 13: Contract Responsibilities

- **Contracts Administration.** Maintain your contract files. Review, comment on and maintain contract modifications; and write, negotiate and maintain subcontract agreements.

- **Closeout.** All non-accounting facets pertaining to closeout of commercial and U.S. Government contracts. Efforts include property closeout sweeps and certification; preparation of release and assignment documentation; labor hour certification for level of effort contracts; and the like. Interface with client's customer closeout personnel to achieve final closeout status.

You really have many options, and you can choose to handle all the contract work in-house or to outsource some or all of it. You can also hire a consultant, like **ConnekServ**, to help you get off the ground, set up your files and even schedule audits to ensure you properly maintain everything.

---

3. GENERAL INFORMATION ABOUT CONTRACT RESPONSIBILITIES

Government Contracting Officers

The government conducts business through authorized agents known as contracting officers **(COs).** Unless you are otherwise advised in writing, *only a CO has authority to bind the government.* We emphasize this authority because you may find yourself in a position where your government technical counterpart (often called contracting officer's technical representative (**COTR**, pronounced Co-Tar [long "O"]), gives what you perceive as "direction" that is counter to your signed contract or outside the scope of your signed contract. You must not—you cannot—take action on the direction without first obtaining approval from the

CO. In most cases, the COTR's job is to direct the work of the technical personnel, and that direction must be in line with and within scope of the signed contract. The key is to fully understand your contract obligations, and when in doubt, meet with your CO to discuss where you are being "redirected."

> **COTRs** and contracting officer's representatives **(CORs)** hold unique and important positions in government contracting. They are designated by the contracting officer to assist in administering specific aspects of a contract. COTRs and CORs typically have initial and most continuous contact with the contractor, and they are the liaisons between the contractor and the contracting officer. Contracting officers rely on the expertise and background of COTRs and CORs to ensure that the technical and financial aspects of the contract are accomplished.

Even contracting officers have limits on their authority; so do not hesitate to make sure of the authority of the person with whom you are dealing.

What can you expect to be included in your contract?

- First, you will find the name of the office that will administer your contract (in most federal agencies, this is usually the same office that awarded the contract). In the Department of Defense, the contract is most often assigned to a special administering office, and the contract will list the address and contact information. If you have any questions about the contract, contact the office of administration at the phone number provided in the contract.

Chapter 13: Contract Responsibilities

- The contract includes all the boilerplate material we mentioned above. It contains, or makes reference to, many general contract provisions unique to the government. These provisions implement various statutory or regulatory requirements that are applicable solely to federal contracts.

- You'll also find ***termination for default and termination for convenience clauses.*** Government contracts provide that the government may cancel (terminate) your contract if you fail to:

    o Make delivery within the time specified in the contract

    o Make progress so as to endanger performance of the contract

    o Perform any provisions of the contract

Some Key Points On Termination:

- Before terminating your contract for default, the CO must give you an opportunity to remedy the defects in your performance.

- If your contract is terminated for default, you are entitled ***only*** to payment at the contract's price for items accepted by the government. If the government still needs the items that you failed to deliver, it has the right to procure the same items elsewhere and, if they cost more, charge the excess costs to you.

- If you can show that your failure to deliver or to make progress is excusable, your contract may not be terminated for default. To be excusable, however, any delay must be beyond your control and not caused by your fault or negligence. If your contract is terminated for default and you can prove that the government's action was improper, the termination may still be treated as one for the "convenience of the government."

- The government may choose to unilaterally terminate all or part of a contract for its convenience. Termination for convenience does not arise from any fault on the part of the contractor but protects the government's interests by allowing it to cancel contracts for products that become obsolete or unnecessary.

- The government must give you written notice of termination for convenience but is not required to give advance notice. The notice of termination will usually direct you to stop work, terminate subcontracts, place no further orders, communicate similar instructions to subcontractors and suppliers, and prepare a termination settlement claim. If you fail to follow those directions, you do so at your own risk and expense.

- After termination for convenience, the government will eventually make a settlement with you to compensate you fully and fairly for the work you have done. A reasonable allowance for profit is also usually included.

Contract Changes

Because the government's needs change over time, government contracts contain a clause authorizing the CO to unilaterally order changes in the specifications and other contract terms. The changes must be "within the general scope of the contract." The contractor is obliged to perform the contract as unilaterally changed by the CO. A change is considered within the scope of the contract if it can be regarded as within the contemplation of the parties at the time the contract was entered into. The government cannot use a change order to change the general nature of the contract. As the contractor, you will be entitled to an equitable adjustment in price and delivery schedule if changes are ordered.

Chapter 13: Contract Responsibilities

Payments

The government is generally obligated to make prompt payments for products delivered or services rendered. Prompt payment is important to the small business since cash flow is critical in day-to-day operations and to the survival of the small business. Your contract will specify the government office responsible for payment and will contain invoicing instructions. The more accurate your invoices, the more quickly you will be paid, so it is important to thoroughly understand the payment process. Prompt payment on all contracts serves the best interest of both the contractor and the government. Under certain circumstances, if the government does not pay promptly, you can submit a request for interest payments.

When you work *fixed-price contracts*, the method of payment can vary with the dollar value of the contract. For relatively small contracts with a single item of work, you will generally be paid the total contract price in one lump sum. Payment is made after the government accepts delivery. For larger contracts with many items, you can invoice and receive partial payments. Larger fixed-price contracts and subcontracts, where the first delivery is several months after award, may contain a clause permitting you to receive progress payments based upon costs you incur as work progresses toward the end product.

> Because progress payments are based on work that is not completed, *you will be expected to repay the government if you fail to complete the work*. Keep in mind that to qualify for progress payments, you must have an accounting system that can accurately identify and segregate contract costs.

Specifications

Specifications describe the government's requirements and are contained in the invitation for bids or RFPs on which you based your bid or proposal. The federal government has very detailed specifications for most of the products and services it buys on a regular basis.

Once an award is made to your company, you are contractually bound to deliver the product or service described in the specifications. Sometimes, the basic specifications will make reference to and incorporate other federal government specifications. You are bound by the terms of these specifications as well as the basic specifications. Failure to deliver a product that meets these terms may result in termination of your contract by default.

> You should never bid on a contract unless you have read and understood all the specifications. Also, you should read the specifications again before you start work under the contract.

Inspection and Testing

Government contracts provide that the government may inspect and test the items you deliver to determine if they conform to contract requirements and specifications. The government will not accept a contractor's product unless it passes inspection. The type and extent of inspection and testing depend largely on what is being procured.

Chapter 13: Contract Responsibilities

The Federal Acquisition Regulations (FAR)

All of the matters we discussed in this chapter are described in various parts of the FAR, which is the essential reference for all government contractors.

Disputes

Disputes between you and the CO may occur. Federal contracts contain a clause setting forth procedures to resolve disputes. If the CO issues a decision that is not satisfactory to you, you must make a timely appeal to the Board of Contracts Appeal or the decision becomes final.

CHAPTER 14: TIME AND LABOR CHARGING

Time and labor charging is such a significant topic that we dedicated an entire chapter to it. Improper time charging can literally kill your company, so you and your employees must understand the importance and procedures of proper time and labor charging. It is also a matter of ethics and company reputation.

As owner, you must set policy standards for time and labor charging and annually remind and retrain your employees on the importance of proper time and labor charging practices. Establish, publish and brief your employees on company values and standards of business conduct, and then maintain a monitoring effort to ensure your employees follow those policies—*daily*. On any program, commercial or government, misuse of time is as wrong as misuse of any of the company's physical assets or resources.

When working on government contracts, correct time charging is the basic element of compliance and a legal, as well as an ethical, responsibility. Accurate time charging establishes a record of the effort necessary to accomplish a task or process. Such a record helps determine not only how employees are paid and customers are billed, but also how contract costs are allocated, costs are estimated for bids on new work, and financial and operational performance is ultimately reported.

1. TIME CHARGING SYSTEMS

You have many options to choose from when selecting a time charging system. Some companies still use paper timecards to track their time, while others have gone to online time charging systems that integrates with their accounting software.

Here is a short list of some systems used by our companies and peers. We do not necessarily recommend these systems, but rather, we offer them as examples of systems that might work for your unique needs.

Unanet Technologies (www.unanet) is a resource management system that helps organizations reliably plan, track and manage people and projects. Unanet provides resource planning, resource management, project management, timesheet management, expense report management, project accounting, billing and workforce collaboration. Their products are available as an Enterprise license (self-hosted) or a cloud-based license.

Replicon (www.Replicon.com) is a cloud-based timesheet system. The default software package includes a Defense Contract Audit Agency **(DCAA)** module that you can enable.

Procas (www.Procas.com) is another popular project accounting and web-based timesheet software tool that many chose to use. It also is DCAA compliant.

Deltek GCS Premier (**www.Deltek.com**) develops software for use by companies that are project focused, such as government contractors (who must, under U.S. government procurement law, track costs by individual contract, and in some cases, by task order or line item). As they grow and can afford the purchase, many companies switch to Deltek software to meet project accounting and web-based timesheet needs. The software also supports DCAA compliance.

Some companies opt out of ready-to-use software and prefer to design and develop their own time-tracking tools. They customize the tools and processes to match their specific needs, and they maintain those systems in-house.

Chapter 14: Time and Labor Charging

Regardless of which system you choose to implement, each employee is responsible for correctly recording time worked and you (or their supervisor) are responsible for overseeing the process and approving the accuracy of the record.

2. EMPLOYEE RESPONSIBILITIES

The primary responsibility for accurately recording time belongs to each individual employee. Each employee responsibility must ensure that their time is recorded correctly and reflects proper labor charges, vacation hours, absent time and any other appropriate adjustments. When employees sign their timesheets each week or report their time electronically, they certify that it accurately reflects how their time was actually spent during that work period. Your reputation, as well as the company's reputation (and future existence), is on the line with every timesheet. All employees should:

- Record their time after it has been worked *every* day.
- Be accurate and precise in charging what they are working on.
- Know where to find documents that authorize their charge numbers (if your company is audited, an auditor may ask employees this type of question).
- Follow procedures for completing timekeeping records and correcting errors.
- Sign their card by hand or use their electronic signature.

You should document policies for your employees to follow, and they should know which manager to ask for clarification or direction.

3. MANAGER RESPONSIBILITIES

Your managers share responsibility with employees for ensuring the accuracy of timekeeping. Specifically, your managers should:

- Regularly review and approve the time-charging records of their employees.
- Ensure that all employees under their supervision, especially new employees, know their correct classification as exempt, non-exempt or hourly and the corresponding differences in reporting.
- Maintain a workplace environment that encourages ethical behavior and makes employees feel free to ask questions if they are not sure about their time-charging requirements.

4. TIMESHEET IRREGULARITIES

Timesheet irregularities generally fall into two categories, namely, falsification and mischarging.

Timesheet Falsification. Timesheet falsification occurs when an individual employee knowingly misrepresents time worked for some personal gain. This could take the form of:

- Falsifying the record of hours worked.
- Improperly using and recording paid benefits (vacation, personal, sick time, etc.).
- Misrepresenting true attendance.

Mischarging. Timesheet mischarging occurs when the proper number of hours may be worked but they are knowingly not charged to the correct contract/charge number. Mischarging can be the act of one or more employees. Mischarging can take the form of:

- A supervisor directing an employee to charge hours to the wrong account. (The employee may or may not be aware it is the wrong account).

Chapter 14: Time and Labor Charging

- Charging labor for an overrun on a fixed-price contract to a cost-plus contract.

- Splitting costs between a number of contracts or accounts without being able to verify the actual time spent on each contract or account.

- Charging a single job when multiple jobs have been worked.

- Charging overhead activity (training, downtime) to a contract or vice versa.

It is important to emphasize that timesheet falsification or mischarging can have a serious impact on your job and career as well as a significant impact on your company.

Accurate time charging depends on *your entire team knowing the policies you have established*, and ensuring that employees and supervisors can affirmatively answer these questions:

- Do the employees know how to complete their timesheet or make an electronic entry accurately?

- Do the employees know the correct charge numbers for the projects assigned to them?

- Do the employees know whom to ask if they have questions about completing their timesheet?

- Do the employees know with whom to speak if they suspect mischarging or timesheet falsification, or if they are directed to incorrectly charge time?

- Do the employees know the rules regarding to compensatory time and how to record it?

5. IMPORTANT TERMS

Total Time Accounting. Means just what it sounds like, accurately recording *all* of the time you work.

Exempt Timesheet. For salaried (exempt) employees. Exempt labor is professional, executive, and certain administrative staff who are paid on a salaried basis with normal scheduled works weeks. They are not eligible for overtime pay and may work uncompensated overtime.

Non-Exempt Timesheet. For hourly (non-exempt) employees. Personnel who do not meet the Department of Labor definitions of exempt labor, are paid on an hourly basis and are paid overtime pay for work in excess of 8 hours in a day or 40 hours in a week.

Dummy Timesheet. This is used when the employee, for whatever reason, is not available to complete the timesheet. With web-based systems, this should be very rarely used or needed.

Correcting Timesheet. Just what it sound like, this is used to correct an incorrectly submitted timesheet. Typos happen, and people can get rushed and make simple mistakes. Sometimes the employee will catch his or her mistake after submitting a timesheet, and other times the manager will notice the mistake and have the employee submit a correcting timesheet. Any corrections to timesheets should be made promptly, checked for accuracy and approved by a manager.

Direct. This is the time worked that you charge directly to a billable contract.

Indirect. This is for (non-direct) time spent on independent research and development, bid and proposal, marketing,

Chapter 14: Time and Labor Charging

management, administration, fringe, unallowable, and other work that is not directly tied to a specific contract.

Unallowable. Time spent on activities that are not reimbursable by the federal government under its contracts, either as a direct or indirect cost. This could include things like, acquisition of companies, lobbying, public relations, certain trade shows, etc.

B&P. Bid and proposal

Uncompensated Time. Exempt employees are paid a standard weekly salary and are not paid for hours worked beyond the standard work-week, usually 40 hours. Uncompensated time, then, includes those hours worked by exempt employees outside their standard work-week.

Key Conclusions about Time and Labor Charging

- Accurate time charging is an important ethical and legal matter; time spent on a task must be charged to that task.
- Time records must be maintained daily.
- Employees legally certify the accuracy of their timesheets when they sign and submit the timesheets.
- Corrections to the timesheets must be prompt, correct and provide accurate documentation explaining the need for the correction.
- Distinctions between categories of labor are important
- Ask for help when you are in doubt
- Ensure you have documented, publicized policies and your employees know where the policies are and what the policies require.

CHAPTER 15: DEFENSE CONTRACT AUDIT AGENCY

According to their website, **www.dcaa.mil**, "The Defense Contract Audit Agency (**DCAA**) provides audit and financial advisory services to Department of Defense **(DOD)** and other federal entities responsible for acquisition and contract administration. DCAA operates under the authority, direction and control of the Under Secretary of Defense (Comptroller)/Chief Financial Officer."

Why is this important and what does it mean to government contractors? For starters, the DCAA is tasked with performing all necessary contract audits for the DOD.

> As a government contractor, you will be subject to audits by the DCAA at virtually any time. You must be prepared for the audit *before* it occurs.

If you are not prepared for such an audit, it can be a major headache for you and your company — and this is one headache you do not want. The best thing to do is get prepared and stay prepared. While most people fear being audited, you can be prepared for audits by reviewing the information in this section and at the DCAA website, and by having an expert on your team who can guide you through the process of getting and staying prepared.

> Our experts at **ConnekServ** can help your organization put the right processes, policies and training in place to make audits less stressful and more successful. If you are a new start, they can help you map out a plan to be audit-ready. If you have already stood up your company, they can evaluate your processes, policies and training material to assess your audit-readiness. The **ConnekServ** team will also work with you to eliminate any deficiencies that would prevent you from successfully surviving an audit by the DCAA.

1. PURPOSE OF THE DCAA

The most basic purpose of the DCAA is to ensure that a contractor's systems and organizational requirements are in compliance with the Federal Acquisition Regulations **(FAR)**. Audits can occur at different times, either pre-award or post-award, and may come in variety of forms, including:

Pre-award Contract Audit Services

- Pre-award Accounting System Surveys
- Contract Price Proposals
- Forward Pricing Rate Proposals

Post-award Contract Audit Services

- Incurred Costs/Annual Overhead Rates
- Cost Accounting Standards **(CAS)** Compliance and Adequacy
- Claims

Chapter 15: Defense Contract Audit Agency

Business System Audits

- Accounting and Billing
- Estimating
- Material Management

Negotiation Assistance

- Fact-finding and analysis of contractor information after audit report is issued
- Attending negotiations to support contracting officer

DCAA will audit your company to ensure that its systems and organizational requirements are in compliance with the FAR.

The DCAA focuses on the timekeeping and accounting systems a company uses while on contract.

Labor is often the largest cost component of a contract, as well as one of the easiest components to manipulate, so timekeeping is often the highest priority when the DCAA performs an audit.

See **Chapter 14** for more detailed information on timekeeping.

---

2. AUDIT PROCESS OVERVIEW FOR CONTRACTORS

DCAA offers a helpful website that provides an overview of the types of their audits with links to checklists and an explanation of what to expect in an audit. The website can be found at:

www.dcaa.mil

DCAA also established a ***small business focal point,*** which can be reached by phone at 937-255-7789 or by email at *DCAA-OAL-SmallBusinessFocalPoint@dcaa.mil*. The DCAA website offers information to help with audit issues that specifically relate to small businesses. From the link above you can learn about:

- Accounting system requirements
- Contract briefs
- Incurred cost submissions
- Real-time labor evaluations
- Monitoring subcontracts
- Provisional billing rates
- Public vouchers

3. BE AUDIT READY

If you plan up front and put the tools in place to correctly segregate and account for your work, you are a long way toward that goal of being audit-ready.

In addition to **ConnekServ**, there are other consultants and dozens of courses available to help further understand DCAA requirements and prepare for an audit.

> *It is well worth the effort and expense to understand DCAA requirements because the agency no longer offers a partial passing grade; you either pass an audit, or you fail it.* If you fail an audit, payments can be withheld until you pass, and the cash flow delay can easily wipe out your company.

How to Become Audit Ready. You must have three main components to your DCAA strategy: *Process, Policies and Training*:

Chapter 15: Defense Contract Audit Agency

1. The Process. You must define your process, which in itself should include many DCAA audit-required components, such as creating a chart of accounts and segregating your *indirect, direct and unallowable costs*. DCAA auditors want to see how you categorize and define your labor costs. You need to create pools of direct and indirect costs.

   a. Indirect Costs. Examples of indirect costs include accounting, billing, payroll and other human resource activities.

   b. Direct Costs. Direct costs are usually clear-cut and include activities immediately related to the contract work, like a machine operator or engineer. You need reports that show indirect and direct labor costs, per contract, and you should have immediate access to such reports.

   c. Unallowable Costs. Examples of unallowable costs are entertainment costs and some advertising costs. Also, travel costs that exceed the lowest available coach fares are not allowed unless they are approved by the contracting agency.

2. The Policies. You need to establish policies to make your processes accurate and accountable, and you should have a DCAA-approved timekeeping system to manage your projects. Your policies should include language that clearly articulates the *employees' responsibility to completely and accurately fill out their timesheets*. DCAA also requires *daily time entry* by the employee along with sign off and approval of that time by a supervisor. Additionally, you must make sure your policies outline clear disciplinary action for employees who fail to comply with your policies.

3. Training. You should provide new-hire training and annual review training on your policies to all employees, so employees have no excuse for being unaware of and complying with company policies. Train your employees to enter work time on a daily basis, not at the end of the week or a later date. Supervisors should be trained on the proper process for approving timesheets. Your training should include requirements for notes and documentations when employees change their timesheet entries.

> **Chances are you will be audited some day. You need to be prepared from day one by putting in place the right processes, policies and training program. Here is a sample checklist (overly simplified, but good for our purposes) to evaluate your DCAA compliance level:**
>
> - Have you put policies in place to make your processes accurate and accountable?
> - Does your written policy include language that instructs employees to completely and accurately fill out their timesheets?
> - Have you created a chart of accounts to segregate indirect, direct and unallowable costs?
> - Have you categorized and defined your labor costs?
> - Do you have immediate access to your cost reports?
> - Did you put an employee timekeeping system in place?
> - Do you require daily timesheet entry by employees?
> - Do your supervisors sign off and approve timesheets?
> - Do your policies provide clear disciplinary steps to follow for failure to comply?

CHAPTER 16: HIRING

You are ready to hire new employees and grow your company, and you want to hire great employees, who will help your business grow, keep your customers satisfied, and love your company so much that they cannot imagine working anywhere else.

> Before you can hire those great employees, you need to think through the entire hiring process and follow some preliminary steps to be prepared to successfully begin hiring. This chapter will help you evaluate options and get organized, so you will be ready to hire and maintain new employees.

1. **Getting Organized to Hire**
2. **Evaluating Independent Contractors Versus Employees**
3. **Finding Good Candidates**
4. **Interviewing Candidates**
5. **Checking Out Candidates**
6. **Hiring New Employees**
7. **Taking Care of Your New Employees**

1. GETTING ORGANIZED TO HIRE

The first thing you need to do in getting organized is to understand the responsibilities of an employer. There are many compliance issues and employment laws to keep in mind. We'll go over some of these, but like we often do in this book, we recommend you consider hiring experts who specialize in compliance, employment laws and benefits to make sure you get your hiring practices off to a good (and compliant) start.

Some first steps (some of the next few paragraphs were borrowed liberally from the SBA.gov site on hiring):

www.sba.gov/category/navigation-structure/starting-managing-business/starting-business/establishing-business/hiring

A. Obtain Your Employer Identification Number (EIN). Before hiring any employees, you need an EIN from the Internal Revenue Service **(IRS).** If you have followed the steps from this book from the beginning, then you have already completed this step. If not, check out the steps in **Chapter 1, Section 9**.

B. Check Whether You Need State/Local IDs. Some state or local governments require separate ID numbers in order to process taxes. Check with your state and local governments to see if this is required in your area.

C. Set up Records for Withholding Taxes. As an employer, you will be required to keep records of employment taxes on file (as of the date of this publishing, the IRS requires four years of records).

Three types of *withholding taxes* you need to know about and keep records of include:

> **Federal Income Tax Withholding (Form W-4).** Every employee must provide an employer with a signed withholding exemption certificate (Form W-4) on or before the date of employment. Employers must then submit Form W-4 to the IRS. Forms can be downloaded from the IRS website.
>
> **Federal Wage and Tax Statement (Form W-2).** On an annual basis, you must report to the federal government

wages paid and taxes withheld for each employee. This report is filed using Form W-2 Wage and Tax Statement.

State Taxes. Depending on the state where your employees are located, you may be required to withhold state income taxes. Visit your state and local tax websites for more information.

D. Register for Unemployment Insurance Tax. Some businesses with employees are required to pay unemployment insurance taxes under certain conditions. It is a good idea to know what your responsibility is in paying these taxes before looking into hiring your first employee.

E. Post Required Notices. You are required by state and federal laws to prominently display certain posters in the workplace that inform your employees of their rights and your responsibilities under labor laws. You can get these posters for free from federal and state labor agencies.

2. EVALUATING INDEPENDENT CONTRACTORS VERSES EMPLOYEES

Will you hire employees or independent contractors **(ICs)**? As many companies grow, they hire a mix of employees and ICs. However, in the early phases, many companies hire only employees or ICs. While most of this chapter focuses primarily on hiring and managing employees, we wanted to give you a brief overview of ICs and remind you that they may be a great option for you to consider.

The distinction between employees and ICs is important because it affects how you withhold income taxes, withhold and pay Social Security and Medicare taxes, and pay unemployment taxes. Misclassification of an individual may result in a number of costly legal consequences, so let's look at ICs and employees more closely:

An IC:

- Operates under a business name
- Hires their own employees
- Maintains a separate business checking account
- Advertises their business services
- Invoices for work done
- May have more than one client
- Possesses personal tools and schedules own hours
- Keeps their own business records

Many small businesses rely on independent contractors for their staffing needs. Benefits of hiring ICs include savings in labor costs, reduced liability, and flexibility in hiring and firing. It is often easier to hire an IC than to hire an employee, especially when the work is temporary or sporadic. Rather than carry an employee on overhead when work requirements run low, you can fill your gaps with ICs and terminate their services as the work tapers off.

Check out the **IRS website** to learn more about how to tell the difference between an IC and an employee for federal tax purposes.

www.irs.gov/Businesses/Small-Businesses-&-Self-Employed/

Hiring an Independent Contractor

We hire ICs all the time, and we use a basic Independent Contractor Agreement (some call it simply a Services Agreement) that outlines the terms of the business arrangement we are seeking. Our agreement opens with a paragraph summarizing the "effective date" and states that the agreement is between our company and the IC supporting us. This paragraph is followed by paragraphs describing things like:

Chapter 16: Hiring

- *Scope of Work* to be performed.
- *Compensation* terms (describe whether this is a retainer, time and materials **(T&M)**, or fixed price).
- *Expense Reimbursement* terms of the agreement (details what is and what is not a reimbursable expense).
- *Non-Disclosure* (this non-disclosure requirement protects us and ensures that our confidential company information will be protected by the IC).
- *Representations and Warranties* of the agreement.
- *Limitation of Liability* for each party.
- *Non-Solicitation* (mutual agreement paragraph that each side will not recruit the workers of the other company).
- *Term of the Agreement and Termination Clauses.*
- *Task Order* (we may have one or more task orders with the same IC, so we often get a basic agreement in place and then assign work via a task order).

The agreement needs to be signed by the IC and a representative from your company, who is authorized to obligate the company with such an agreement.

> You can download sample IC agreements by doing a simple web search.

3. FINDING GOOD CANDIDATES

When you first start out and cannot afford to hire a recruiter, you still have many options available to help find great candidates for your company openings. We use some of the following options:

Your Network

When you are the only employee in the company, you will probably do what most small businesses do—use your network to find good candidates. Networking actually works no matter how large your company grows, but it is particularly effective when you're starting out. We use email to get out the word when we have openings, and we use LinkedIn and other networking sources to post our job opening descriptions. In some cases, we also post job openings on our websites. We find that friends often send us resumes or contact information of potential candidates. We will often call our friends in business and ask them for by-name referrals. When we make these calls, we do not focus solely on people who are currently looking for a job. Instead, we ask our friends for the names of candidates who have the requisite skills and who they would personally recommend. This approach has proved very effective for our companies.

Referrals from Your Employees

As we grow and hire employees, we rely on current employees to help us find new candidates. We share job opening descriptions with employees and ask them the same questions that we ask our business friends: Do you know someone with the requisite skills? Who would you recommend we pursue? Some companies make it clear that scouting and recommending new hires is part of every employee's job responsibilities. We actually go one step further: We expect current employees to help us find great new hires, but we also pay a referral fee for each new candidate we hire that an employee first referred to us. We maintain a database of all incoming resumes because we never know when we may have a need for the candidate's skills. And as mentioned above, *we do not focus only on candidates that are looking for a job. We routinely go after people who are happily employed somewhere else. It does not hurt to ask them if they are open to consider a new option.*

Chapter 16: Hiring

> ### More on Referral Fees
>
> While we have a standing referral fee amount set for each of our companies, we sometimes raise our referral fee amount depending on the urgency of filling the position. We also offer higher referral fees to employees when they help us fill positions that require a candidate with skills that are unique or hard to find, or if the position requires special clearances (such as a Secret, Top Secret, or Top Secret with a polygraph).
>
> ### Referral Fees Are a Form of Bonus
>
> We typically pay referral fees 90 days after a new candidate has been employed with the company. That 90-day period allows time for the employee not only to begin working for our company but also to begin generating revenue for it—before the referral fee is paid. Other companies opt to pay referral fees as part of an annual bonus arrangement. Of course, you should determine a timeline for payout that works for your company and cash flow situation.

Resume Job Boards

You can subscribe to one or more resume job boards, so you can compare your job opening to available resumes. The resume job boards are all very easy to use, allowing you to set up search filters based on key words, location, salary, type of clearance, etc. For example, if you are looking for candidates to fill a position that requires a specific certification and a full polygraph to work onsite in Reston, VA, you can set the criteria to filter out any candidates that do not meet the requirements.

The job board will then provide a list of candidates who meet those requirements. We typically set our resume job board filter criteria to look for candidates within a 30-mile radius of the work location. If we do not get enough potential candidates from the search, we open the filter to 50 or more miles. You can try out different job boards by paying an annual fee, and then you can renew—or not—based on your success with each resume job board.

> **Here are some resume job boards we recommend:**
>
> **ClearedJobs: www.ClearedJobs.net**
>
> **Monster: www.Monster.com**
>
> **Career Builder: www.CareerBuilder.com**
>
> **Recruit Military: www.RecruitMilitary.com**

Besides being very easy to use, some resume job boards allow you to post a limited number of job openings (usually three or four) for free as part of your annual fee. You can also pay a fee to post additional job postings beyond your baseline annual agreement. You should get to know the people who run the resume job board and establish a point of contact with them. They can help you get the most out of the service, and some will also work with you on the price, especially if you are a repeat customer year after year.

There are many different resume job boards, and you can do a web search and find them all. It pays to search out, compare and understand their different offerings before signing up.

Chapter 16: Hiring

4. INTERVIEWING YOUR CANDIDATES

In the early stages of your business, your employees may come from a pool of people that you already know or have worked with in previous jobs. As the business grows, it will become necessary to reach beyond this comfort zone and consider candidates that you may have never met or even heard of. As this happens, you need to become comfortable with — in fact, you need to become skilled in — the process of interviewing candidates. If interviewing job prospects begins to interfere with your other primary responsibilities, you will need to engage a hiring manager — someone who will be able to find the best candidates to join your business team.

Regardless of who conducts the interviews, you must be aware of two fundamental areas of concern. First, you must know your legal responsibilities as an interviewer. It is essential that you know exactly what questions you legally can and cannot ask candidates, otherwise you could end up in the uncomfortable situation of dealing with a lawsuit. The list of taboo subjects includes everything from the candidate's age to family life to nationality, and we will discuss these in more detail.

Second, once you are familiar with the legalities of what you can and cannot ask, it is imperative to know the best interviewing practices to generate the information you need to make an informed hiring decision. This affects how you prepare for an interview, what kinds of questions you ask during it and how you evaluate candidates both during and after the interview. Let's begin by looking at some of the legal do's and don'ts of interviewing candidates.

A. Legal Do's and Don'ts

According to the Equal Employment Opportunity Commission **(EEOC)**, it is illegal to discriminate against a job applicant due to their race, color, religion, sex (including pregnancy), national origin, age (over 40), disability or genetic information. While asking specific questions related to these topics is not always explicitly illegal, they are best avoided as asking them opens you up to allegations of discrimination based upon answers given, or not given, by candidates.

> The best rule of thumb to follow when interviewing candidates is to stick to questions that relate directly to job performance and to avoid personal questions. Here are some examples of questions that you should not ask and also some suggestions of questions you can ask to obtain similar, pertinent information.

Race and National Origin

Don't ask questions that require candidates to divulge information about their national origin. This includes asking whether they are U.S. citizens, what their native language is, or how long they have lived at their current residence. Instead, ask questions that relate directly to their ability to perform the job.

Do: You can ask if a candidate is authorized to work in the United States. If it is applicable to job performance, you can ask what languages the candidate is fluent in. Regarding residency, only ask questions about their current situation, such as their current address and if they are willing to relocate.

Religion

Don't directly ask candidates what their religion is, what holidays they observe, or what clubs/social organizations they belong to.

Chapter 16: Hiring

> **Do:** One reasonable concern that relates to religion is that it can affect the schedule an employee will be able to keep throughout the week or year. Instead of directly asking about their religion, ask candidates which days they are able to work or ask if they are able to keep your required schedule.

Involvement in certain organizations can be considered a desirable quality in applicants when these organizations are related to the work that they perform. To avoid indirectly asking them to reveal information about their religion, ask candidates directly if they are in professionals groups that are relevant to your industry.

Gender

Almost universally you will be able to tell the gender of a candidate based on their name or their appearance upon meeting them. The important thing to remember here is that you do not make any assumptions about the candidate based upon this knowledge.

> **Don't** ask candidates any questions that directly relate to their gender or about working with other men or women.

> **Do** ask general questions like do they feel they are able to perform the work required or what do they have to offer the company.

Age

Age can be a tricky subject when it comes to evaluating candidates. On one hand, it is important to know that a candidate is of legal age to work. On the other hand, you cannot discriminate against older candidates for any reason, including the possibility of their retirement in the near future.

Don't ask how old they are, what their date of birth is, or when they plan on retiring. Also, avoid using terms like "boy," "girl" or "young" when describing or advertising a job position so as not to discriminate against people over the age of 40.

Do ask whether the candidate is over the age of 18. If you are curious about candidates' plans for the future, ask more general questions like what their long-term career goals are.

Disability, Health and Physical Issues

From the physically demanding aspects of a specific job to concerns about an employee's drug or alcohol use affecting their performance, there are a wide variety of reasons that an employer may be mindful about the health and physical fitness of a candidate. Once again, while interviewing a candidate, it is important to focus on questions directly pertaining to the candidate's ability to perform and to avoid asking personal questions.

Don't ask the candidate if they smoke, drink or do drugs.

Do: It is OK to ask if the candidate has ever been disciplined for violating company policies in the past. If they have not, then it is reasonable to assume that life-style choices such as these do not interfere with their ability to perform.

Don't ask specific questions about a candidate's height, weight or disabilities.

Do: Instead, ask them if they are able to perform the tasks necessary to complete the job. You can even ask them if they can perform specific tasks required for the position, such as lifting a box that weighs 50 pounds.

Chapter 16: Hiring

Family and Marital Status

Don't ask questions about candidates' family life or marital status. Topics such as whether they are married, have children, are pregnant or plan on becoming pregnant are inappropriate to broach during an interview.

Do: In order to perform background checks, it is permissible to ask if the candidate has worked or earned a degree under any other name. This step often comes after the interview, but if you must know during the interview, be sure *not* to ask whether the name is their maiden name, as this inevitably reveals marital status.

Having children can obviously place a strain on an individual's time, both on a day-to-day basis and in the long-term in the case of a pregnancy. Still, as an employer, you cannot make assumptions about any candidate in terms of how these things will affect their performance or work schedule. Instead of approaching these personal topics directly, ask more job-focused questions like whether they are able to work overtime or travel, if required. You can also ask more general questions like what the candidate's long-term career goals are.

B. How to Perform an Effective Interview

Once you have a solid understanding of what you legally can and cannot ask during an interview, you need to develop an understanding of questions you should ask in order to get the best information possible from a candidate. If you hire the wrong candidate, it can be very costly both financially and in terms of wasted time. Invest your time — and money — in getting hiring right the first time.

Preparation

Before you sit down with a candidate, you want to be well prepared and have a game plan for the interview.

Don't just "wing it." If you skip preparing to interview candidates, you may often find that you forget to address important issues. Also, if you interview multiple candidates, you will find it much more difficult to objectively compare them and make the best decisions.

Do draft a list of questions that you plan to ask potential candidates, or at least a pool of questions to choose from, depending on how the interview is going. The benefit is two-fold. First, you can be sure to ask candidates everything that you want to ask. Second, preparation ensures that you ask different candidates more or less the same set of questions. This practice will make it much easier to compare and contrast how the different candidates respond to similar questions and situations.

Interviewing

Interviews can take on a wide variety of looks and feels, whether it is a more casual meet and greet at a coffee house or a more formal interview in an office space. The tone and setting of an interview should reflect your personality and management style, as well as the type of position to be filled. Here are a handful of do's and don'ts to keep in mind during the interview process:

Do:

- Focus on past performance. Avoid asking candidates a question like "What would you do in this situation?" because you allow them to imagine an ideal resolution to the scenario. You may not get a realistic idea how they would truly behave or react. Instead, ask candidates about how they have handled specific, similar situations in the past.
- Tailor your interview to the position to be filled and be aware of what qualities fit that position well. For example, if you are filling a sales position, then you want a candidate

Chapter 16: Hiring

who is outgoing and well-spoken. After all, if the candidate cannot sell himself or herself, then how will they be able to sell your product? On the other hand, if the open slot is for an engineer or a tech person, then you will be more focused on if candidates are technically proficient enough to perform the required tasks.

- Be aware of the urgency with which the position needs to be filled. Sometimes companies interview to build a pool of potential candidates for slots that will open up in the future. In this case, you can take time, be selective, and find the best possible candidates. In other cases, businesses need to quickly find candidates to bid against an open position. In this case, you do not necessarily have time to be highly selective. After all, it is much better to bid a candidate who meets 85% of the qualifications and has a decent chance of being picked up than it is to wait and not bid any candidates at all.

- Ease the candidate into the interview. Make introductions and general small talk (without getting too personal, of course) to set the tone. Once settled, you should explain to the candidate how the rest of the interview process will proceed.

- Feel free to include different types of tests in the interview process. If the position involves a great deal of math, then testing their capabilities will quickly let you know if they are not as qualified as they might say. If the position involves a lot of writing, ask candidates to prepare a writing sample for you. You could even ask them give a short presentation if it will help you evaluate how they perform on the job.

> Take notes, especially if you are interviewing multiple candidates. Notes help you remember questions and situations that the candidates handed well or maybe not so well. As soon as the interview ends, add any other observations that you did not have time to write down during the interview. Do not rely on your memory alone.

Don't:

- Let initial biases or assumptions cloud your judgment. Just because an applicant has one small typo on their resume or is not dressed as well as you would like does not mean you should immediately dismiss them as a candidate. You never know what the possible explanations might be for situations like these, and you may inadvertently dismiss the perfect candidate.

- Forget that these are people that you will work with on a regular basis. When contracting with the government, you generally will look for people who best fit the requirements of the contract itself. While this often means that you will not necessarily have final say on whether the candidate gets the job, you should not blindly pick the best candidate "on paper." Make sure you hire people that fit well with the culture of your company and that you will not clash with in the future.

- Be afraid to dig a little deeper. Often, candidates will not give you the answer you are looking for, or they will not paint the whole picture when answering a question. Make sure to ask follow-up questions until you are satisfied that you have all of the information you need.

- Let the candidate control the flow of the interview, but at the same time, do not be afraid to the let candidate ask you questions during or at the end of the interview. This can greatly help you to get a feel for their mindset and for what they are looking for.

Chapter 16: Hiring

- Dominate the interview or talk too much. Remember, you are there to evaluate them as a potential candidate, not necessarily to sell yourself or your company.

Evaluation

If you prepare well and adhere to your game plan, evaluating your candidates will not be difficult. You may find using a scorecard or rating system can be very useful in evaluations. Determine the main factors that are important to performing a job and rate candidates on each of those factors. A rating system can help a great deal when deciding between candidates that might be very similar in their qualifications. Differentiating between candidates is one of the main reasons it is important that you conduct interviews in similar manners and ask candidates the same types of questions. If you do not, then you will end up trying to compare apples to oranges, which will only makes your job more difficult.

5. CHECKING OUT YOUR CANDIDATES

When you are hiring employees, you may need more information about a candidate than what you learn from an interview or resume. However, you do not have unlimited rights to investigate an applicant's background and personal life. Employees maintain a right to privacy in certain areas. If this right is violated, they can take legal action against you. Therefore, it is important to know what is permitted when following up on a potential employee's background and work history.

The following list includes the types of information that employers often consult as part of a pre-employment check, and the laws governing access and use for making hiring decisions.

Credit Reports. Employers must obtain an individual's written consent before seeking that person's credit report. See the United States Department of Labor website for more details on your requirements and on the rights retained by you and the individual:

www.dol.gov/compliance/laws/comp-flsa.htm-UKASKqUqHPY

Criminal Records. Consult a lawyer before attempting to access a candidate's criminal records. The extent to which you can consider an applicant's criminal history varies greatly from state to state.

Verify Degrees. Over the years, we have seen many candidates list colleges, and even specific programs like "Electrical Engineering," on their resumes only to discover in the interview or when we checked with the college that the person did not graduate from that college. They may have attended, but they did not actually graduate. You should verify a degree before you hire an individual for a position that clearly requires a degree. As you place employees in government contracting positions, you will find the positions usually have education requirements that must be met. (Sometimes the education requirements are "required," meaning the candidate must have that education or cannot be considered for the position. Other times, the education requirement is "desired," meaning a candidate can be considered if they do not meet that requirement but has other sufficient experience to be able to perform the work.)

Verify Employment History. Verify the employment history listed on your candidates' resumes. Government contracts typically require candidates to have a minimum number of years of relevant experience to be considered for a position, so you need to verify their employment history before submitting them for consideration.

Chapter 16: Hiring

Verify Clearances. Make sure the candidates' security clearances are current and have not expired. Government contracting positions often require clearances to perform the work, and some positions require candidates to have passed a counterintelligence polygraph ("CI poly") or a lifestyle polygraph ("full poly" or "poly"). If the candidate currently works in an environment that requires the same clearance your position requires, then you can feel pretty safe that the individual can be cleared to perform the work for the new position (if they meet the technical qualifications).

Much like false or embellished degrees, we have seen several candidates list a security clearance on a resume, but they have not worked in that secure environment for years and were "read out" (debriefed) when they left the program. You must ask candidates if they are actively working in a secure environment and using their clearances in their current job. You should also ask them if their clearances are current or if they have been debriefed, and then also verify their clearances are still active. See **Chapter 17** on hiring a security specialist for more information. The whole security process takes a long time to learn and stay on top of, so we always outsource our security function to a consulting company that specializes in it.

Ask for References. You should ask candidates for at least three to five references. Then, as you talk to each of those references, you can ask them for additional references for your candidate.

Ask Your Employees. We ask our employees if they know the candidate, and if they do, we ask them to tell us if they would hire the candidate if they owned the company.

This section overlaps with the next section, "Hiring New Employees," so be sure to read them together.

6. HIRING NEW EMPLOYEES

While we tried to write this book so you could read from front to cover or skip around and read chapters in the order you prefer, some of the material that follows could have been included in the last section "Checking out Your Candidates." There is some overlap in the subject matter, so make sure you read that section as well before reading this section.

As in the previous section, some of this material we borrowed liberally from the SBA.gov website since it is so complete and detailed.

Employee Eligibility Verification (Form I-9). You are required by federal law to verify an employee's eligibility to work in the United States. You must examine the forms of documentation supplied by the employee to confirm their citizenship or eligibility to work in the United States, and within three days of hire, you must complete an Employment Eligibility Verification Form, Form I-9 (often simply called the I-9 form). You do not need to file the I-9 with the federal government, but you must keep the form on file for three years after the date of hire or one year after the date of the employee's employment termination, whichever is later.

You can download the Form I-9 form from the U.S. Citizenship and Immigration Services website:

www.uscis.gov/i-9

You also can use information taken from the Form I-9 to verify electronically the employment eligibility of newly hired employees through **E-Verify**.

www.uscis.gov/e-verify

Paying Employees and Setting up Payroll. Whether you have one employee or 50, setting up a payroll system not only

Chapter 16: Hiring

streamlines your ability to stay on top of your legal and regulatory responsibilities as an employer, but it can also save you time and help protect you from incurring costly Internal Revenue Service **(IRS)** penalties. You may want to outsource your payroll function. You can contact **ConnekServ** (**www.ConnekServ.com**) for help with this decision and for help in picking the right outsource company.

Take Care of Employees' Paperwork. When you hire new employees, they are required to fill out Federal Income Tax Withholding Form W-4 and return it to you, so that you can withhold the correct amount of federal income tax from their pay.

Decide on a Pay Period. You may already have a preference for this, but the two most common pay periods are biweekly (once every two weeks) or semimonthly (twice a month). A semimonthly pay period is often preferred by employers, as it means two fewer pay periods to process per year and is easier to align with monthly financial reporting processes. On occasion businesses adopt weekly, monthly or even bimonthly pay periods, but these are far less common. Before making a final decision, make sure you are in compliance with your state and local laws regarding this matter.

Carefully Document Employees Compensation Terms. When you set up payroll, consider these factors:

- Will you provide paid time off **(PTO)?**
- Will employees be paid a salary or an hourly wage?
- How will you track the hours that your employees work?
- How will you handle overtime?

Additionally, you should set up a payroll system that includes benefits components such as health plan premiums and retirement contributions. These monies should be withheld from employee earnings and directed to the appropriate vendors.

Choosing a Payroll System. You have two primary options for running payroll for your employees, managing payroll in-house or outsourcing it to a company that specializes in processing payroll. As a small business owner, your time is both valuable and limited, and managing your own payroll can be tedious and time-consuming. For these reasons, it is often worth the expense to outsource the task. If you outsource, keep in mind that you want a payroll service that integrates easily with your accounting software. You also need to decide whether to use a "full-service" payroll system that withholds and pays taxes for you or if you want to handle these tasks in-house.

Running Payroll. Once you have all your forms and information collected, you can start running payroll. Depending on which payroll system you choose, you will either enter it yourself or give the information to your payroll company.

Be Proactive and Diligent in Your Recordkeeping. Recordkeeping is another example of the importance of being organized when running a business. You will save yourself a lot of headaches if you keep good records on file and easily accessible. With regards to employees, you are required by state and federal law to keep certain records for specific periods of time. For example, you must keep employees' W-4 forms on file as long they are employed and for three years after they are terminated. You must also keep W-2s, copies of filed tax forms and the date and amount of all tax deposits.

Report Payroll Taxes. One more thing you will need to know is what your obligations are in terms reporting payroll taxes. There are several different reports that you need to file on either a quarterly or annual basis. The IRS has an Employer Tax Guide; found at (**www.irs.gov/publications/p15/index.html**)

Chapter 16: Hiring

that details your responsibility for reporting federal taxes. Visit your state agency's website for information about reporting state taxes. Once you have properly set up payroll processing, much of the tax reporting will be done by your payroll service.

The Offer Letter. We always personally present or email offer letters to successful candidates, and we keep an offer letter for our files. We encourage the new candidate to keep a copy for their records as well. We utilize firm (non-contingent) and contingent offer letters. If we have a funded position and all of the contractual authorizations lined up to hire, we present the candidate with a firm offer letter stating various things like title, start date and special incentives (if any are to be paid out). Other times we hire candidates for positions on a government contract, but we are waiting on contract authorization to proceed **(ATP)** to bring the candidate onto the contract. We line up candidates by having them sign a contingent offer letter that clearly states the same items listed in the firm letter, but this letter includes clauses that the position is contingent upon us receiving ATP before we hire them. For positions requiring clearances, we also add a contingency clause that states that the position is offered contingent upon verification that their clearances be can processed over to work on the new contract. In these contingency situations, we encourage the candidate to not give notice to their current employer (not to resign) until we are can give them a firm offer letter.

> *The following is an example of a simple contingent offer letter. Be sure to put it on your company letterhead (for firm offer letters for funded positions, simply delete the contingency language).*

Start Grow Sell

Candidate's Name

Mailing Address

Dear "Candidate Name",

It is my pleasure to extend a Contingent Offer of employment as a Senior Systems Engineer with "your company name goes here". Details of the offer are provided below.

Salary: Your base compensation will be $XX,XXX.00 with paid annual leave that is accrued on a monthly basis starting with X weeks each year.

Contingencies: (*list any contingencies here*)

Authorization to Proceed. Employment with "your company name goes here" is contingent upon authorization to proceed (ATP) from the prime contractor allowing you to begin work on the contract. A firm offer with a firm start date will be sent to you as soon as the contingencies are met. Your estimated start date is Month Day, Year.

Clearances. Applicant must be eligible for, or able to obtain, the appropriate personnel clearance required for this position.

We look forward to you joining the team. This is an exciting time for "your company name goes here", during which we anticipate tremendous growth. As we grow, our goals are simple—to provide world-class engineering and consulting support to our customers while never compromising our integrity or that of our customers. Each employee will be able to take great pride in working in a corporate environment which, above all else, values and promotes integrity through our actions! We are excited with the prospect of you joining us in our endeavors.

Very Respectfully,

[signed]
Printed Name
CEO
Company Name

Upon acceptance of this Contingent Offer, please sign and return one (1) copy of this letter within 7 days of the postmarked date.

_____   _____
Signature   Date

Chapter 16: Hiring

Benefits Summary. We also try to ensure the benefits we offer our employees are well advertised because we believe strong incentives are a huge recruitment factor. When we meet with candidates, we usually provide them with a copy of the benefits we offer (always on company letterhead, of course).

Below is a sample format you can use to prepare your own benefits summary, which should be tailored to reflect the benefits you offer.

Company Benefits Summary

Salary/Compensation: "Your company name goes here" provides annual performance evaluations and salary reviews at the employee's anniversary date. Spot bonuses AND annual bonuses may also be provided to recognize outstanding performance or special achievements.

Annual Leave: Paid annual leave is accrued on a monthly basis with a maximum of (X) weeks each year. The company also supports a flexible work schedule and encourages employees to coordinate this as an option with their contract supervisors.

Disability and Life Insurance: Short- and long-term disability insurance covers serious illnesses. Life insurance is also offered as part of our comprehensive benefits package. We also encourage our employees to work with their own or "your company name goes here" referred broker to establish additional personal insurance plans/programs to suit each individual's specific requirements.

Paid Holidays: "Your company name goes here" observes all ten (10) regularly scheduled government holidays.

> ***Retirement Plan:*** "Your company name goes here" contributes as a match up to 6% of an employee's contribution to a 401K Plan (administered by Transamerica). "Your company name goes here" historically has made contributions to employees retirement through additional profit sharing contributions.
>
> ***Health and Dental Insurance*** (if offered by your company): Health and dental insurance is provided with the premium paid entirely by "your company name goes here." (Or, you may choose a cost-sharing approach to health and dental—if so, state this here.)
>
> ***Comprehensive Vision Care:*** Vision care is also provided with the premium paid entirely by "your company name goes here."

Employment Agreement. In general, we limit the use of employment agreements, but you should be informed about them. There are some hiring scenarios in which employment agreements are absolutely appropriate.

Employment agreements are documents that you and your employee sign setting out the terms of your relationship. You do not have to enter into a written contract with every employee you hire. In fact, written employment contracts are generally the exception rather than the rule. In some situations, however, it makes good sense to ask new employees to sign an employment agreement. For example, it could be a good idea to enter into an employment agreement, or contract, when you want to clearly define what the employee is going to do for you (the job itself) and what you are going to do for the employee (the salary the employee will receive). There are also many other aspects of the employment relationship that you may want to clearly define, such as:

Chapter 16: Hiring

- Duration of the job (a specific time frame or even "indefinitely")
- Information about the employee's responsibilities
- Specific information about benefits (such as medical and dental insurance, vacation [or paid time off], disability)
- Grounds for termination
- Limitations on the employee's ability to compete with your business once the employee leaves (also called non-compete clause)
- Protection of your company trade secrets and/or client lists
- Your ownership of the employee's work products
- A method for resolving any disputes that arise about the agreement

Remember, the employment agreement is not a one-way street; the agreement binds both you and the employee, so it can limit your flexibility as well as theirs.

Salary Surveys and Online Salary Data Options. How do you determine a fair salary to offer potential new employees on government contracts? You can get help from your mentors or business partners, who can offer historical trend data. You also can research salary survey data or turn to websites like Salary.com, glassdoor.com or indeed.com. On these sites, you can search based on job title and zip code to find comparable salaries paid for similar jobs. These are all good resources as you start and grow your company.

Regardless of which salary service or website you choose, you rarely will find a perfect match for the position you are filling because the service/survey or websites offer only "representative data." You will find that sometimes their descriptions are actually spot on, and other times they are only somewhat close to the type of job you are trying to fill. In general we find that these websites are very helpful to get a feel for what others in industry are paying in a specific geographic location.

Salary.com and glassdoor.com, for instance, offer salary ranges and median salary data (and similar benefit pay), which can be helpful. You should also factor in any unique aspects of the job, such as clearances required, special technical certifications required, etc., and adjust the salary offerings accordingly.

One example of a free salary survey is the annual ClearanceJobs Compensation Survey (go to ClearanceJobs.com). This survey is geared towards those positions requiring a security clearance, but it is very helpful for staying on top of trends in salaries earned by job description and identifying top earning jobs by geographic location, clearance level, polygraph level, and more. If you want to pay for a customized salary survey to meet specific job description criteria, ClearanceJobs also offers a compensation survey query tool online. You can run custom queries for the current and previous years, so you can see actual data and trend data. This approach may be helpful if you are trying to determine salaries to bid on a large number of labor categories. On many occasions, we have put together bids where we had to propose salary data for up to 100 different labor category descriptions. This scenario sounds unreal, but it is not uncommon to have a large number of labor categories in one bid, and it takes time to develop salary data for each labor category.

7. TAKING CARE OF YOUR EMPLOYEES WITH BENEFITS AND INCENTIVES

To provide benefits or not to provide benefits? If you provide benefits, how much will your company pay, and how much will you expect your employees to pay? Will you provide for just your employees' benefits or provide for benefits for your employees' families? Those are big questions facing employers these days, and they are questions that require analysis and planning. If you decide to provide benefits (beyond those required by law), you must decide which benefits to provide, which benefits the company will pay for outright and which benefits you will provide in a cost-share approach with employees.

The more benefits you provide at no cost to employees, the happier your employees will be. On the other hand, if you pay for more benefits, those costs can result in higher rates to your customers—and higher rates impact your cost competitiveness. Only you can evaluate the tradeoff between benefits and costs. In other words, you must determine your overall expenses (all costs) and overall benefits expenditures to strike the right balance, so the rate you charge customers does not make you uncompetitive or unprofitable.

You should also keep in mind that employee benefits play an important role in the lives of employees as well as their families. The benefits you choose to offer can be a big deciding factor in whether a candidate chooses to accept your offer and work for your company.

There are two types of employee benefits. First, benefits the employer must provide by law; and second, benefits the employer offers as an option to compensate employees. Those benefits required by law include Social Security and workers' compensation insurance. Optional benefits include healthcare insurance and retirement benefits. Since both required and optional benefits have legal and tax implications for employers, you need to understand the options and find the right balance of what to offer.

When starting a new company, we prefer to partner with an independent agency that will provide advice for the best coverage at the lowest prices. An independent agency does not try to push their own products, but will look across the various vendors and conduct plan comparisons to tailor a solution to meet your needs. Your independent agent has the expertise to offer advice on which plans will best serve your company and employees. The agent will educate you on what seems to be an endless set of acronyms, such as PPO, HMO, POS, HSA, HRA, etc., as well as self-funded and fully-funded plans. The agent can explain the benefits of each plan, so you can make a well-informed, cost-effective decision. From plan design to administrative assistance to expedited underwriting, your agent can guide you through the maze of employee benefits packages.

Let's take a look at some required and optional benefits that you can provide to employees.

A. Required Benefits. As of the date of this writing, U.S. employers are required to provide these benefits (each are further explained in the following paragraphs):

- Social Security Taxes
- Unemployment Insurance
- Workers' Compensation Insurance
- Disability Insurance (some states)
- Leave Benefits under the Family and Medical Leave Act **(FMLA)**
- Family and Medical Leave

Social Security Taxes. Employers must pay Social Security taxes at the same rate paid by their employees. The Social Security Administration **(SSA)** website offers guidance on your responsibility in filing.

www.socialsecurity.gov/pgm/business.htm

Every employer that engages in a trade or business who pays for services performed by an employee, including non-cash payments, must file a Form W-2 for each employee (even if the employee is related to the employer) from whom income, Social Security, or Medicare tax is withheld. The Social Security website gives a comprehensive guide to filing Form W-2 with

Chapter 16: Hiring

the SSA (employers may file electronically). Check out the following website to learn more:

Employer W-2 Filling Instructions and Information

www.ssa.gov/employer

Unemployment Insurance. As you hire new employees, your business will be required to pay unemployment insurance taxes under certain conditions. If your business is required to pay these taxes, you must register with your state's workforce agency. To help you determine your state requirements, the **SBA** has a good set of links to each state agency:

www.sba.gov/content/learn-about-your-state-and-local-tax-obligations

That same link will direct you to your state requirements regarding workers' compensation insurance.

Workers' Compensation Insurance. Businesses with employees are required to carry workers' compensation insurance coverage through a commercial carrier, on a self-insured basis, or through the state workers' compensation insurance program.

Disability Insurance. Some states require employers to provide partial wage replacement insurance coverage to their eligible employees for non-work related sickness or injury. Currently, you are required to purchase disability insurance if your employees are located in any of the following states: California, Hawaii, New Jersey, New York, Puerto Rico and Rhode Island.

Leave Benefits. The majority of common leave benefits offered by employers are not required by federal law and are offered to employees as part of the employer's overall compensation and benefits plan. These leave benefits include holiday/vacation, jury duty, personal leave, sick leave and funeral/bereavement leave. However, employers are required to provide leave under the Family and Medical Leave Act **(FMLA).**

Family and Medical Leave. The **Family and Medical Leave Act** provides an entitlement of up to 12 weeks of job-protected, unpaid leave during any 12-month period to eligible, covered employees for any of the following reasons:

1. Birth and care of the eligible employee's child, or placement for adoption or foster care of a child with the employee.
2. Care of an immediate family member (spouse, child, parent) who has a serious health condition.
3. Care of the employee's own serious health condition. FMLA requires group health benefits to be maintained during the leave as if employees continued to work instead of taking leave. FMLA applies to private employers with 50 or more employees, and to all public employers. The following resource provides employers with information on how to comply with FMLA:

   Family and Medical Leave Act: Compliance Assistance

   www.dol.gov/whd/fmla

Consolidated Omnibus Budget Reconciliation Act (COBRA) Benefits and Administration. COBRA provides certain former employees, retirees, spouses, former spouses and dependent children the right to temporarily continue health coverage at group rates. Businesses are required to provide COBRA when employees are terminated or laid off. Your independent agent will assist you in educating your employees and lowering your risk for compliance fines.

From the **US Department of Labor Website:**

www.dol.gov/dol/topic/health-plans/cobra.htm - .ULDfJ6UqHPY

Chapter 16: Hiring

"The Consolidated Omnibus Budget Reconciliation Act **(COBRA)** gives workers and their families who lose their health benefits the right to choose to continue group health benefits provided by their group health plan for limited periods of time under certain circumstances such as voluntary or involuntary job loss, reduction in the hours worked, transition between jobs, death, divorce and other life events. Qualified individuals may be required to pay the entire premium for coverage up to 102% of the cost to the plan.

COBRA generally requires that group health plans sponsored by employers with 20 or more employees in the prior year offer employees and their families the opportunity for a temporary extension of health coverage (called continuation coverage) in certain instances where coverage under the plan would otherwise end.

COBRA outlines how employees and family members may elect continuation coverage. It also requires employers and plans to provide notice."

It is important to understand your requirements as an employer to avoid penalties and fines. As the rules continue to change, meet with your independent agent to stay abreast of the latest rules and make sure your procedures are set up in such a way that you can comply with COBRA correctly on day one and as you grow.

The U.S. Department of Labor offers a booklet that summarizes COBRA continuation coverage and explains the rules that apply to group health plans. Information contained in the booklet is intended to assist employers that sponsor group health plans comply with COBRA.

An Employer's guide to Group Health Continuation Coverage Under Cobra

www.dol.gov/ebsa/publications/cobraemployer.html - .UMSOi6W_Coc

That same U.S. Department of Labor website offers a Frequently Asked Questions **(FAQs)** section for employers and employees about COBRA Continuation Health Coverage that is very useful.

COBRA Continuation Health Coverage Frequently Asked Questions

www.dol.gov/ebsa/FAQs/faq_compliance_cobra.html

B. Optional Benefits. Before we dive into specific individual benefits, we want to talk a little bit about benefits in general.

As you start and grow your company, you should think about having your benefits agent conduct an annual **benchmarking analysis**, which will compare your benefit offerings to those offered by peer companies and help ensure that you are offering competitive benefits.

You want to attract the best candidates to your company, but you also want to be competitive. In other words, you want to not only think about the employee and what benefits you are offering, but you also need to be competitive in the rates you bid on contracts. Obviously, the more benefits you offer for free to the employee, the higher your rates, and the higher your rates, the less competitive your company becomes. You must perform a balancing act as you consider what type and how many benefits you offer and the resulting effect on your rates.

If you set up your annual budget correctly, you can take the tailored benefit figures provided by your agent and plug them into your annual budget and run "what-if" drills to see the bottom line impact on your budget, profit, and rates you will have to charge customers.

Chapter 16: Hiring

> If you need help creating an annual budget or evaluating the impact of various levels of benefits offerings on rates and profit margins, our company, **ConnekServ (www.ConnekServ.com)** offers a proprietary budget tool that allows you to easily plug in the tailored cost figures from your benefits agent and run what-if drills to see the bottom-line impact on your budget, rates and profit margins.

We believe benchmarking analysis is essential to a successful company. Your independent agent can assist in recognizing the deficiencies and overages in your current benefits offerings to ensure you are on target with your numbers. In benchmarking, the agent will explain about trends in healthcare, dental and vision plans; paid time off **(PTO);** human resource policies; outsourcing; retirement plans; and more. Another benefit of benchmarking is that you can look into the out-year (the next year of your fiscal budget) and project rates and profit margins, while making sure you are staying competitive in benefits offerings. While there is no way to truly know how much the cost of providing benefits will change year-over-year, your independent agent will have much more insight into the out-year costs than you will, and that perspective will make your out-year planning numbers much more realistic.

Build Your Benefits Package. After your benchmarking analysis, it is time to set up your benefits package. Your employees will appreciate a comprehensive benefits package that includes medical, dental, vision, life insurance, short- and long-term disability insurance and other options, usually at minimal costs. They will feel appreciated, and in the long run, will be happier, more productive employees.

Custom Open-Enrollment. Once you have set up your benefits package, your independent agent can provide a customized open-enrollment packet to all employees. This packet includes these items and more:

- Medical Benefit Highlights
- Dental Benefit Highlights
- Vision Benefit Highlights
- Income Replacement
- Retirement Plans
- Life Insurance
- Disability Insurance (short- and long-term)

Understanding Retirement Plans and How to Select Them. We recommended this earlier in the book, but we want to emphasize it again: You should work with an independent agent to guide you through the maze of retirement plans and options. Working with an agent will save hours and hours of frustration as you start your company and as you grow and need to put in place more and more benefits to keep those valued employees.

If you decide to try to figure it out yourself, the U.S. Department of Labor's Employee Benefits Security Administration **(EBSA)** provides an interactive question-and-answer tool to help self-employed individuals and small business employers determine which type of retirement plan is most appropriate for their businesses.

Small Business Retirement Savings Advisor

www.dol.gov/elaws/pwba/plans/start.asp

They also offer a pamphlet describing the retirement savings options available to small businesses and comparing the features of each option at the following website:

Choosing a Retirement Solution for Your Small Business

www.dol.gov/ebsa/pdf/choosing.pdf

Chapter 16: Hiring

They offer tips to help an employer comply with Employee Retirement Income Security Act **(ERISA)** fiduciary responsibility provisions when selecting and monitoring a service provider for its plan.

Tips for Selecting and Monitoring Service Providers for Your Employee Benefit Plan

www.dol.gov/ebsa/newsroom/fs052505.html

Types of Benefits to Consider for Your Employees

The following is not meant to be an exhaustive list of benefits, and it is not in any order of priority. It is representative of some of the most common benefits offerings.

Medical and Dental. One of the most talked-about topics in the news, medical care insurance may be the most significant benefit for employees. Medical coverage can be very costly to offer, especially if your company covers the entire premium for the employee, but a lack of medical benefits — or inferior benefits — may mean that potential employees do not even consider your company for employment.

Your independent agent can investigate and get quotes for the types of products and services that will be available your company. Some examples of the companies they may suggest include Aetna, Anthem, CareFirst, Kaiser Permanente, UniCare, and United Health Care. Your agent can do a complete analysis and comparisons on emerging health plans, such as health savings accounts **(HSA)** and health reimbursement accounts **(HRA),** so you can understand the offerings and the costs.

Comprehensive Vision Care. Have your agent look into quotes from several providers to help you understand what the cost would be to the company. With that information, you can decide if you will provide this coverage or not.

Disability and Life Insurance. You may want to offer short- and long-term disability insurance to cover instances of serious illnesses. You could also offer life insurance as part of your comprehensive benefits package. At company startup, these benefits are very limited or very costly to provide.

Simplified Employee Pension (SEP). If you would like a low-cost retirement plan, you may want to consider a SEP. A SEP plan provides employers with a simplified method to make contributions toward employees' retirement and, if self-employed, their own retirement. Contributions are made directly to an Individual Retirement Account **(IRA)** or annuity set up for each employee (a SEP-IRA).

SEP plans can provide a significant source of income at retirement by allowing employers to set aside money in retirement accounts for themselves and their employees. A SEP does not have the startup and operating costs of a conventional retirement plan and allows for a contribution of up to 25% of each employee's pay.

The SEP is available to any size business. The employee is always 100% vested in (or, has ownership of) all SEP-IRA money.

To learn about SEPs, their advantages and how to establish, operate, contribute and terminate a plan, check out the following website:

Simplified Employee Pension (SEP) Retirement Plans for Small Business

www.dol.gov/ebsa/publications/SEPPlans.html

Savings Incentive Match Plan for Employees (SIMPLE). Another retirement plan option is the SIMPLE IRA. From the U.S. Department of Labor:

Chapter 16: Hiring

"[The] SIMPLE plan offers great advantages for businesses that meet two basic criteria. First, your business must have 100 or fewer employees (who earned $5,000 or more during the preceding calendar year). In addition, you cannot currently have another retirement plan. If you are among the thousands of business owners eligible for a SIMPLE IRA plan, read on to learn more.

A SIMPLE IRA plan provides you and your employees with a simplified way to contribute toward retirement. It reduces taxes and, at the same time, attracts and retains quality employees. And compared to other types of retirement plans, SIMPLE IRA plans offer lower start-up and annual costs . . . they are just simpler to operate."

Check out the following website to learn more:

SIMPLE IRA Plans for Small Businesses

www.dol.gov/ebsa/Publications/simple.html - .UMSB0KW_Coc

Payroll Deduction IRAs for Small Businesses. If you do not want the responsibility of an employee benefit plan, but you want to help your employees save for retirement, you may want to consider this option. From the U.S. Department of Labor website:

"A payroll deduction individual retirement account **(IRA)** is an easy way for businesses to give employees an opportunity to save for retirement. The employer sets up the payroll deduction IRA program with a bank, insurance company or other financial institution, and then the employees choose whether and how much they want deducted from their paychecks and deposited into the IRA. Employees may also have a choice of investments depending on the IRA provider.

Many people not covered by an employer retirement plan could save through an IRA, but do not do so on their own. A payroll deduction IRA at work can simplify the process and encourage employees to get started.

Under Federal law, individuals saving in a traditional IRA may be able to receive some tax advantages on the money they save, up to a certain amount, and the investments can grow tax-deferred. If the individual selects a Roth IRA, the employee's contributions are after-tax and the investments grow tax-free.

Advantages of a payroll deduction IRA:

- The payroll deduction IRA is a simple and direct way for employees to set up an IRA and save for their retirement.
- The employee makes all of the contributions. There are no employer contributions. By making regular payroll deductions, employees are able to contribute smaller amounts each pay period to their IRAs, rather than having to come up with a larger amount all at once.
- There is little administrative cost and no annual filings with the government.
- There is no requirement that an employer have a certain number of employees to set up a payroll deduction IRA.
- The program will not be considered an employer retirement plan subject to Federal requirements for reporting and fiduciary responsibilities as long as the employer keeps its involvement to a minimum.
- Providing a payroll deduction IRA for employees may assist an employer to attract and retain quality employees."

See the following website for more information:

Payroll Deduction IRAs for Small Businesses

www.dol.gov/ebsa/publications/PayrollDedIRAs.html

Chapter 16: Hiring

401(k) Plans. More and more companies are offering 401(k) plans to their employees, and these plans can be a powerful tool in promoting financial security for retirement. From the U.S. Department of Labor website:

"Employers start a 401(k) plan for a host of reasons:

- A well-designed 401(k) plan can help attract and keep talented employees.
- It allows participants to decide how much to contribute to their accounts.
- Employers are entitled to a tax deduction for contributions to employees' accounts.
- A 401(k) plan benefits a mix of rank-and-file employees and owners/managers.
- The money contributed may grow through investments in stocks, bonds, mutual funds, money market funds, savings accounts, and other investment vehicles.
- Contributions and earnings generally are not taxed by the federal government or by most state governments until they are distributed.
- A 401(k) plan may allow participants to take their benefits with them when they leave the company, easing administrative responsibilities."

See the following website to learn more about establishing and operating a 401(k) plan:

401(k) Plans For Small Businesses

www.dol.gov/ebsa/publications/401kplans.html

The term **401(k)** comes from subsection 401(k) of the Internal Revenue Code Title 26. A 401(k) plan is a "defined contribution plan" with a limit on annual contributions. Contributions are "tax-deferred," meaning contributions are deducted from paychecks before taxes are taken out, and then taxes are paid when a withdrawal is made from the 401(k) account later. Depending on the employer's program, a portion of the employee's contribution may be matched by the employer.

A well-designed 401(k) plan can help attract and keep talented employees. It allows participants to decide how much to contribute to their accounts. Employers are entitled to a tax deduction for their contributions to employees' accounts. The money contributed may grow through investments in stocks, bonds, mutual funds, money market funds, savings accounts and other investment vehicles. Contributions and earnings are generally not taxed by the federal government or by most state governments until they are distributed. As mentioned above, one of the key benefits of the 401(k) plan is that it may allow participants to take their benefits with them when they leave the company.

If you decide to offer a 401(k) match, you will also need to determine how much you will match of your employee's contribution to a 401(k) plan. "Matching" means that you will make contributions to your employee's 401(k) when the employee does the same, up to a certain percentage of their gross income. This can be dollar-for-dollar matching or proportional matching. For example, if you employ a 50% match up to the first 6%, then you will contribute 50 cents to the 401(k) for every dollar that the employee contributes, up to 6% of their gross salary. It is common practice to match up to 4%, 6%, 8% and higher, but remember, more benefits translate to higher rates charged your customers. As with all optional benefits, calculating the best 401(k) match rate will factor into balancing the simultaneous goals of keeping great employees and maintaining competitive rates and healthy profit margins.

Flexible Spending Accounts (FSA). A Flexible Spending Account **(FSA),** also referred to as a Flexible Spending Arrangement, is another type of tax-advantaged financial

Chapter 16: Hiring

account that may be used for specific purposes that have been approved by the IRS. FSAs are most commonly used for medical expenses that are not covered by insurance, but they can also be used for other approved expenses, such as childcare services. The primary benefit of an FSA is that contributions are made with pretax dollars and therefore not subject to payroll taxes, which can noticeably reduce the tax burden of your employees. One drawback of an FSA, however, is the "use it or lose it" nature of the account. Unlike retirement plans such as an IRA or 401(k), money contributed to an FSA does not roll over from year to year. Any money contributed to an FSA must be used within that plan year or the money is forfeited.

Your independent agent can work with you to establish FSAs and ensure that the process of reimbursements and deposits works smoothly for you and your employees.

Profit Sharing. You may also want to consider a profit sharing plan as part of the benefits package. Contributions to a profit sharing plan are discretionary. You can choose when and how much to contribute. Contributions and earnings generally are not taxed by the federal government or by state governments until they are distributed. A profit sharing plan benefits a mix of rank-and-file employees and owners/managers. The money contributed may grow through investments in stocks, mutual funds and other investment vehicles.

Paid Time Off (PTO), Vacation Days and Annual Leave. You need to determine how many PTO days to offer your employees. Usually companies scale PTO by the employee's length of employment with the company or by their seniority.

For instance, many companies offer two weeks PTO to new employees or employees who recently graduated from college or only have a few years of work experience. As people stay longer with your company or are hired with many years of experience, you would probably increase their PTO to three to four weeks. Some companies offer five or six weeks of PTO to employees who have many years of experience or have worked for the company for many years.

> For example, you can consider your employees' years of experience and classify them with increasing years as entry-level, mid-level, senior-level and expert-level. You may offer a PTO schedule like this:
>
> Entry (0 to 4 years of experience): 2 weeks of PTO
> Mid (5 to 10 years of experience): 3 weeks of PTO
> Senior (11 to 20 years of experience): 4 weeks of PTO
> Expert (21 or more years of experience): 5 to 6 weeks of PTO
>
> Of course, you can set up PTO as you like and via a model that you think will best encourage people to join and stay with your company.

Advance Leave. Sometimes employees need more leave than they have accrued (this happens mostly in the first year of employment or in the case of prolonged family member illnesses). In those cases, you will have to decide if you will "advance" the employee the leave time or if they will have to take leave without pay. When the employee takes advance leave, they run a negative leave balance until they have worked with you long enough to make up the leave shortfall. If you offer advance leave to employees, you should set and publish guidelines for it, so your employees know what to expect. The policy should state the maximum number of advance leave hours they can expect before they must go on leave without pay.

Sick Leave Days. You may want to offer sick leave days in addition to regular PTO. Sick leave days allow employees to take time off when they are sick, have medical appointments, or need to care for a family member who is sick or has medical appointments.

Chapter 16: Hiring

We typically offer every employee three sick leave days per calendar year in addition to PTO. In general, those sick leave days do not roll over into the next calendar year — the days are "use-it-or-lose-it" days. At the end of the calendar year, if an employee has not used their sick leave, the employee forfeits those days. In reality, we allow our employees 24 hours (three days worth) of sick leave, so if they need a few hours off from work to run to a family medical appointment, they can charge just those few hours to sick leave time and work the rest of the day. This flexibility allows employees to take a whole day if necessary, or just take off the amount of time they need that day, thus stretching their sick leave hours throughout the year. Your employees will appreciate flexible work schedules like this.

Flextime–Flex Schedule. Flextime is a variable work schedule that allows employees to choose when they want to work within certain parameters. Typically, there will be a core work period that all employees are expected to be at work, such as 9:00am to 3:00pm. Employees can then choose what eight-hour window they would like to work around that core period. For example, some employees could choose to work from 6:00am to 3:00 pm or maybe 9:00am to 6:00pm (allowing an hour for lunch). The great benefit for employees is that this flexibility allows them to work around traffic, school schedules, etc.

Another variation of flextime, often seen in IT industry, is one that allows employees to vary how many hours they work per day. For example, an employee can choose to work four 10-hour days (as opposed to five 8-hour days) and is able to take Monday or Friday off every week. In another popular model, employees work for 9 hours Monday through Thursday and then take off every other Friday.

While employees often prefer flexible work schedules, the type of work that your company performs is often a decisive factor in whether or not flextime is a viable option.

Government Holidays. As a government contractor, we typically consider the 10 government holidays as days off work for our employees, which results in 10 more PTO days for every employee each year. In most cases our government is shut down, and our employees are not able to get into the closed government space, so it becomes a day off work. The federal government typically takes these 10 annual holidays (sometimes 11 days in inauguration years):

- New Year's Day
- Birthday of Martin Luther King, Jr.
- Washington's Birthday or Presidents' Day
- Memorial Day
- Independence Day
- Labor Day
- Columbus Day
- Veteran's Day
- Thanksgiving Day
- Christmas Day

You can find the government holiday list for the current year at the **U.S. Office of Personnel Management website:**

www.opm.gov/operating_status_schedules/fedhol/2013.asp

C. Benefits to Consider for Co-Owners, Key Personnel or Executives. There are many additional benefits to consider offering to co-owners, key personnel and executives that can be critical to your continued success. Here are a few benefits you may want to consider offering or putting in place. The company can pay for these benefits, but like all benefits, the costs affect the bottom-line rate you charge customers and your profit margins.

Chapter 16: Hiring

Buy-Sell Agreements. If you start your company with one or more partners, we strongly recommend you set up and sign a buy-sell agreement "up-front," that is, as you start your company. You must know the terms inside and out! A buy-sell agreement defines how an owner's interest is to be distributed if he or she dies or becomes permanently disabled. This agreement helps ensure that a business or professional practice can continue after the death or disability of one of the owners or partners. It does this by requiring each owner or partner to sell his or her interest to the remaining owners, or to the business entity itself, under terms defined in the agreement. The agreement equally obligates the remaining owners or the business entity to purchase the deceased or disabled owners interest, and it stipulates the formula by which the price will be determined. The formula is negotiated, in advance of the event, by a mutual agreement and the document is signed by the owners or partners.

Key-Person Insurance. The main purpose of key-person insurance is to provide a death benefit to the business in the event of the premature death of an essential employee, but it can also be used as a way to provide the key person with supplemental non-qualified retirement benefits. With key-person insurance, a business purchases life insurance on the life of an essential employee to help the company survive financially if something happens to that individual.

Disability Buy-Out Plans. Disability buy-out insurance, which ensures a disabled business owner receives fair market value for his/her interest in the business, should be part of any business continuation or succession plan. A disability buy-out insurance plan provides the funds needed to purchase an owner's or partner's interest in the business if they become disabled. At the same time, the insurance protects all the business owners from the threat that a disability could impose on the company by allowing them to buy out the disabled owners interest — at an agreed upon price set forth in a well-designed buy-sell agreement.

Deferred Executive Compensation. Non-qualified deferred compensation arrangements allow employers to reward selected executives without taking on the administrative burdens of qualified plans. In many cases, deferred compensation is used in addition to qualified retirement plans, and other broadly based employee benefit plans.

Executive Long-Term Care. An executive long-term care plan can be used when a business decides to reward a specific group of executives by purchasing a long-term care insurance policy for each member in the group. These executives usually are considered essential to the success of the business.

Executive Bonus Agreement. Employers usually find retaining and rewarding existing key employees more cost-effective than recruiting and training new employees. A properly structured executive bonus agreement can be an excellent tool for recruiting, retaining and rewarding key employees.

We have covered a lot of material in this chapter — from getting organized to hire to taking care of employees to providing ways to continue business if key personnel become unable to work. Your main goal in this process is to hire great employees that will help you grow, keep your customers satisfied and love your company so much that they do not want to work anywhere else. Take your time and put the right hiring processes in place, interview plenty of candidates to make sure you have selected the right candidate — and then take care of those valuable assets by providing them with the right benefits.

CHAPTER 17: HIRING A SECURITY SPECIALIST

> If your company is small and you plan to do classified work, we recommend you hire a security consultant firm and outsource the bulk of the work. We promise, you will be glad you did! In-house or outsourced, you need a designated Facility Security Officer **(FSO)** in your company, who will be responsible for developing and implementing your facility security plan, and having a knowledgeable security consultant train and guide you through the process will save tons of hours and frustration. You can always hire in-house personnel to perform this work after you grow to the point where your budget allows for additional staff.

A security consultant can take care of things like (each topic will be explained in more detail):

1. **Design, develop and implement a compliant industrial security program**
2. **Prepare for annual security inspections**
3. **Process clearances**
4. **Establish and maintain a clearance roster**
5. **Conduct pre-employment screening and security assessments**
6. **Conduct pre-polygraph consultations**
7. **Provide proposal support**
8. **Prepare security management plans**
9. **Educate you and your team on security protocols**
10. **Interpret physical security requirements**

11. **Establish automated information system security plans and procedures**
12. **Prepare security reports**
13. **Prepare and organize security files**
14. **Provide overall security advice**

Your security consultant can help you in many ways, and you will appreciate them even more as they demonstrate their value over the years. Let's take a closer look at the tasks they can perform:

1. DESIGN, DEVELOP AND IMPLEMENT A COMPLIANT INDUSTRIAL SECURITY PROGRAM

- Assist you in implementing a security program that will meet all National Industrial Security Program Operating Manual **(NISPOM)**, Director of Central Intelligence Directives **(DCID)** and Intelligence Community **(IC)** Directives **(ICD)** security requirements.
- Conduct an internal "self-inspection" at your office to evaluate procedures, methods and facilities used in support of classified contracts.
- Provide written results of the self-inspection along with suggested action items for improvement of your security program.

2. PREPARE FOR ANNUAL SECURITY INSPECTIONS

- Assist you in preparing for annual Defense Security Service **(DSS)** and IC security inspections. Preparations could include:
- Reconcile Joint Personnel Adjudication System **(JPAS)** records with company security files
- Review Department of Defense Contract Security

Chapter 17: Hiring A Security Specialist

Classification Specification form **(DD Form 254)**

- Prepare Request for Information **(RFI)** sent by DSS representatives
- Prepare classified contract listings
- Update Key Management Personnel Lists **(KPML)**
- Conduct self-inspections
- Organize corporate security files, etc.

The Federal Acquisition Regulation **(FAR)** requires that a DD Form 254 be incorporated into each classified contract. DD Form 254 provides the contractor (or subcontractor) with the security requirements and classification guidance that would be necessary to perform on a classified contract.

3. PROCESS CLEARANCES

- Perform the administrative functions involved in submitting your personnel for the required security clearances and accesses in support of current contracts and contracts awarded.
    - Prepare the security portions of the required forms to include all JPAS processing and review all SF86 "Questionnaire for National Security Positions" records for completeness and accuracy prior to submission to the government.
    - Remain in close contact with the government throughout the clearance process to check the status of processing; supply any additional information requested; coordinate polygraph schedules, security orientation briefings, special access program briefings and badge appointments.

4. CLEARANCE ROSTER

- Establish and maintain, in your security file, an up-to-date clearance roster.
    - This roster will include each individual's name, Social Security number, date and place of birth, clearance date, background investigation date, polygraph date, badge number and expiration date, access request submission and approval dates, and all relevant comments.

5. PRE-EMPLOYMENT SCREENING

- Conduct non-confrontational security assessments and pre-employment screening interviews with applicants who are candidates to work on classified contracts.
    - These interviews will include a behavioral and deception analysis of the applicant's responses to a structured set of questions designed to elicit information related to the government's adjudicative criteria and the applicant's integrity, honesty and suitability.
    - Following the screening interview, they will provide you with the applicant's predicted probability of successfully completing the governments' security clearance process.
    - This assessment will be based on the applicant's attitude, behavior, admissions, omissions and/or falsification of records.
    - The results of the interview are intended to provide you with additional information with which to make an informed decision concerning the applicant's suitability for a position requiring a high-level security clearance.

Chapter 17: Hiring A Security Specialist

6. PRE-POLYGRAPH CONSULTATIONS

- Conduct individual pre-polygraph consultations with the employees scheduled to take a government polygraph examination.
    - The purpose of these sessions will be to familiarize the employee with the polygraph process, to answer any questions concerning the process and to help the employee develop the required degree of confidence in his/her answers to the sample questions to successfully complete the polygraph examination.

7. PROPOSAL SUPPORT

- Review the security requirements contained in Requests for Proposal **(RFPs)** and prepare security management volumes for inclusion in your proposals.
    - These plans will contain detailed procedures for implementing the requirements stated in the RFPs.

8. SECURITY MANAGEMENT PLANS

- Prepare a detailed security management plan for your active classified contracts in accordance with NISPOM.

9. SECURITY EDUCATION

- Prepare a security education program for your company.
    - At a minimum this program will include an annual security education/awareness briefing for all cleared employees and periodic written reminder memorandums.
- Brief senior management or other corporate groups on security policies and procedures at your request.

- Written records of security briefings and education programs will be maintained in your company security files.

10. PHYSICAL SECURITY

- Assist you in interpreting the physical security requirements of the NISPOM, the DCID or ICDs, and other related standards as they pertain to facilities.

- If requirements dictate classified storage at your facility, they will assist in the design of the facility and will prepare the necessary physical security checklists (i.e.; DCID 6/9 Fixed Facility Checklist) for submission to the government.

- They can also provide advice and assistance during the construction/modification phase and will act as a liaison with the government to clarify requirements for the facility.

- Assist in preparation of any additional paperwork required for facility or SCIF accreditation.

11. AUTOMATED INFORMATION SYSTEM SECURITY

- Assist you in establishing automated information system security plans and procedures for protecting classified and/or proprietary materials in accordance with the applicable computer security requirements required by the government.

12. REPORTS

- Prepare and submit all required security reports to the U.S. Government.

- Examples of required reports include changes in personal status, contact with foreign nationals, foreign travel, adverse information, requests for information from

Chapter 17: Hiring A Security Specialist

unauthorized persons, improper security practices, security violations, compromises and potential compromises.

13. SECURITY FILES

- Prepare and organize your company security files to include copies of the DOD Security Agreement, Classified Contracts Listing, Key Management Personnel List, DOD Contract Security Classification Specification, and any other related correspondence and forms.
- Organize and maintain personnel security files, which will include copies of each individual's JPAS Person Summary, SF312 and related forms.

14. SECURITY ADVICE

- Work directly with you and your company's senior management to effectively implement all required government security procedures.
- Provide input on all security-related issues and processes implemented at your facility.

We mentioned this at the beginning of the chapter, and it is worth repeating—if you plan to do classified work, at least while your company is small, we recommend you hire a security consultant firm and outsource the bulk of the work. As your company and budget grows, you can add staff and bring the work in-house, but for now, save time and frustration by accessing the experience and resources of an experienced security consultant.

CHAPTER 18: INTELLECTUAL PROPERTY RIGHTS

In business, protecting your assets is essential. It's why companies opt to do business as a Limited Liability Company **(LLC)** or Corporation and why they purchase insurance to cover everything from company vehicles to the very lives of the owners. As a business owner, you have many assets besides the physical ones that may come to mind, such as money, real estate or machinery. You also have the right to protect your intellectual property **(IP),** intangible assets that your business owns and controls, from your name and logo to a secret recipe or even a unique business process. In this chapter we will discuss the various types of IP and the means of protection available.

The different forms of IP tend overlap, but they are typically grouped into two main categories, **functional** and **non-functional**. Functional IP includes **utility patents** and **trade secrets;** non-functional IP includes **trademarks and service marks, design patents, copyrights, and trade dress.** The best way to think about it is that functional IP rights protect those aspects of a product or idea that actually make it *functional*. On the other hand, non-functional IP rights protect those aspects that are purely aesthetic and do not improve actual function in any way.

For example, you develop a new refrigerator. If you develop a new technology that improves the temperature regulation and reduces energy expenditure, then you could protect this highly *functional* aspect through a utility patent. On the other hand, the aesthetic aspects such as the sleek handle design or even the name would be protected through the *non-functional* IP protections of design patents and trademarks, respectively.

Now that you have a basic understanding of what separates the two sides of IP, let's break it down further as we introduce each of the individual aspects of IP rights.

1. FUNCTIONAL

As a reminder, functional IP is designed to protect the *functional* aspects of a product and includes utility patents and trade secrets.

A. Utility Patents

According the U.S. Patent and Trademark Office **(PTO)**,

www.uspto.gov/web/offices/ac/ido/oeip/taf/patdesc.htm

Utility patents are "issued for the invention of a new and useful process, machine, manufacture, or composition of matter, or a new and useful improvement thereof . . . ." This grants the patent owner the *exclusive right to make, use and sell the invention for up to 20 years*. It also gives the owner the legal right to seek damages from anybody who violates the patent by making, using or selling the invention.

The types of inventions that qualify for a patent are as follows:

- **Process.** A unique and definable series of steps that can be followed to achieve a certain result.

- **Machine.** A piece of equipment that achieves results through the interaction of its different parts.

- **Manufacture,** also referred to as an **Article of Manufacture.** This can refer to one of two different types of objects. The first is a single object that simply does not have any moving parts like a paperweight or bookend. The second is an object that has moving parts that are not essential to the usefulness of the object. An example of this

Chapter 18: Intellectual Property Rights

would be a folding knife, where the ability of the knife to cut, its intended use, is independent of its ability to open and close.

- **Composition of Matter.** A specific combination of chemicals or materials, such as household cleaners or lubricants.

- **Improvements.** A specific improvement on a previous invention of one of the previous listed types

In order to receive a patent, an invention must meet three criteria. It must be:

- **Useful,** and the purpose of the invention must not be illegal or deceptive.

- **Novel,** as in it must truly be an invention and not something that is already known about or used by other people.

- **Non-obvious,** perhaps the most subjective and hardest criterion to define. Generally speaking, it must be something that others in the field would not necessarily expect or maybe even think could be achieved.

Patents generally are considered one of the most powerful aspects of IP because of the potential licensing power. We will cover licensing more in depth later, but it is important to note that it is a primary method of capitalizing on your ideas. The process of obtaining a patent is known as **prosecution**. You must file a written application that thoroughly describes the invention so that someone who is educated in the field may reasonably duplicate it. While under review at the patent office, the invention is referred to as "patent pending." Once granted, the patent is considered prosecuted.

Obtaining and maintaining a patent can be expensive—to the

tune of tens of thousands of dollars. Costs can escalate because prosecution often calls for the services of patent lawyers, and once gained, patents require yearly fees to maintain. You should weigh all the costs and benefits of a patent before beginning the prosecution process.

B. Trade Secrets

Trade secrets are governed in the United States by the Uniform Trade Secrets Act **(UTSA)**. According to the UTSA, "**Trade secret** means information, including a formula, pattern, compilation, program, device, method, technique, or process, that:

a. Derives independent economic value, actual or potential, from not being generally known to, and not being readily ascertainable by proper means by, other persons who can obtain economic value from its disclosure or use, and

b. Is the subject of efforts that are reasonable under the circumstances to maintain its secrecy."

In other words, a trade secret is information used by your business to gain an economic advantage over the competition. Unlike a patent, where you are required to publicly disclose the invention and how it works, trade secrets demand that you make all reasonable efforts to keep the important information private and undisclosed. Once you have willfully disseminated the information to the public, that information loses its status as a trade secret.

As you are expected to preserve your trade secret, there is no application process similar to that of obtaining a patent. Instead, you are expected to protect the trade secret through physical, technological and legal means (such as using non-disclosure agreements **[NDA]**). Your protection comes through the ability to seek legal action against those who acquire your trade secret through improper means. According to the UTSA, "**Improper means** includes theft, bribery, misrepresentation, breach or

Chapter 18: Intellectual Property Rights

inducement of a breach of a duty to maintain secrecy, or espionage through electronic or other means."

This standard puts the burden of proof on the original holder of the trade secret to show that they had taken reasonable measures to ensure the protection of their trade secret, and also that it was actually stolen through improper means. Unlike with a patent, the UTSA provides no protection for trade secrets when these criteria are not met. This approach means that if somebody else legitimately reverse engineers or independently invents your trade secret, then you lose all protection.

2. NON-FUNCTIONAL

As a reminder, non-functional IP protects those aspects of a product that are purely aesthetic and includes trademarks and service marks, design patents, copyright, and trade dress.

A. Trademarks and Service Marks

As with patents, trademarks are controlled by the U.S. Patent and Trademark Office. According to the **PTO**, "A **trademark** is a word, phrase, symbol, and/or design that identifies and distinguishes the source of the goods of one party from those of others. A **service mark** is a word, phrase, symbol, and/or design that identifies and distinguishes the source of a service rather than goods. The term 'trademark' is often used to refer to both trademarks and service marks."

www.uspto.gov/trademarks/basics/definitions.jsp

There are several important things to know about trademarks that set them apart from other forms of IP. First, trademarks are not related to the creation of a product or idea so much as they are related to one's ability to sell their goods and services. As the main goal of a trademark is to identify the source of a product being sold, you must actually sell or advertise your product in order to obtain legal protection. The only way to obtain trademark protection without selling or advertising a product is to file an **Intent-to-Use Registration**, in which case, you must be able to show that you intend to use the trademark in federally regulated commerce in the near future.

Second, trademarks do not have to be registered to gain legal protection. Trademarks are regulated at the federal level as opposed to the state level. This means that you must use your trademark in federally regulated commerce, for instance, internationally or even just across state lines, in order to register with the PTO. Even then, the question of whether or not to register your trademark is up to you. If you only sell your goods or services within a single state or if you simply choose not to register, then your mark will still be protected under common law.

The benefits of registering include use of the registered trademark symbol ®, as well as creating the assumption that you have the right to use that mark nationally. The downside to registering is that you have to pay fees and renew the registration periodically. If your trademark is unregistered, then you must use the symbol ™ for trademark or ℠ for service mark.

Third, trademarks are primarily controlled by the right of first use as opposed to being controlled by registration. To put it simply, you gain legal protection of a trademark the very first day that you use it in commerce. This means that if somebody else comes along and registers a mark that is the same as or very similar to yours after you have been using it, you will retain the right to use the mark even though they registered and you did not. You simply have to be able to show that you were using the mark first, in which case you can petition to cancel the other company's registration or even take them to court to pursue legal action.

Finally, it is important to note that there is no time limit for

Chapter 18: Intellectual Property Rights

trademark protection. As long as you use the trademark in commerce, you will continue to enjoy the legal protections and the exclusive right to use that trademark.

B. Design Patents

Design patents are very similar to utility patents, and are also controlled by the U.S PTO. The primary difference is that design patents exist to protect the purely aesthetic, or ornamental, aspects of an otherwise functional or utilitarian design. To acquire a design patent, the design must be new, original and ornamental. For example, if you designed a children's television that looked like a monkey, you could obtain a design patent for the monkey design as it is purely ornamental and does not affect the functionality of the television itself. Design patents last 14 years and must be filed within a year of the date that you first begin selling the product.

C. Copyright

In the United States, the Copyright Act of 1976 primarily governs copyright law. Generally speaking, the purpose of the copyright law is to protect and encourage the creation of artwork. It does so by granting the author of original art the exclusive right to reproduce and sell the artwork. As listed in the **Copyright Act**, the following categories of art and expression are eligible for copyright protection:

- Literary works
- Musical works, including any accompanying words
- Dramatic works, including any accompanying music
- Pantomimes and choreographic works
- Pictorial, graphic and sculptural works
- Motion pictures and other audiovisual works
- Sound recordings
- Architectural works

www.copyright.gov/title17/92chap1.html#102

As a government contractor, you probably will not be selling artwork to the government, so we will not go into detail in regards to copyright. It is important to note that, like design patents, there are aspects of products that you may want to garner copyright protection for, such as packaging or artwork included on the invention itself or in advertising. Copyright protection generally last quite a long time. For individual creators, a copyright will last for the duration of their lives plus 70 years. For copyrighted material created by a company, protection lasts for 95 years after first publication or 120 years after creation, whichever is longer.

D. Trade Dress

Trade dress, very similar to trademark and copyright law, prevents people from packaging products in ways that mimic the goods of another product. The protection strives to benefit the original maker of a product and also to safeguard customers from purchasing one item when they believe it is actually another item.

As with trademarks, you do not have to register with the PTO to gain protection, but you may do so if you choose. In order to gain protection, the design must be distinctive, that is, easily identifiable. It must also convey a "secondary meaning" in that the design creates an association with the producer in the mind of the consumer.

3. LICENSING AND ASSIGNMENTS

Now that you have a good idea of the various forms of IP, let's explore different ways of monetizing your ideas. If you have invented a product or created a piece of art, the most obvious and simple way to make money would be to obtain a patent or copyright and sell the products yourself. For various reasons,

Chapter 18: Intellectual Property Rights

this is not always the easiest thing to do. Perhaps you do not have the time or resources to efficiently produce, market and sell the product yourself. Fortunately, odds are, there is someone out there who does have the resources necessary to accomplish this.

A. Licensing

Licensing makes this exchange possible. Simply put, a **license** is a contract in which you grant someone else the permission to use or produce and sell your invention for a specific period of time. In exchange for the rights to your invention, the **licensee** pays you, the **licensor**, fees known as royalties. As with any contract, licensing agreements can be written or oral, although written contracts are always recommended so as to avoid confusion later.

Licensing agreements can take on many forms and run the gamut from very simple to very complicated. Entire books are devoted to ways to write and implement licensing agreements. The contract can last for a certain amount of time or into perpetuity (or at least for as long as you retain protection under IP laws). An agreement can even be limited to certain geographic areas. For example, you can have a licensing agreement with one person to sell your product in California and an agreement with somebody else to sell it in Texas.

There are also many ways to arrange for payment of royalties, and every method comes with inherent risks and benefits for each side. For instance, a single **lump sum** payment at the beginning could be risky for both sides. If the sum is too small and the product takes off, then the licensor could lose a lot of potential profit. If the sum is too high and the product is not successfully marketed, then the licensee could end up with no return on a large investment.

With **per-unit** payment, the licensee pays a set amount of money per unit sold. This is also risky because either side could lose out depending on market fluctuations. For example, if the per-unit royalty is $5 and the profit margin only turns out to be $4, then the licensee not only loses money on each transaction but also loses incentive to sell the product. This scenario would be especially unfortunate because nobody would be making money even though the potential for profit exists.

The most popular licensing agreement allows for payments based on **net sales**. For each unit sold, the licensor receives a royalty payment as a percent of the profit from that sale. This method tends to be the best balance of risk and reward for both sides, as neither is taking too large of a risk and both sides have the potential to make a lot of money if the product sells well. There are more payment models, and if you find yourself in the position of licensee or licensor, you should research the options and weigh the risks and rewards carefully.

B. Assignment

One last option to keep in mind is **assignment.** When you assign your rights to an invention, you permanently transfer those rights to another person. If we equate licensing to renting your house to a tenant for a specific period of time in exchange for rent money, then assignment is the equivalent of permanently selling your house and transferring your ownership rights to another person. This practice is not as common as licensing, though you may sometimes see the two terms used interchangeably. In legal terms, licensing and assignment are actually different, so when you hear the two terms, be sure to know which one is truly meant.

In the world of business, it is very important that you protect your assets. Oftentimes your intangible assets are far more valuable than your tangible ones, and your intangible assets are the real basis for your potential to earn a profit. Hopefully by reading this chapter, you will start to get an idea of where you might be vulnerable and what steps you need to take to protect your product and your business.

Chapter 18: Intellectual Property Rights

> If you have read through the first two parts of our book and followed our guidance, you have figured out what company structure you need, filed all of the necessary paperwork and stood up your company. We hope you launched a website, and have already marketed and captured your first contract. At this point, you are successfully managing your contract and meeting all of the contract requirements—so the customer will keep asking you for more support.
>
> But what if you are thinking about selling your company or you have already decided to sell your company? Well then, you are ready for **Part 3,** *Sell Your Company*.

PART 3: SELL YOUR COMPANY

> You may be wondering why we included material on selling your company when this book focuses primarily on how to start and operate a government contracting business. The reason for this is that you should think about starting and growing your company with the "end" in mind. Too many entrepreneurs start their business and focus only on getting the company running and then acquiring their first contract. Then they get tied up trying to grow their company, or they end up operating in survival mode. All of that is important, but you can save yourself, and your partners, loads of grief if you plan your exit options from the beginning and put some key files in place early on.

This chapter is not intended to be a comprehensive discussion on selling your company. It's included to help you think through some important details while you start and grow your company so that you will not have regrets when the time comes to sell. For example, often people start their company with one or more partners, or give away (or sell) some ownership in the company after startup. They are focused on startup, so they do not give any thought to official legal paperwork that addresses what to do if an owner decides to make an exit—or if you decide that you want them out of the company. The time to plan an exit is at the very beginning. It is not something you want to put off and then have to deal with later, when the exit is under unfriendly circumstances.

You are not obligated to formulate an exit strategy at startup. In fact, you can ask your lawyers to draft the paperwork at any time, but it is helpful to consider possible scenarios—and come to an agreement—up front. You may find it useful to get something like a *buy-sell agreement* written (usually prepared by a lawyer using the key terms the owners have agreed to) and signed by all the owners, preferably **before** you give away ownership to anyone else (more on buy-sell agreements in this chapter).

1. REASONS FOR SELLING (OR EXITING)

Entrepreneurs tend to set up a company because they see a business opportunity, and they want to exploit that opportunity. They do not tend to think about selling out or about planning their exit strategy as they start the company. There are myriad reasons you may want to sell your company, or sell out to your partners, for example:

- It is time to retire!
- You want to take your company public.
- You have become disabled or face health issues.
- There are serious conflicts between the owners, and someone needs out of the business.
- It is just time to call it quits.
- A divorce.
- Estate tax reasons.
- Financial decline, bankruptcy or a decline in the market.

- You received a purchase offer that is too good to pass up.
- You need funds to start your next company or your next career.
- And on and on . . .

If you are thinking about selling, it is natural that you begin asking yourself and your advisors several questions. For example:

- Why *should* I sell? (see previous list)
- Is this the *best time to sell*? If not *now*, then when *is* the best time to sell?
- What *process* will I need to go through to sell?
- What are some *possible obstacles* that I may face in selling?
- What is my *ownership worth*?
- Who might be some *potential buyers*?
- Will I want to work for the new buyer? Or leave the company altogether and move on to the next phase of my life?
- And on and on . . .

2. THE BUY-SELL AGREEMENT

If you do your planning up front (like we do), you already put in place a buy-sell agreement—drafted by your lawyer and signed by all key personnel (owners), including the person taking new ownership.

The buy-sell agreement clearly identifies things like:

- Company name
- Owners and their share of ownership
- Date of the agreement

- Terms of the ownership offer
- Any restrictions that need to be documented
- Acceptance period before expiring
- Purchase price
- Details of the closing (It is similar to buying a house. Once everyone reads the documents and agrees to the terms, they gather and "close" by signing all the key documentation.)
- Termination of employment terms
- Consideration upon Death or Other Purchase for Consideration (This is important because you may not want a deceased owner's spouse or estate to own stock in your company. They may know nothing about the day-to-day business and could not be a contributing owner, like the person who just passed away. Instead, you can ensure a "buy out" with cash, insurance proceeds, or whatever consideration everyone agreed to upfront.)
- *Buy-Sell Insurance* terms (As the company grows and its value increases, you should obtain buy-sell insurance in order to buy out the spouse or estate of a deceased owner. Depending on its value, the company may not have enough cash on hand to buy out the estate, and you certainly do not want to put your company at risk. We purchase buy-sell insurance policies, paid for by the company, to buy out the estate should an owner pass away. This insurance keeps cash in the company and reduces risk of a situation in which the company is strapped for cash because the funds were needed to buy out an estate.)

Many other items can go into the buy-sell agreement, and we hope you have rounded out your team by including a lawyer, accountant and tax advisor. These professionals can craft a buy-sell agreement for your unique needs and help protect you and your company against any circumstance that you may face.

Part 3: Sell Your Company

> Make sure you document everything through your board of directors and meeting minutes. Keep *official records* of all company resolutions to add owners, add a buy-sell agreement, remove owners, sell the company, etc.

Also, remember that if your business is a partnership, limited liability company **(LLC)** or corporation, you and your co-owners must make the decision to dissolve the entity according to the guidelines established in your articles of organization. Remember to document the final decision with a written agreement.

3. PROTECTION FOR YOU, YOUR FAMILY AND YOUR BUSINESS

In addition to buy-sell insurance, another part of planning for your exit should be to protect you, your family and your company through appropriate retirement plans and insurances policies, such as life insurance and disability insurance. We covered the details of retirement plans and disability insurance in earlier chapters. As a reminder—and a strong recommendation—making ongoing contributions to your retirement plan and putting life insurance and disability insurance plans (long- and short-term plans) in place can be extremely important to your survivors should the worst case happen.

4. TWO SIDES TO EVERY SELL

If you and your partners decide to sell your company outright, keep in mind that every deal involves two sides—with competing perspectives. On one hand, you engage in the seller's acquisition strategy and process. Meanwhile, someone else walks through the buyer's acquisition strategy and process. Let's briefly look at both perspectives in the Merger and Acquisition **(M&A)** process.

A. The Seller's Perspective

Whatever your reason for selling, you have much work to do to be ready to sell. In addition to your usual business team—lawyer, accountant, tax advisors, etc.—you now need people who have M&A experience. These people should be able to advise and help you through the process of preparing to sell, finding buyers, providing them with the information they need to make a bid/no-bid decision, and helping you close the deal.

If you have the right team already, then great! You are ahead of the game. If not, you may want to hire an *investment banker* to assist you with the sale of the company. Your investment banker should have extensive knowledge of the industry, a demonstrated track record of M&A successes and a database of potential buyers. Additionally, investment bankers should have a good database of recent sales, so they can guide you in determining a fair price for your company. Here are some things an investment banker can do for you or assist you in:

- **Determine Company Value.** Since they have access to databases of recent comparable sales, they can help you set your asking price. They can also suggest actions you can take to garner the highest asking price possible.

- **Time the Sale.** Timing really is everything, and investment bankers know and track the market. They will advise you of the best time to put your business up for sale. Timing and market conditions drive the sale price that buyers are willing to offer. Unless you have a solid understanding of these issues, you should rely on your investment banker.

- **Prepare to Sell.** Your investment banker will guide you, step by step, through the process and advise you on specific actions needed, so you will get the best price for your business. Also, since they know how serial acquirers work, and may know your buyer very well, they often can advise you on the buyer's habits and help tailor your package to be more attractive to the buyer.

Part 3: Sell Your Company

- **Develop Selling Methodology.** They will advise you on what method to follow to sell your company. Will you sell to one buyer? Get multiple bids? Go through an auction? The investment banker will advise you on the best approach based on timing and market conditions.

- **Put Together Your Offering Memorandum.** The primary tool used to communicate the value of your business to buyers, an offering memorandum is not usually a comprehensive document. The memorandum gives insight into your business without revealing all the private details. It provides an overview that offers buyers information about your company's history of growth, products, intellectual property, number of employees and other assets, profit record, growth potential and more. The memorandum may also include things like an investment summary, business and industry overviews, management team profiles, and an overview of financials (past five years or more plus the next few years' projections).

- **Prepare Your Data Room.** This is the place where the copies of your files are made available to prospective buyers. The data room can be a specific location with hard copies of files, or it can take the form of a completely digital space, where files can be downloaded for review.

- **Handle Logistics of Meetings.** The banker can coordinate all meetings between the buyers and the sellers. The banker can also serve as the "go-between" or "buffer" between you and prospective buyers. In fact, if you prefer to keep the potential sale of your company private or low-profile, the banker can filter prospective buyers by providing key company data without specifically citing your company name (until you are ready for your name to be shared).

- **Advise on Negotiations.** Since really good investment bankers have insight into other recent sales and current market conditions, they are well suited to offer you advice on key terms to get the best deal and close the sale.

Not every sale requires an investment banker's expertise, and you should know that it can be quite expensive to use the full suite of investment banker services. Some bankers require a monthly retainer on top of a percentage of the sale price, so the costs can really add up over time.

Sometimes, depending on the size of the company being acquired, number of employees, number of contracts, diversity of location, etc., a sale could take place without an investment banker. A private buyer, who is willing to work the deal within the respective management teams—while going through the appropriate due-diligence process, of course, may approach you. In that scenario, you can save the cost of an investment banker's services. In most cases, you still need a lawyer to help structure the sale. Lawyers, like investment bankers, often require a monthly retainer, so the longer your sale takes, the more legal expenses will rack up. Therefore, the more terms you can resolve within your management teams, the more you can potentially save in terms of support team costs.

B. The Buyer's Perspective

The buyers are in the market for their own reasons, and they want to get the best price possible, but only after they have done their due diligence. The typical buyer's process includes:

- **Research Target Companies.** This is pretty a straightforward process. Buyers usually have done their homework and decided *where* they want to expand their business. Now they need to decide which company best meets their requirements for expansion. Often they have their sights on companies they can personally contact. Other times they use public information, investment bankers, personal contacts and third-party sources to line up potential acquisition targets. Often buyers have been watching the acquisition market and tracking acquisitions in their workspace, so they know the going sale multiples to target. On the other hand, this information is usually pretty closely held for private company sales, which is why third-party sources or investment bankers can come in handy. They have access through their business dealings to many of the details of recent acquisitions.

- **Make the Initial Contact.** (This could be direct contact or contact by a third party). These conversations usually occur at a pretty high level, and basically are an opportunity for key players on each side to meet and start discussions to better understand what the seller has to offer and what the buyer is looking for. There may be a series of meetings before the parties are ready to get serious and enter discussions that include protections for each side via a formal document called a *non-disclosure agreement.*

- **Sign a Non-Disclosure Agreement (NDA).** An NDA allows the buyers and sellers to share confidential information, which gives the buyers access to details, so they can decide whether to sign a letter of intent. Under the NDA, the seller will provide confidential information to give you insight into their company financials (historical and forecasted) and summary-level key company files to shape an appropriate offer.

- **Sign a Non-Binding Letter of Intent or Term Sheet.** Once the buyer goes through the NDA process, they can review in detail the historical and forecasted financial data and key company documentation to put together a purchase agreement (purchase offer) in the form of a non-binding letter of intent or term sheet. Usually, the buyer asks for an exclusivity period (the target company commits to deal only with you and not continue to shop around for other buyers). This letter of intent provides a baseline from which the real negotiations happen (up or down) depending upon the results of the due diligence phase.

- **Enter the Due Diligence Phase.** This is the formal phase where the buyer investigates the financial, legal, operational and other aspects of the target company. The buyer examines the selling company's detailed financials (historical and forecast), contracts, products, etc., against their high-level data in the offering memorandum. The due diligence phase can be rather lengthy and usually involves bankers, lawyers, accountants and key management from both the buyer and the seller. The more prepared the seller is going in to the due diligence phase, the quicker this period can be completed. If the seller must create or gather data after this phase begins, it can take months just to pull together materials for the buyer's team to review.

- **Begin Final Negotiations.** Based on the findings during the due diligence phase, the buyers will decide what they believe the company is worth and put together their initial offer. This offer reflects the buyers' valuation of the company and also their attempt to get the best possible deal—that is, the lowest possible price. On the other side, the sellers have their own idea of what the company is worth and are trying to get top dollar for the business that they have worked so hard to grow. Often, the true value of the business falls somewhere in the middle, so the two sides must negotiate. They have the option of negotiating directly or communicating through bankers, lawyers or another third party.

- **Close the Sale.** Again, much like buying a house, the key players meet in an office and sign the closing documents.

There is much more involved in buying and selling a company, or even just partial ownership of a company, but this gives you a high-level understanding of the buyers' and sellers' perspectives and the basic steps they go through during an acquisition.

Part 3: Sell Your Company

5. PLAN YOUR EXIT—SOME WEBSITES TO KNOW

IRS

If you have more specific questions about exiting your business, be sure to check out the **IRS' guide to closing a business.**

www.irs.gov/Businesses/Small-Businesses-&-Self-Employed/Closing-a-Business

SBA

The SBA provides a good section entitled **"Getting Out"** that covers getting out for all kinds of companies. It contains good information plus links to other helpful sites.

www.sba.gov/category/navigation-structure/starting-managing-business/managing-business/getting-out

SCORE

SCORE's recommended five steps to succession planning can help provide you with some practical succession planning direction.

www.score.org/resources/developing-succession-plan

> It may sound counter-intuitive, but the best time to think about exiting your business is at the beginning, when you are starting it. Lawyers should be hired to work out all the paperwork and you may change your plans later—but think through and talk through your exit strategy and terms up front and get those terms documented and signed by all involved parties.

> Whether you are just thinking about starting a company or already have started one, we can help you consider your exit options. Additionally, we can consult with you as you grow your company and eventually go through your exit process. Send us an email at *info@TheUnconventionalStrategist.com*.

You have reached the end of the main part of the book. The rest is hopefully useful material as well. Good luck! Whether you have gone through this entire book or just read select sections and chapters that piqued your interest, we hope it helped you understand the processes we have gone through over and over. We wish you all the success you hope for!

ABOUT THE AUTHORS

Tom Keith

I love what I do, and if you are willing to work hard and to think unconventionally, then you, too, can escape the 8-to-5 grind, create your own path, and start and grow your own business(es). Here is an in-depth look at my background and work experience. My hope is that by knowing more about me and my work, you will not only understand why I wrote this book and believe that I am qualified to write it, but you will also understand the experiences that ultimately shaped my business strategies and drove me to write the book.

My background includes 20 years in the Air Force as a systems acquisition expert followed by 20+ years as a government contractor, business owner and business consultant. After retiring from the Air Force, I served in executive management positions with annual revenues of up to $160 million, including Corporate Vice President at SAIC, President and COO of McClendon Corporation, and President at **ICES**, providing support to various U.S. government agencies.

In 2013, I started **The Unconventional Strategist** to provide one-on-one business and management consulting services to companies of all sizes. My specialties and background include business startup and consulting, executive consulting-coaching, systems engineering, and systems integration in the commercial market as well as the Department of Defense **(DOD)**, and Intelligence Community **(IC)** sectors.

I consult primarily as a business coach and mentor. The company name says it all; I work with you, or with you and your executive team, to help strategize and think "unconventionally" about growing personally and professionally. I can help you map out a plan to start, grow and even sell your company—if that is your goal.

Additionally, I have ownership in multiple businesses that operate in the commercial, DOD and IC markets. You can own one or more companies, too, if that is what you chose to do. I admit, it takes hard work, and it takes time. It also requires putting together a strategy, which is just one of the things I can help you with through **The Unconventional Strategist**.

When I look back over my early years in the Air Force, I never gave much thought to owning my own business, let alone owning more than one. Instead, I focused on doing the best I could in whatever job I had. When I became a contractor, I started to get the entrepreneurial bug and to think about owning my own business and setting my own agenda. Here's a little more about how I made the leap from Air Force veteran to the owner, and in many cases, founder, of multiple companies.

How My Air Force Experience Shaped Me

I spent the last years of my time in the Air Force working on the systems acquisition side, where I used my Bachelor's and Master's degrees in electrical engineering to work on and oversee multiple engineering projects. I was not satisfied to simply do my job and go home. I learned everything I could about the systems acquisition process, contracts, finance, specifications, statements of work, etc., so that I could deliver the best programs to our airmen and service partners and get the best bang for the buck for the taxpayers. I took my job seriously, and I took my on-the-job education seriously, too. I treated every day as continuing education—as a chance to learn something new.

About The Authors

> *We have an innate desire to endlessly learn, grow, and develop. We want to become more than what we already are. Once we yield to this inclination for continuous and never-ending improvement, we lead a life of endless accomplishments and satisfaction.*
> *(Chuck Gallozzi)*

One thing that stood out to me in the Air Force systems acquisition field was that there was so much to learn, and there was no way I could ever learn it all. I decided to focus on understanding everything I could about the big picture of systems acquisition, that is, the process (or basic, repeatable steps, from beginning to end) of turning a concept or an idea into a fielded system.

I also learned that good leaders know themselves—their strengths and weaknesses—and they rely on other people who complement those capabilities and shortcomings. You can spend all of your time trying to reinvent the wheel, or you can learn enough to work with and oversee others who specialize in things you do not know, and together you can accomplish far more than you ever could alone. Let the experts in their fields do their job and do not try to do it all yourself!

> *The way of a fool seems right to him,*
> *but a wise man listens to advice. (Proverbs 12:15)*

I focus on being really good at what I do—I'm a big picture guy—and I outsource or delegate everything else. I continue to learn, and I look ahead to understand the changing landscape, but I hand off everything I do not want to do, do not like to do or am just not good at. After many years in this business, I know myself pretty well—I know what I am good at and I know what I am not good at.

> *He who knows others is learned.*
> *He who knows himself is wise. (Lao Tse 604-531 BC)*

How My Contractor Experience Shaped Me

After the Air Force, I joined SAIC (Science Applications International Corporation), a very entrepreneurial company. I loved SAIC because the managers I worked for were entrepreneurs. They had a "you kill it, you eat it" approach to business and were happy to reward employees that shared this spirit. In plain English, that means if you devise an idea for new business, market it, chase and eventually win that work, they will let you manage it and will reward your hard work.

My managers' attitude was, if you have an idea and it makes business sense, we will provide you with the support resources you need to be successful — and they did. I came up with the concepts/ideas, wrote white papers (also called concept papers) and submitted them to customers recommending ways to do things better, smarter, faster. My SAIC managers provided technical experts to review the white papers, contracts and finance experts to review or write their sections, and we grew and grew as we chased more and more work.

Essentially, my managers empowered me; they provided expertise I did not have (in the form of other staff and other experts); and they rewarded me for the work that I created (killed), they let me oversee (eat) the work. By the time I left SAIC, I was a corporate vice president and our last business unit had grown to a $160 million unit. I got the entrepreneurial bug!

I was recruited and became President of McClendon Corporation, a company with about 120 employees and annual revenue of about $18 million. The owners were thinking seriously about retirement, and they wanted to put others in charge, who could help grow their company. (The owners wanted to eventually sell the company, which they did, for about $66 million.)

Going to such a small company, after working at SAIC, which had many thousands of employees, was quite a change. But the McClendon Corporation owners had big goals and wanted to grow their company rapidly. We hired great employees, incentivized them and provided them back-office support so they could focus on being great at their job—and the company grew and grew. Just a short 14 months later, the company had over 220 employees and an annual revenue stream that had almost doubled.

Since I had worked in the government (Air Force) and as a contractor, I had a solid understanding of how the government side of business worked, and I had a solid understanding of how the contractor side of business worked. At McClendon, I learned a lot about working in the small business world, and those lessons melded well with what I learned in the Air Force and at SAIC.

I got the small business bug—big time! I knew I would enjoy operating in the small and medium business environment where bureaucracy was not the norm. I hate bureaucracy—it probably stems from my years in the Air Force, working classified programs where we were always understaffed and had tight timelines to meet. Our daily mantra was to press on to get the mission done with as little bureaucracy as possible. The nice thing about the small business world is that bureaucracy is not the norm; in fact, bureaucracy is pushed aside to enable performance.

I left McClendon Corporation after 14 months and joined with two partners to grow the newly formed **ICES (Intelligence Consulting Enterprise Solutions, Inc**.), another government contracting company. Yes, there were just the three of us, but let it be noted that **ICES** is still a flourishing company—even as we write this book.

In summary, after leaving the Air Force, I went from a 40,000+ person company, where I had a nice big corner office with a nice title of corporate vice president; to a 120-employee company, with a modest corner office; to a three-person company, where we worked out of our homes. To some people, maybe to most people, it might appear that I moved backward in my career. In reality, my Air Force career and my subsequent contractor jobs shaped and prepared me to do what I do today—and I am doing what I love to do.

Mentoring and Consulting

Over the years, people often asked me how to network, to take an idea from the idea stage to an end product, to start a company, to grow a company, to get contracts, to strategize, and more. I was always hearing people say that they would love to start their own company, but they just did not know how to go about it. I began mentoring individuals in those skills and on many additional topics, like how to build rates to propose to the customer, to write a whitepaper, to respond to a request for proposal, to write proposals, and much more.

In other words, I was always mentoring and consulting and helping people to strategize. The most exciting thing is that I really loved mentoring and consulting and strategizing, so I decided it was time to get paid for my consulting work. I decided it was time to shape my own strategy and my own vision and to act on that vision.

My Business Concept and Vision

Several years ago I started working on a personal business concept, in which I would work with other entrepreneurs to start several new businesses to do different kinds of technical specialties, like systems engineering, security engineering, information technology **(IT),** network engineering, etc. I would also start a series of businesses to provide those companies the services and back-office support they need, so they can focus on being really great at their technical expertise. My thought was, much like at SAIC, if talented and entrepreneurial people could start their own companies but outsource all of the work they do not want to do, do not know how to do, or are not good at, then they could put all of their energy into their core (or specialty) skills where their passions lie. They could grow their company and be successful in their technical specialty (without the burden of learning the details of things they really did not need to learn or have the time to learn).

There were several elements to my original business concept, some of those key elements, while rough, included:

- Start one company, grow it, incentivize someone to run it. Move on to start another company of my own, while serving on the board of directors of each startup company.

- Find entrepreneurs who have specific technical skills to sell and who want to start a company (but do not know how to start or run a company), and partner with them for some percentage ownership.

- Work with my companies to grow until they are recognized in an industry and have a strong record, and then target small business set-aside prime contracts requiring their skills.

- Repeat the first three steps over and over each year.

- Start companies that provide all the back-office services (contracts, finance, budget, program controls, human resources, administration, etc). that any small- or medium-size company needs to be successful. Encourage my technical companies to outsource all back-office functions, so the entrepreneurs of the technical companies could then focus on their technical specialties and grow the company.

- Reduce the cost of doing business and be extremely competitive by allowing small businesses to outsource back-office functions and only pay for the specific services they need. In other words, they do not have to hire back-office personnel when they can hire only the level of support they need when they need it.

- Become a recognized expert in business startup and growth. Consult to and mentor small business owners.

- Build a strong network of experts in various types of specialties, so I could connect the companies I own and those I consult to with proven experts (be the person others call for just about any business topic—start, grow, or sell).

- Start a company that provides startup services to others where anyone who has an idea, wants to start a company and wants to know how to go about it can come to our company for consultation and guidance.

- Help others expedite their company growth by providing them with tools, processes, procedures, templates, etc., so they do not have to reinvent the wheel.

- Provide training services.

- Write "how-to" books.

- Network my company executives with others in my network, so they become better connected and can therefore grow faster by working together.

- Become a recognized expert in helping others to sell their companies.

- Learn all about the process of acquiring companies and become a go-to person (recognized acquisition expert) when others want to buy a company or sell their company.

- Buy companies using the profits of my companies.

- Give back personally of my time and resources.

- Foster an environment of giving back—of our profits, time and resources (both technical and people).

These notes are actual bullet points that I brainstormed in my early, private planning sessions. Over the years I have refined the original concepts a few times, just as I have refined my overall business concept every year to what it is today.

Targeting Set-Aside Contracts

A big part of my strategy was to target government set-aside contracts. Each year, the federal government sets aside money in their many agencies for prime contracts for small businesses with different certifications, such as veteran-owned small business **(VOSB),** service-disabled veteran-owned small business, **(SDVOSB),** woman-owned small business **(WOSB),** minority-owned small business, etc. We started partnering and launching companies with those different small business certifications with the goal to have ownership in one or more companies with just about every small business certification possible, so that over time, we could strategically target contracts set aside for small business in each agency.

For example, I cannot personally target WOSB set-aside contracts, but I *can* find a woman entrepreneur who has marketable capabilities and who wants to start her own company. I can partner with her (she must have at least 51% ownership) and help her launch, market and grow the company. She gets my startup knowledge, business experience and contacts. I get an entrepreneurial partner with small business certifications that I do not qualify for by myself. It makes for a great partnership!

Once we get the company launched, the strategy is to grow to the point of being able to target prime set-asides. I also work hard to get my companies to work together to leverage their unique capabilities to partner and pursue work together. The companies will all grow through this synergistic teaming approach.

My business concept may not have been entirely unique, but who ever said that your business idea has to be unique to be successful? I want to use my expertise and connections to continue to start new specialty companies with small business certifications and offer services not only to my companies, but to other businesses as well.

Extending My Vision through Strategic Partnerships

We started companies to do technical work, and we created companies to do the back-office services that take the burden off of the technical workers. In some cases, there already were companies in existence that perform the functions we were considering doing in our new starts. We created strategic partnerships with them rather than create a new company that would compete against them. This allowed us to create the exact same diversified dynamic without having to go through the sometimes tedious process of standing up a new company and finding the right people to work for it.

The Future

The bulk of my early career focused on systems engineering and systems integration work, either in the Air Force or as an employee of a contractor company. I have spent the past several years starting and growing companies and diversifying my ownership into business, management and startup consulting, real estate investment (rehab, rentals), staffing and recruiting, contracts and finance services consulting, and marketing and branding.

Sounds like quite a leap doesn't it? To go from serving in the Air Force to working as an employee for others to owning one company to being the owner in multiple companies! The thing that is most important to me is that I choose my own path; I set my own agenda; and I control my own schedule.

And I am not done! I have several companies in the queue that I will start over the next few years. I am confident, since I love what I do, I will start even more companies until I finally decide to retire, if that day ever comes.

My pastor gave me a compliment, when in a sermon in 2012 he said,

> *"Tom Keith is one of the most driven, goal-oriented, get-it-done persons I have ever been around in my life!"*

I do not know if I deserve all of that praise, but I am driven. I do set lofty goals, and I press on regardless of the roadblocks. I treat roadblocks as learning experiences.

> *I am not afraid of storms for I am learning how to sail my ship. (Louisa May Alcott)*

I believe in having big visions. I have a vision for my businesses and my personal life. I know that I will run into roadblocks, but I also know that I will continue to march towards my vision.

> *If your vision doesn't scare you, then both your vision and your God are too small. (Brother Andrew)*

I hope that you will be bold in your thinking, your vision and your efforts, and I hope you will take action today, to get started towards your vision.

> *Whatever you do, or dream, begin it now. Boldness has genius, power and magic in it. Begin it now. (Goethe)*

About The Authors

Ryan Keith

At the age of 29, my experience in the world of business is fairly limited but has been rich in quality and diversity. I graduated from The Ohio State University in 2008 with a BS in business administration and a specialization in economics. As my time at school ended, I faced the same decision that all students eventually confront: What do I want to do with my life? I was going through the process of interviewing with different companies and exploring various career fields. The idea of getting a regular 8-to-5 job and climbing the corporate ladder was not terribly appealing to me, but there did not seem to be many other options available.

That is when Tom came to me with a different idea. I was on a break from school and preparing for an interview with a financial company in Charlotte, NC, when he suggested that I come to work for him. I honestly only had a vague idea of exactly what he did for most of my life. I knew he had an engineering and operations management background (which I do not), and he generally worked in the classified government contracting world. Surprisingly, one of his business ideas was to start a real estate business, flipping and managing investment properties and the like. Again, this was an area in which I had little to no experience, but the idea of running a business was highly intriguing to me.

This idea stuck with me throughout my visit to Charlotte, as I went through the various stages of interviews and was introduced to the corporate culture I might join. Looking back, there was never really a decision to be made. Taking on the challenge of helping to start a new business and learning the ins and outs of running it was an opportunity I could not pass up.

The day after graduation, I packed up my stuff, said my farewells, and moved back to the Northern Virginia area to begin RazoRealty, LLC. I got my real estate license, and we immediately began scouting potential investment properties.

The general goal was to buy depressed properties, fix them up by putting in sweat equity and then rent them out to further build equity with the intention of selling much later down the road. This became my full-time job. Meanwhile Tom continued working primarily in the world of government contracting, and he helped out with the houses in the evenings and on weekends.

For a few years we successfully rehabbed and rented houses that we still own and manage. I spent a great deal of time wearing a tool belt, tearing down walls, installing cabinets, building fences and the like. At the same time, I was learning valuable lessons about how to run and manage a business and about the importance of diversifying my business, financial interests and investments.

Handling the day-to-day accounting, I learned the importance of keeping costs low and efficiencies high, all while trying to add value to the properties, and therefore the business. We took on all the projects that we could do ourselves but contracted the bigger projects that we knew were out of our scope. This helped me to learn the importance of prioritizing time and delegating tasks that we were not particularly well suited for. Over the course of those two years, I learned a great deal about fixing up and maintaining a home, but more importantly I built foundational knowledge of what it takes to run a business.

After a few years, Tom's consulting business began to ramp up. We decided to put the real estate business on hold (i.e., not buy or flip, but simply manage the existing properties), so I could transfer my focus and work for with him in the government contracting arena. Since then, it has been a whirlwind of activity. In the beginning I learned the ins and outs of, and began guiding others through, the process of officially standing up a new company. I still handle the day-to-day accounting for some of our smaller companies and help out with everything from building websites, recruiting, building salary justifications and submitting candidates to contracts—and everything in between.

About The Authors

Several people, who have known and worked with Tom for a long time, told me that in working with him, I would learn more than I ever could from most MBA programs. It did not take me very long to realize just how true this was. The goal of this book is to try to impart some of this same, invaluable knowledge onto you.

THINK LIKE THE UNCONVENTIONAL STRATEGIST

As mentioned before, we started and have ownership in several small businesses. (If you have not read the previous sections, which offer background information on our companies, and us please take a moment to do so before continuing this chapter.) Our approach may not be the right approach for you, but we share this information to get you thinking *unconventionally* about how to grow your business.

Part of the strategy we set in motion a few years ago was to start one or more businesses each year with different core competencies and in different market spaces (Department of Defense **[DOD]**, Intelligence Community **[IC]**, local and state government, etc.). The next building block in the strategy is to regularly gather the company leaders and business development leaders from each business to explore ways to work together by targeting contracts that they could team together on. They synergistically support each others' business development efforts by sharing information about upcoming bids that the other companies may want to pursue.

As the businesses grow, take on larger projects and need subcontractors, they bring on some of the other companies to perform the additional work or the work that falls in their particular specialty. Meanwhile, as we implement this multi-year strategy of growing companies and working together, we continue to leverage our various small business certifications to grow each individual company.

For example, **ICES**, a veteran-owned small business **(VOSB)** that offers consulting, analysis and engineering services, recently won a prime contract to perform systems engineering work in an IC agency. **ICES** subcontracted some of the work to **LOTO,** a woman-owned small business **(WOSB)** that provides information technology solutions, engineering and project management. Through this arrangement, each company is able to grow, and in the course of time, to expand into new customer spaces. **ICES** opened the door of the IC agency to **LOTO**. **ICES** will, in turn, look for opportunities to perform subcontract work when **LOTO** eventually bids on prime contracts in their primary customer space.

Oftentimes, small business owners think that they have to do it all; they try to handle their own contracts, finance, security, marketing, recruiting, etc. The problem with this approach is that you spend time and energy to perform support functions — time that you could be investing in expanding your product or service or reaching out to your core market. To keep costs down, we rely heavily on outsourcing functions that other businesses could do much better or more quickly.

For example, we outsource contracts, finance, human resources, and recruiting to our companies — like **ConnekServ** and **ConnekTek** — that specialize in those functions. By outsourcing, we pay only for the services we need at the time we need them. As a result, none of the companies spend time recruiting support personnel or spend money to pay for full-time employees to perform those back-office and support functions. **ConnekServ** and **ConnekTek** provide services to companies outside our family of businesses, too.

We believe the business model we have chosen is highly unconventional but also has a lot of built-in advantages. This model will not work for everybody, but at our core, we believe it is important to think outside the box and look for opportunities and advantages where others may not see them.

Think Like The Unconventional Strategist

Once your business is up and running, it can be all too easy to focus solely on your initial goals and the primary purpose of your business and to forget about planning and strategizing for the future. Growth is not guaranteed and is certainly not always easy to obtain. Oftentimes your best opportunities for growth come from unexpected areas, and they can quickly pass you by if you do not know to look for them. If nothing else, we hope this material will help you recognize the need to be forward looking — to think *unconventionally* — and to see that there is a wide array of opportunities to grow that you might not have even considered before.

APPENDIX A: KEY TERMINOLOGY

Acceptance: The legal obligation by a party to the terms and conditions **(T&C)** of a contract.

Acquisition: The act of acquiring goods and services (including construction) for the use of a governmental activity through purchase, rent or lease. Includes the establishment of needs, description of requirements, selection of procurement method, selection of sources, solicitation of procurement, solicitation for offers, award of contract, financing, contract administration and related functions.

Acquisition Plan (AP): An administrative tool in which agency program offices report their upcoming formal contract actions and planned procurement. It is designed to assist the program and procurement offices in planning effective and efficient accomplishments of an assigned product.

Acquisition Planning: The process by which the efforts of all personnel responsible for a procurement are coordinated and integrated through a comprehensive plan for fulfilling an agency's needs in a timely manner and at a reasonable cost. It includes developing an overall acquisition strategy for managing the acquisition plan.

Addendum: An addition or supplement to a document (e.g., items or information added to a procurement document).

Advantage! (GSA Advantage): Where federal agencies and employees can view and purchase products and services provided by General Services Administration **(GSA)** Schedule contractors. (**www.gsaadvantage.gov/**)

Affiliates: According to the Small Business Administration **(SBA),** affiliation exists when one business controls or has the power to control another or when a third party (or parties) controls or has the power to control both businesses. Control may arise through ownership, management or other relationships or interactions between the parties.

Agreement: A duly executed and legally binding contract; the act of agreeing.

Amendment: A written modification to a contract, purchase order or other agreement that becomes binding once it is signed.

Appropriation: Sum of money from public funds set aside for a specific purpose.

Award: Any instrument, signed by a contracting officer **(CO),** that provides government funds or other resources to an offeror and permits expenditure of such government funds or the use of such government resources.

Basic Ordering Agreement (BOA): Written agreement between a buyer and a seller outlining the terms, specifications and prices of services or goods to be supplied. A BOA is not a contract. A BOA is a written instrument of understanding, negotiated between an agency, contracting activity, or contracting office and a contractor, that contains (1) terms and clauses applying to future contracts (orders) between the parties during its term, (2) a description, as specific as practicable, of supplies or services to be provided, and (3) methods for pricing, issuing and delivering future orders under the basic ordering agreement.

Best and Final Offer (BAFO): For negotiated procurements, a contractor's final offer following the conclusion of discussions.

Best Value (BV): The expected outcome of an acquisition that, in the government's estimation, provides the greatest overall

Appendix A: Key Terminology

benefit in response to a requirement; a term applied to comparing proposals and ranking them from best to worst, not only on price but on all factors stated in the solicitation.

Bid Decision (or Bid/No-Bid Decision): A process companies go through (usually documented and briefed up the management chain) to evaluate Request for Proposal (**RFP**) opportunities to decide if they should pursue the opportunity, and whether they should pursue it as a prime or as a subcontractor. Some companies go through a very formal process where they weigh numerous factors to decide if they have a high probability of winning **(Pwin)** — or at least a high enough Pwin to invest their precious and often limited business development dollars in trying to win the opportunity.

Bid Protest: Challenge by a bidder against the awarding of a government contract.

Blanket Order (BO): A contract under which a vendor agrees to provide goods or services on a purchase-on-demand basis. The contract generally establishes prices, terms, conditions and the period covered (no quantities are specified). Shipments are to be made as required by the purchaser.

Blanket Purchase Agreement (BPA): A simplified way to fill anticipated repetitive needs for services or products. BPAs are "charge accounts" that ordering offices establish with General Services Administration **(GSA)** Schedule contractors to provide themselves with an easy ordering tool.

Broker: A business that carries no inventory and has no written ongoing agreement with any manufacturer or manufacturer's authorized distributor to sell the products of the manufacturer. You may use an insurance broker or benefits broker who will represent your company and get quotes for you to consider.

Budgeting: The process of translating approved expenditures into funding allocations for a specified period of time.

Business: A contractor, subcontractor, supplier, consultant or provider of technical, administrative or physical services organized as a sole proprietorship, partnership, association, corporation, or other entity formed for the purpose of doing business for profit.

Business Concern: The Small Business Administration **(SBA)** defines a business concern as a for-profit organization that: has a place of business in the United States or makes a significant contribution to the U.S. economy through payment of taxes or use of American products, materials or labor; is independently owned and operated; and is not dominant in its field on a national basis.

Capability Statement: A document that summarizes a company's background, certifications, experience, capabilities, expertise, past performance and pertinent codes such as Data Universal Numbering System **(DUNS)** number.

Central Contractor Registration (CCR): Formerly a primary vendor database for the federal government. Companies or individuals were required to be registered in the CCR to be awarded government contracts. Functionality has been replaced by the System for Award Management **(SAM).**

Certificate of Competency (COC): A certificate issued by the Small Business Administration **(SBA)** stating that the holder is "responsible" (in terms of capability, competency, capacity, credit, integrity, perseverance and tenacity) for the purpose of receiving and performing a specific government contract.

Certified 8(a) Firm: A business that is owned and operated by a socially or economically disadvantaged individual(s) and therefore eligible to receive government contracts under the Small Business Administration's Business Development Program.

Appendix A: Key Terminology

Change Order (CO): Written instructions issued by the government to a contractor to modify contractual requirements within the general scope of the contract. Unilateral written change orders are typically limited to changes to the drawings, designs, specifications, method of shipment or packing, or place of delivery.

Code of Federal Regulations (CFR): The codification of the general and permanent rules published in the Federal Register by the departments and agencies of the federal government.

Commercial and Government Entity (CAGE) Code: A five-character identification number that identifies government contractors. Automatically assigned as part of registration with the System of Award Management **(SAM)**.

Commercial off-the-Shelf (COTS) Products and Services: Commercial goods and services that are sold to the general public.

Commitment: The reservation of funds for obligation at the time the contract is signed by an agency's warranted contracting officer **(CO)**.

Commodity: A transportable article of trade or commerce that can be bartered or sold.

Competition: A procurement strategy where more than one contractor that is capable of performing the contract is solicited to submit an offer for supplies and services. The successful offer is selected on the basis of criteria established by the agency's contracting office and the program offices for which the work is to be performed.

Consideration: Something of value given or done as recompense that is exchanged by two parties; that which binds a contract.

Contract: A mutually binding legal relationship obligating the contractor to furnish the supplies or services and the agency to pay for them. It includes all types of commitments that obligate agencies to an expenditure of funds that, except as otherwise authorized, are in writing. In addition to bilateral instruments, contracts include (but are not limited to) awards and notices of awards; job orders or task letters issued under basic ordering agreements; letter contracts; orders, such as purchase orders, under which the contract becomes effective by written acceptance of performance; and bilateral contract modifications. Contracts do not include grants and cooperative agreements covered by 31 United States Code **(USC)** 6301.

Contract Action: An action resulting in a contract, a modification to a contract, or a delivery order **(DO)** placed against an indefinite-delivery, indefinite-quantity **(IDIQ)** contract.

Contract Administration: All the activities associated with the oversight of a contractor's performance of a contract, from award to closeout.

Contract Award: Occurs when the contracting officer **(CO)** has signed and distributed the contract to, or notified, the contractor.

Contract Requirements: In addition to specified performance requirements, contract requirements include those defined in the Statement of Work **(SOW);** specifications, standards, and related documents; management systems; and contract terms and conditions **(T&C).**

Contracting: Purchasing, renting, leasing or otherwise obtaining supplies or services from non-federal sources. Contracting includes the description of supplies and services required, the selection and solicitation of sources, the preparation and award of contracts, and all phases of contract administration. It does not include grants or cooperative agreements.

Appendix A: Key Terminology

Contracting Office: The office authorized by an agency's senior procurement executive that awards or executes contracts for supplies or services.

Contracting Officer (CO): A person with the authority to enter into, administer and/or terminate contracts and make related determinations and findings.

Contracting Officer's Technical Representative (COTR) / Contracting Officer's Representative (COR): The COTR and COR are designated by the contracting officer **(CO)** to assist in administering specific aspects of a contract and typically have the initial and most continuous contact with the contractor while acting as liaisons between the contractor and the contracting officer. COs rely on the expertise and background of the COTR and COR to ensure that the technical and financial aspects of the contract are accomplished.

Contractor: Entity that performs the service mandated by a contract with a federal agency. In some cases, the service will actually be performed by a subcontractor, subject to the approval of and conditions set by the contracting agency. In other cases, subcontracting is not permitted under the contract. Contractors are usually for-profit companies, but they also include universities, independent non-profits, hospitals and other types of entities.

Contractor Team Arrangement: An arrangement in which (a) two or more companies form a partnership or joint venture to act as potential prime contractor; or (b) an agreement by a potential prime contractor with one or more companies to have them act as its subcontractors under a specified government contract or acquisition program.

Cooperative Agreement: An assistance instrument used when substantial involvement is anticipated between the federal government and the state or local government or other recipient during performance of the contracted activity.

Cooperative Purchasing: The combining of requirements of two or more governmental units to obtain the benefits of volume purchases and/or reduction in administrative expenses.

Cost Accounting Standards (CAS): CAS were designed by the General Accounting Office **(GAO)** to achieve uniformity and consistency in the measurement, assignment and allocation of costs to government contracts. The standards were based on examinations of common cost accounting practices throughout the industry. CAS establishes limits and constraints on what is considered appropriate, allowing the CAS to meet the goal of providing consistency and uniformity in cost accounting.

Cost Analysis: The review and evaluation of the separate cost elements and proposed profit of a contractor's cost or pricing data. Cost analysis always includes price analysis.

Cost Data or **Pricing Data:** Factual and verifiable data that includes (1) direct costs, (2) indirect costs, (3) profit or fee, (4) vendor quotations, (5) information on changes in production methods and in production or purchasing volume, and (6) information on management decisions that could have a significant bearing on costs.

Cost Plus Fixed Fee (CPFF): (FAR 16.306) A cost-reimbursement contract that provides payment to the contractor of a negotiated fee that is fixed at the inception of the contract. The fixed fee does not vary with actual cost, but may be adjusted as a result of changes in the work to be performed under the contract. This contract type permits contracting for efforts that might otherwise present too great a risk to contractors, but provides the contractor only a minimum incentive to control costs.

Cost Reimbursement Contracts: Contracts based on payment by an agency to a contractor of allowable, reasonable and allocable costs incurred in the contract performance to the extent prescribed in the contract. These contracts may not require completion of the contract work but rather the best efforts of the

Appendix A: Key Terminology

contractor. The types of cost-reimbursement contracts include (1) cost, (2) cost sharing, (3) cost-plus-fixed fee **(CPFF)**, (4) cost-plus-incentive fee **(CPIF)**, and (5) cost-plus-award fee **(CPAF)** contracts.

Cradle-to-Grave: The total concept of a procurement, from inception through development, procurement, performance and final disposition.

Current Year: The fiscal year in progress. Also called execution year.

DD Form 254: Department of Defense Contract Security Classification Specification. The intention of a DD Form 254 is to convey security requirements, classification guidance and provide handling procedures for classified material received and/or generated on a classified contract. The DD Form 254 is a resource for providing security requirements and classification guidance to a contractor. The Federal Acquisition Regulation **(FAR)** requires that a DD Form 254 be integrated in each classified contract. The DD Form 254 provides the contractor (or a subcontractor) security requirements and the classification guidance that is necessary to execute a classified contract.

A DD Form 254 Preparation Guide can be found at:

www.cdse.edu/documents/cdse/DD254.pdf

Dealer: A business that maintains a store, warehouse or other establishment in which a line or lines of products are kept in inventory and are sold to the public on a wholesale or retail basis. Also called a jobber or distributor.

Debarment: The disqualification of a person to receive invitations for bids, requests for proposals or the award of a contract by a government body for a specified time commensurate with the seriousness of the offense, failure, or inadequacy of performance.

Default: Failure by a party to fulfill a contract or to comply with the requirements set in the contract.

Defective Pricing: Inadequate cost/pricing data, to include delivery orders placed against Federal Supply Schedules **(FSS)**, certified by a contractor to be accurate, current and complete.

Defense Contract Audit Agency (DCAA): Responsible for performing all contract audits for the Department of Defense **(DOD)** and providing accounting and financial advisory services regarding contracts and subcontracts to all DOD components responsible for procurement and contract administration.

Defense Contractor: Any business organization, individual or other entity that enters into a contract with the United States for the production of material or for the performance of services for the national defense.

Deliverable: A report or product that must be delivered to the government by the contractor to satisfy contractual agreements.

Direct Cost (DC): Any cost specifically identified as a final cost objective for a particular contract action. Includes cost factors such as direct labor materials.

Direct Labor (DL): Labor required to complete a product or service; includes fabrication, assembly, inspection and tests for constructing an end product. Also, the labor expended by contractor personnel in performing contractual requirements.

Direct Materials (DM): A direct material cost is the cost of material used in making a product and includes raw materials, purchased parts and subcontracted items required to manufacture and assemble completed products.

Appendix A: Key Terminology

Disbursements: In budgetary usage, gross disbursements represent the amount of checks, cash or other payments issued, less refunds received.

Discriminators (proposal discriminators): Aspects of a proposal that are clearly different from the competitors' proposals and are acknowledged to be important by the customer.

D-U-N-S (Data Universal Numbering System) Number: A DUNS (or D-U-N-S) number is a unique nine-character identification number provided to entities interested in contracting with the federal government. These numbers are distributed by the private company Dun & Bradstreet **(D&B)**. Companies interested in contracting with the government must have a separate DUNS number for each physical location and different address in the company, as well as each legally distinct division that may be co-housed at the same address or location. You do not have to pay for a DUNS number as a government contractor.

Effective Competition: A market condition that exists when two or more contractors, acting independently, actively compete for an agency's business in a manner that ensures that the agency will be offered the lowest price or best technical design to meet its minimum goals.

Electronic Data Interchange (EDI): Transmission of information between computers using highly standardized electronic versions of common business documents.

Emerging Small Business: A small business concern whose size is no greater than 50% of the numerical size standard applicable to the North American Industry Classification Systems **(NAICS)** code assigned to a contracting opportunity.

Employee Retirement Income Security Act (ERISA): (from the US Department of Labor website) ERISA, protects the assets of millions of Americans so that funds placed in retirement plans during their working lives will be there when they retire.

ERISA is a federal law that sets minimum standards for pension plans in private industry. For example, if an employer maintains a pension plan, ERISA specifies when an employee must be allowed to become a participant, how long they have to work before they have a non-forfeitable interest in their pension, how long a participant can be away from their job before it might affect their benefit, and whether their spouse has a right to part of their pension in the event of their death

Equity: An accounting term used to describe the net investment of owners or stockholders in a business. Under the accounting equation, equity also represents the result of assets, less liabilities.

Evaluation Criteria: Standards that are used to evaluate an offeror's technical and operational effectiveness.

Expenditure: A charge against available funds, evidenced by a voucher or claim. Expenditure represents the actual payment of funds.

Facility Security Officer (FSO): Responsible for designing and implementing the facility security plan.

Fair and Reasonable Price: A price that is fair to both parties, considering the agreed-upon conditions, promised quality, and timeliness of contract performance. "Fair and Reasonable" price is subject to statutory and regulatory limitations.

FedBizOpps (FBO): Online entry point for government procurement opportunities over $25,000. Buyers are allowed to publicize their opportunities directly at the web site (**www.fbo.gov**).

Appendix A: Key Terminology

Federal Acquisition Regulations (FAR): The body of regulations that is the primary source of authority governing the government procurement process. The FAR, which is published as Chapter 1 of Title 48 of the Code of Federal Regulations, is prepared, issued and maintained under the joint auspices of the secretary of defense, the administrator of the General Services Administration **(GSA)** and the administrator of the National Aeronautics and Space Administration **(NASA)**. Actual responsibility for maintenance and revision of FAR is vested jointly in the Defense Acquisition Regulatory Council **(DARC)** and the Civilian Agency Acquisition Council **(CAAC)**.

Federal Acquisition Regulation (FAR) Council: Governing body that makes FAR interpretations and rulings.

Federal Fiscal Year: The federal government operates on a fiscal year that begins on October 1 and ends the following September 30. Fiscal years are typically notated with FYXXXX or FYXX. The year notates the calendar year when the fiscal year will end. For example, fiscal year 2007 (FY07) runs from October 1, 2006 through September 30, 2007.

Federal Supply Schedule (FSS) Program: A simplified process for procuring commonly used supplies or services by placing delivery orders against FSS contracts that have been awarded by the General Services Administration **(GSA)** for use by all agencies.

Federal Supply Service (FSS): The FSS provides federal customers with the products, services and programs to meet their supply, service, procurement, vehicle purchasing and leasing, travel and transportation, and personal property management requirements. FSS is one of the General Services Administration's **(GSA)** three services. It provides a source for virtually every commercial product or service an agency might need.

Fiscal Year: The 12 months between one annual settlement of financial accounts and the next; a term used for budgeting and so forth. The fiscal year for the U.S. government is October 1 to September 30, but many companies choose to use the calendar year **(CY)** as their fiscal year.

Fixed Price (FP) Contract: A type of contract that provides for a firm price or, under appropriate circumstances, for an adjustable price for supplies or services being procured

Forward Pricing Rates (FPR): A written agreement negotiated between a contractor and the government to make certain rates available during a specified period for use in pricing contracts and/or modifications. These rates represent reasonable projections of specific costs that are not easily estimated for, identified with, or generated by a specific contract, contract end item, or task. These projections may include rates for such things as labor, indirect costs, material obsolescence and usage, spare parts provisioning, and material handling.

Fraud: Acts of fraud or corruption or attempts to defraud an agency or to corrupt its agents; acts that constitute a cause for debarment or suspension under Federal Acquisition Regulations **(FAR)** 9.4062(a) and 9.407-2(a); and acts that violate the False Claims Act, 31 U.S. Code **(USC),** sections 3729 to 3731, or Anti-Kickback Act, 41 USC, Sections 51 and 54.

Fringe Benefits: A collection of benefits provided by an employer, which are exempt from taxation as long as certain conditions are met. Fringe benefits may include things like health insurance, group term life coverage, education reimbursement, childcare and assistance reimbursement, cafeteria plans, employee discounts, and personal use of a company-owned vehicle.

Read more: www.investopedia.com/terms/f/fringe-benefits.asp - ixzz2DtsPNups

Appendix A: Key Terminology

Read more: www.investopedia.com/terms/f/fringe-benefits.asp - ixzz2Dts8pUJ9

Full and Open Competition or **Full and Open Contract:** Refers to the rule that all appropriate suppliers may compete for a contract.

Full and Open Competition after Exclusion of Sources: A term indicating that all responsible sources that meet certain criteria, such as business size or location in a labor surplus area, are permitted to compete. These competitions are specifically authorized by the Competition in Contracting Act **(CICA).**

Fully Burdened: A rate, proposed by an offeror, to cover direct labor (salary), indirect costs (overhead, general and administrative **[G&A],** fringe), and a fee/profit under a service contract.

General Services Administration (GSA): Independent agency that establishes procurement policy and secures the buildings, products, services, technology and other workplace essentials for government agencies. The GSA is a centralized federal procurement and property management agency created by Congress to improve government efficiency and help federal agencies better serve the public. It acquires, on behalf of federal agencies, office space, equipment, telecommunications, information technology, supplies and services. In 2014, the GSA was comprised of 4,000 associates and provided services and solutions for the office operations of over one million federal workers located in more than 8,000 government-owned and leased buildings in 2,000 U.S. communities.

General Services Administration (GSA) Schedule: A GSA schedule is an unfunded, long-term contract that lists the prices the federal government has agreed to pay for a product or service provider's commercial goods and services. There are 62 categories of products and services from which GSA buys; those are known as "Schedules."

General Services Administration (GSA) Smartpay: Method of paying for goods or services with a charge card, which enables online ordering; formally called pCard.

Government Property or **Government Furnished Property (GFP)** or **Government Furnished Equipment (GFE):** Equipment and facilities furnished by the government to a contractor or recipient or acquired by a contractor or recipient at the government's expense for use during the performance of a contract or assistance agreement.

Governmentwide Acquisition Contracts (GWACs): GWACs are defined in the Federal Acquisition Regulation **(FAR)** as task orders or delivery order contracts for information technology **(IT)** established by one agency for government-wide use.

Grant: An award of financial assistance in the form of money, or property in lieu of money, by a funding agency. The grantee is required to account for spending the money in the manner specified by the grantor. A federal grant is also an authorized expenditure to a non-federal entity for a defined public or private purpose in which services are not rendered to the federal government. This classification of spending comes in two types: "formula grants" and "project grants."

Historically Underutilized Business Zone (HUBZone): The HUBZone Empowerment Contracting program provides federal contracting opportunities for qualified small businesses located in distressed areas.

Improper Influence: An influence that induces or tends to induce a federal employee to consider awarding a federal contract or purchase on any basis other than its merit.

Incremental Funding: Used if the total task order is awarded and the dollar amount of the work is more than the client has available at the desired start time. Pricing for the project is totaled and assigned on the contract, but the pricing is charged

Appendix A: Key Terminology

incrementally as it becomes available. The overall scope of work and pricing does not change from the original proposal. The incremental funds are added by modifications, but the modifications should not add time to the period of performance or add money to the full amount of the contract.

Incumbent: Usually refers to the company doing the work today, so when Company X is called the incumbent, they hold and are executing the current contract. When you are chasing a re-compete or a new contract vehicle, it is important to look at the incumbents, so you can posture which team to join or whether to go after the work yourself. Additionally, you should find out if the government customer is happy with the incumbent or dissatisfied with their work and factor that answer into your decision to pursue — or not pursue — the contract.

Incumbentitis (also "Incumbent-itis"): A mentality that some companies have, in which they think they cannot lose a competition because they are doing the work today and believe the customer wants them back. They believe they cannot lose a competition or re-compete. This state of mind can hurt a company because it may not put forth the best winning proposal and therefore can lose the competition to another company.

Indefinite Delivery Indefinite Quantity (IDIQ) Contracts: Also known as multiple award IDIQ task order contracts. These provide a broad range of information technology **(IT)** support services and resources for administrative, research, development and operational activities.

Interagency Order: Includes Intragovernmental and Federal Supply Schedule orders written by a military department or defense agency purchasing office.

Interested Party: A prime contractor or an actual prospective offeror whose direct economic interest would be affected by the award of a contract or by the failure to award a contract.

Intermediary Organization: Organizations that play a fundamental role in encouraging, promoting and facilitating business-to-business linkages and mentor-protégé partnerships. These can include both non-profit and for-profit organizations such as: chambers of commerce; trade associations; local, civic, and community groups; state and local governments; academic institutions; and private corporations.

Intragovernmental Order: Orders written by a military department or defense agency purchasing office requesting that a non-defense federal agency furnish supplies or services from its stocks, in-house manufacturing facilities, or contracts.

Invitation for Bid (IFB): Method used to accept a sealed bid and includes a description of the product or service to be acquired, bidding instructions, packaging, delivery, payment, contract clauses and deadline.

Invoice: A list of goods or services sent to a purchaser that shows information including prices, quantities and shipping charges for payment.

Joint Venture (JV): The temporary association of two or more businesses to secure and fulfill a procurement bid award.

Key Personnel Management List (KPML): This form lists the essential personnel in a company, their full names, titles, positions in the company, Social Security numbers, dates and places of birth, citizenship, the facility address and facility cage code. The form is signed and dated by an official in the company to certify that the information is complete and accurate.

Kickback: Any money, fee, commission, credit, gift, gratuity, thing of value, or compensation of any kind that is provided, directly or indirectly, to agency procurement or program officials by any prime contractor employee, subcontractor or subcontractor employee for the purpose of improperly

Appendix A: Key Terminology

obtaining or receiving favorable treatment.

Lead Time: The time that it would take a supplier to deliver goods after receipt of order.

Life-Cycle Costing: A procurement evaluation technique that determines the total cost of acquisition, operation, maintenance and disposal of the items acquired; the lowest ownership cost during the time the item is in use.

Line Item (LI): An item specified in a solicitation for which the vendor must specify a separate price.

Location of Work: The place where an item is to be manufactured, assembled or otherwise supplied by the prime contractor; the place where the service is to be performed; or the site of a construction project.

Lowest Price, Technically Acceptable (LPTA): A source selection method that is used by the government when evaluating proposals. The LPTA source selection process is appropriate when best value is expected to result from selection of the technically acceptable proposal with the lowest evaluated price.

Mandatory: Required by the order stipulated (e.g., a specification or specific description that may not be waived).

Marketing Partner Identification Number (MPIN): A personal code that allows contractors to access government applications such as the Past Performance Information Retrieval System **(PPIRS)**. The MPIN acts as a password in these systems, and it should be guarded as such. The MPIN is a mandatory data element that contractors create when registering in the System for Award Management **(SAM)**. It must have nine characters, including at least one letter (upper or lower case) and one number. No spaces or special characters are permitted.

Mentor: Individual or business who creates a program to advance strategic relationships with a less-experienced business.

Military Interagency Purchase Request (MIPR): A funding-source document accessed through the Information Technology Solutions Shop **(ITSS)** for all branches of the military. Check to be sure that the amount on the MPIR is more than or the same as the contracted amount.

Modification: Authorized changes to a contract after contract award. The following lists possible types of modifications:

- *Administrative Change:* A unilateral contract change that does not affect the contractual rights of the parties (e.g., a change in the paying office).
- *Change Order:* A written order, signed by the contracting officer **(CO),** directing the contractor to make a change authorized by the "changes clause." A change order is issued without the consent of the contractor.
- *Supplemental Agreement:* A contract modification that is accomplished by the mutual action of both parties.
- *Bilateral Modifications:* A contract modification that is signed by the contractor and the CO; used to make negotiated adjustments resulting from the issuance of a change order, for definitive letter contracts, or to reflect other agreements of the parties modifying the terms of contracts.
- *Unilateral Modification:* A contract modification that is signed only by the CO; used to make administrative changes, to issue change orders, or to make changes authorized by something other than a "changes clause."

Multiple Award Contracts (MACs): Contracts awarded to more than one supplier for comparable supplies and services. Awards are made for the same generic types of items at various prices.

Multiple Award Schedules (MAS) Program: Awarding of contract to more than one vendor for comparable goods or

Appendix A: Key Terminology

services. The most common example of this is the General Services Administration **(GSA)** Schedule program.

Negotiation: Contracting through the use of either competitive or other-than-competitive proposals and discussions. Any contract awarded without using sealed bidding procedures is a negotiated contract.

Net Price: Price after all discounts, rebates and other price factors have been allowed.

Net Value (NV): The net amount of debit and credit procurement actions recorded during the period.

No Bid: A response to a solicitation for bids stating that the respondent does not wish to submit an offer. It usually operates as a procedure consideration to prevent suspension from the vendors list for failure to submit a response.

North American Industry Classification System (NAICS): Classification of businesses established by the type of activity for the purpose of facilitating the collection, tabulation, presentation and analysis of data collected by various agencies of the U.S. government, state agencies, trade associations and private research organizations for promoting uniformity and comparability in the presentation of statistical data relating to those establishments and their fields of endeavor; formerly known as the Standard Industrial Classification **(SIC)** code.

Offer: A response to a solicitation that, if accepted, binds the offeror to fulfill the resulting contract. Responses to Invitations for Bids **(IFB)** are called bids or sealed bids; responses to Requests for Proposals **(RFP)** are referred to as offers or proposals; and responses to Requests for Quotations (**RFQ**) are designated as quotes.

Office of Small and Disadvantaged Business Utilization (OSDBU): A part of all federal agencies, OSDBUs serve as small business advocates within the agency.

Options: A clause contained in a contract that gives an agency the unilateral right to extend the term of the contract or obtain additional quantities of products or services at the prices contained in the contract for that option period or additional quantity of products or services.

Orders: Work orders against an existing contract for hardware/software.

Organizational Conflict of Interest (OCI): Activities or relationships with other persons that interfere with the ability of a contractor or contractor employee to render impartial assistance or advice to an agency.

Partnering: A mutually beneficial business-to-business relationship based on trust and commitment and that enhances the capabilities of both parties.

Per Diem: By the day.

Performance Work Statement (PWS): Similar to the Statement of Work **(SOW),** the PWS is a formal document that captures and defines the work activities, deliverables, services, tasks and timeline a vendor must execute in the performance of specified work under a contract for a client. The PWS, typically provided with the Request for Proposal **(RFP),** usually includes detailed requirements and pricing, along with standard regulatory and governance terms and conditions.

Price Agreement: A contractual agreement in which a purchaser contracts with a vendor to provide the purchaser's requirements at a predetermined price; usually involves a minimum number of units—orders placed directly with the vendor by the

Appendix A: Key Terminology

purchaser—and limited duration of the contract. See **Blanket Order** and **Requirements Contract.**

Price Analysis: The process of examining and evaluating a proposed price by comparing it with other offered prices or prices previously paid for similar goods or services.

Price Competition: Two or more bids or offers are received under formal advertising or negotiated methods of procurement, and the award is made to the lowest responsive and responsible bidder or offeror.

Price Fixing: An agreement among competing vendors to sell at the same price. The general purpose of price fixing is to maintain or push prices to an unnaturally high level to increase profits for the vendors. This is considered highly unethical and is a criminal offense under the Sherman Antitrust Act.

Prime Contract: A contract awarded directly by the federal government.

Prime Contract Award: A legally binding agreement executed by a department or an agency to obtain supplies or services.

Prime Contractor (PC): Individual or business contracted to perform a specified piece of work.

Procurement Action: An action involving the obligation or de-obligation of funds which officially awards or changes a prime contract. This may include the award of a new prime contract, a debit or credit change to an existing prime contract, or an order written against an indefinite delivery-type contract or basic ordering agreement.

Procurement Automated Source System (PASS): A database managed by the Small Business Administration **(SBA)** that contains information on over 230,000 small businesses. The PASS database must be queried and reviewed by agency personnel to locate potential contractors. Not all small businesses are included in the PASS database, but it does represent a good sampling of the availability of business in a particular industry. One of the primary reasons for using the PASS search is that if any sources are found, the results are included in the "Justification for Other than Full and Open Competition" **(JUFOC)**.

Procurement Center Representative (PCR): Employees of the Small Business Administration **(SBA),** who are assigned to larger government buying offices. The primary purpose of a PCR is to assist small businesses in obtaining federal contracts.

Procurement Official: Any civilian, military official or employee of an agency who has participated personally and substantially in any of the following activities for a particular procurement:

1. Drafting a specification or a statement of work
2. Reviewing or approving a specification or statement of work developed
3. Preparing or developing procurement or purchase requests
4. Preparing or issuing a solicitation
5. Evaluating bids or proposals
6. Selecting sources
7. Negotiating to establish the price or terms and conditions of a particular contract or contract modification
8. Reviewing and approving the award of a contract or contract modification (Federal Acquisition Regulation **[FAR]**, 3.104-4[h][1])

Procurement Technical Assistance Center (PTAC): The PTAC mission is to generate employment and improve the general economy of its geographic area. The PTAC assists companies seeking to do business with the Department of Defense **(DOD),** and state and local governments.

Appendix A: Key Terminology

Proprietary: The only items that can perform a function and satisfy a need. This should not be confused with "single source." An item can be proprietary and yet available from more than one source. For example, if you need a camera lens for a Nikon camera, and the only lens that will fit is a Nikon lens; then, this lens is proprietary. However, the Nikon lens is available from more than one source; thus, it is not single source.

Protégé: An individual or developing business who cooperates with another more experienced individual or business to improve its capabilities.

Protest: Written objection by an interested party to a procurement action conducted by an agency.

Public Law 10650 (PL 106-50): Also know the **Veterans Entrepreneurship Act.** A federal law passed in 1999 that sets as a goal that 3% of the value of all federal contracts and subcontracts shall be awarded to service-disabled, veteran-owned small businesses. This law also created the Veterans Corporation.

Public Law 108-183 (PL 108-183): The **Veterans Benefit Act of 2003.** This law enables service-disabled veteran-owned small businesses **(SDVOSBs)** to receive sole source and restricted competition contracts for goods and services used by the U.S. government. Congress enacted this statute after data collected from more than 60 federal departments and agencies over a period of three years showed that half of them reported no procurement dollars expended with SDVOSB companies.

Purchase Order (PO): An offer made by an agency to buy certain supplies or non-personal services from commercial sources and based on specified terms and conditions. The aggregate amount shall not exceed the small purchase limits — $100,000 as of 2014.

Purchase Request (PR): A document that is used to initiate a procurement action. Whether referred to as a PR, a requisition, or a procurement directive, it provides the necessary authorization to proceed with a procurement.

Qualified Vendor (QV): A vendor that is determined by a buying organization (agency) to meet minimum set standards of business competence, reputation, financial ability, and product quality for placement on the vendors list; also known as a responsible vendor. Agencies often make Qualified Vendors Lists **(QVL)** for certain categories of work. Know your agency and know whether or not they have QVLs. Oftentimes the agency will send companies on the QVL notices of vendors' conferences, Requests for Information **(RFIs)** and other advertisements, which help contractors stay abreast of the acquisitions and strategies of that agency.

Ratification: The process used by an agency's contracting officers **(COs)** to approve and legitimize an otherwise proper contract made by an individual without contracting authority.

Reachback: A customer often wants to know if a contractor has "reachback," that is, can the contractor "reach back" into its company (or companies) to provide extra resources and extra skills as the requirements change or surge requirements require extra personnel to complete their mission.

Request for Bid: A solicitation in which the terms, conditions and specifications are described, and responses are not subject to negotiation

Request for Information (RFI): An RFI is a precursor in the procurement process to a Request for Proposal **(RFP)** or Request for Quotation **(RFQ),** and is used by the government to obtain written information about the capabilities of potential suppliers. This information is usually received in a standardized format for ease of comparison, and the government will use the

Appendix A: Key Terminology

information to help in making decisions about future steps in the process.

Request for Proposal (RFP): Government document outlining the criteria and requirements to evaluate offers. When the value of a government contract exceeds $100,000 and necessitates a highly technical product or service, the government may issue an RFP. In a typical RFP, the government requests a product or service and solicits proposals from prospective contractors on how they intend to carry out that request, and at what price. Proposals in response to an RFP can be subject to negotiation after they have been submitted.

Request for Quote (RFQ): When the government is merely checking into the possibility of acquiring a product or service, it may issue an RFQ. A response to an RFQ by a prospective contractor is not considered an offer, and consequently, cannot be accepted by the government to form a binding contract. The order is an offer by the government to the supplier to buy certain supplies or services upon specified terms and conditions. A contract is established when a supplier accepts the offer.

Requirements Contract: A form of contract that is used when the total long-term quantity required cannot be definitely fixed but can be stated as an estimate or within maximum and minimum limits with deliveries on demand.

Requisition: An internal document that a program office sends to the purchasing department detailing products or materials required to fulfill a specific need.

Responsible Bidder: A bidder whose reputation, past performance, and business and financial capabilities are such that the bidder would be judged by an appropriate authority as capable of satisfying an organization's needs for a specific contract.

Responsive Bidder: A bidder whose bid does not vary from the specifications and terms set out in the invitation for bids.

Sealed Bid: A method determined by the commissioner to prevent the contents from being revealed or known before the deadline for submission of responses.

Senior Procurement Executive: An executive for an agency who is appointed by the agency head pursuant to section 16(3) of the Office of Federal Procurement Policy **(OFPP)** Act (41 U.S. Code**[USC]** 414[3]) and who is responsible for managing the agency's procurement activities.

Sensitive Compartmented Information Facility (SCIF): A facility that provides formal access controls. This is typically an enclosed area within a building that is used to process classified information.

Service Corps of Retired Executives (SCORE): SCORE Counselors to America's Small Businesses is a non-profit association dedicated to providing entrepreneurs with free, confidential, face-to-face and email business counseling. Business counseling and workshops are offered at 389 chapter offices across the country. The 12,400-member volunteer association, sponsored by the Small Business Administration **(SBA),** matches volunteer business management counselors with present prospective small business owners in need of expert advice. (**www.SCORE.org)**

Services: Unless otherwise indicated, both professional or technical services and services performed under a service contract.

Service-Connected: Refers to a disability or the resulting death that was incurred or aggravated in the line of duty in the active military service.

Appendix A: Key Terminology

Service-Disabled Veteran: Veteran with a disability that is service-connected.

Service-Disabled, Veteran-Owned Small Business (SDVOSB): A small business that is at least 51% owned and controlled by a service-disabled veteran of the military.

Single Source: An acquisition where, after a search, only one supplier is determined to be reasonably available.

Simplified Acquisition Procedures (SAP): May be used for contracts up to $100,000. Methods prescribed for making purchases of supplies or services using imprest funds, purchase orders, blanket purchase agreements, government-wide commercial purchase cards, or any other appropriate authorized methods.

Small and Disadvantage Business Utilization (SADBU): A less-used term meaning the same thing as Office of Small and Disadvantaged Business Utilization **(OSDBU).**

Small Business Administration (SBA): An independent agency chartered to protect the interests of small businesses and maintain free competitive enterprise.

Small Business Development Centers (SBDC): SBDCs offer a broad spectrum of business information and guidance as well as assistance in preparing loan applications.

Small Business Innovative Research (SBIR) Contract: A type of contract designed to foster technological innovation by small businesses with 500 or fewer employees. The SBIR contract program provides for a three-phased approach to research and development projects: technological feasibility and concept development; the primary research effort; and the conversion of the technology to a commercial application.

Small Business Liaison Officer (SBLO): A person working in an agency or company tasked with assisting small businesses in doing business with that agency or company.

Small Business Owned and Controlled by a Service-Disabled Veteran: A business must qualify as small under the SBA rules and not less than 51%-owned by one or more service-disabled veterans or, in the case of any publicly owned business, that is not less than 51% is owned by one or more service-disabled veterans; and whose management and daily business operations are controlled by one or more service-disabled veterans or, in the case of a veteran with permanent and severe disability, the spouse or caregiver of such veteran.

Small Disadvantaged Business Concern: A small business concern that is at least 51% owned by one or more individuals who are classified as both socially and economically disadvantaged. This can include a publicly owned business that has at least 51% of its stock unconditionally owned by one or more socially and economically disadvantaged individuals and whose management and daily business are controlled by one or more such individuals.

Sole Source (SS): A procurement where only one source is practicably available for the goods or services required. Competition is not available in a sole source procurement thus distinguishing it from a proprietary procurement where the product is restricted to that of one manufacturer, but is sold through distributors and competition between them can be obtained.

Sole Source Procurement (SSP): A contract for the purchase of supplies or services that is entered into by an agency after soliciting and negotiating with only one source. Such procurements must be fully justified to indicate the reasons why competition is not possible:

Appendix A: Key Terminology

Solicitation: A formal document that elicits proposals for acquisition or financial assistance awards. Solicitation instruments include Invitations for Bid **(IFBs)**, Requests for Proposals **(RFPs)**, and for small purchase actions, Requests for Quotations **(RFQs)**.

Source Selection Committee (SSC): The SSC evaluates responses to a Request for Proposal **(RFP)**. The government selects qualified government employees and contractors to evaluate each proposal and make recommendations that go into the award decision. They follow the instructions and criteria provided to them in the Source Selection Plan **(SSP)**.

Source Selection Plan (SSP): A document that explains how proposals from offerors will be evaluated. The plan includes the evaluation factors to be considered, the relative weight of the factors, and the methodology to be used by evaluators in judging proposals.

Special Item Number (SIN): A group of generically similar (but not identical) supplies or services that are intended to serve the same general purpose or function.

Specifications: Often abbreviated as Spec or Specs. A concise statement of a set of requirements to be satisfied by a product, material or process that indicates, whenever appropriate, the procedures to determine whether the requirements are satisfied. As far as practicable, it is desirable that the requirements are expressed numerically in terms of appropriate units, together with their limits. A specification may be a standard, a part of a standard, or independent of a standard.

Standard: An item's characteristic or set of characteristics generally accepted by the manufacturers and users of the item as required for all such items.

Standard Industrial Classification (SIC) Code: A code representing a category within the Standard Industrial

Classification System administered by the Statistical Policy Division of the U.S. Office of Management and Budget. The system was established to classify all industries in the U.S. economy. A two-digit code designated each major industry group, which was coupled with a second two-digit code representing subcategories. The SIC systems is no longer in use and has been replaced by the North American Industry Classification Systems **(NAICS).**

Statement of Objectives (SOO): Government's required performance objectives, which are included in the solicitation; potential vendors propose a method and metric system for achieving the objectives (often in a Work Breakdown Structure **[WBS])**

Statement of Work (SOW): A detailed statement describing the buyer's requirements, including, if necessary, what products, services and methods will be used to fulfill the need.

Subcontract (SC or S/C): A contract between a prime contractor and another source to obtain outside supplies or services that the prime contractor needs to perform the contract requirements. Subcontracts include any agreement, other than employer-employee relationship, into which a prime contractor enters for the purpose of fulfilling a government contract.

Subcontractor: An individual, business or corporation hired by a prime contractor to perform a specified piece of work required as part of an overall contract. Occasionally referred to as a **Second-Tier Contractor.**

System for Award Management (SAM): A one-stop shop for government acquisition and award support systems, where businesses can register with the government, look for opportunities, or support subcontract information.

Task Order (TO): A task, delivery or call order for supplies and or/services placed against an established contract, blanket

Appendix A: Key Terminology

purchase agreement **(BPA)** or basic ordering agreement.

Taxpayer Identification Number (TIN): A number assigned to a business by the Internal Revenue Service **(IRS)**. A TIN is needed to complete registration in the System for Award Management **(SAM)**. Also referred to as an **Employer Identification Number (EIN).**

Technical Direction (TD): The direction or guidance of the scientific, engineering and other technical aspects of a project, as distinguished from the administrative and business management aspects.

Terms and Conditions (T&C): A phrase generally applied to the rules under which all bids must be submitted and the stipulations included in most purchase contracts; often published by the purchasing authorities for the information of all potential bidders.

Themes (proposal themes): A central idea that is subsequently supported or proven within a proposal, often by discriminators. Themes are often highlighted and used as the first sentence of a paragraph. In many proposals there will be a theme in every paragraph and every graphic.

Third-Tier Subcontractor: When a subcontractor has a contract with another contractor (their prime), who is also a subcontractor to another contractor (their prime). In other words a subcontractor who reports to a company that is a subcontractor reporting to a prime contractor who reports to the government. The government is moving away from third-tier subcontractors.

Time and Materials (TM or T&M): A type of contract in which payment is based on a) direct labor costs, usually at fixed hourly rates b) actual cost of materials and c) a fixed sum added on as a fee.

Title: The instrument or document whereby ownership of property is established.

Tort: A wrongful act, other than a breach of contract, such that the law permits compensation of damages.

Uniform Commercial Code (UCC): A comprehensive modernization of various statutes relating to commercial transactions, including sales, leases, negotiable instruments, bank deposits and collections, fund transfers, letters of credit, bulk sales, documents of title, investment securities, and secured transactions.

Unsolicited Proposal (UP): As defined in Federal Acquisition Regulation **(FAR)** 2.101, an unsolicited proposal is a written proposal for a new or innovative idea that is submitted to an agency on the initiative of the offering company (i.e. a contractor) for the purpose of obtaining a contract with the government, and that is not in response to an RFP, broad agency announcement, or any other government-initiated solicitation or program. Some agencies accept unsolicited proposals, which allow contractors to submit new and innovative ideas that may not fall within the scope of an ongoing or upcoming new acquisition. When preparing an unsolicited proposal, refer to FAR Subpart 15.6 Unsolicited Proposals, to ensure the proposal meets the government requirements.

www.acquisition.gov/far/html/Subpart 15_6.html

Value Analysis: An organized effort directed at analyzing the function of systems, products, specifications, standards, practices and procedures for the purpose of satisfying the required function at the lowest total cost of effective ownership consistent with requirements for performance, reliability, quality and maintainability.

Appendix A: Key Terminology

Vendors List: A list of the names and addresses of suppliers from whom bids, proposals and quotations might be expected. The list, maintained by the purchasing office, should include all suppliers who have expressed interest in doing business with the government.

Veteran: Individuals who served on active duty and have a discharge other than dishonorable after a minimum of 90 days of service during wartime or a minimum of 181 continuous days during peacetime.

Veteran-Owned Business (VOB): A business that is at least 51% owned and controlled by a veteran of the military.

Veteran-Owned Small Business (VOSB): A small business that is at least 51% owned and controlled by service veterans.

Warranty: The representation, either expressed or implied, that a certain fact regarding the subject matter of a contract is presently true or will be true. This is not to be confused with a guarantee, which is a contract or promise by one person to answer for the performance of another person.

Woman-Owned or Minority Business Enterprise (WMBE): A small business that is at least 51% owned and controlled by a woman or minority. Specific criteria for consideration as a "minority" can be obtained through the Small Business Administration **(SBA).** The business must be owned and at least 51% controlled by one or more minorities or women.

Women-Owned Small Business (WOSB): A small business that is at least 51% owned and controlled by a woman.

Wrap Rate (WR): Generally refers to labor rates that are calculated to include all costs, such as salary, fringe benefits, overhead, general and administrative **(G&A)** costs and profit. In some cases, they also include a pro rata share of other direct costs **(ODC)** and/or material costs. Often, a wrap rate can be calculated by dividing (a) total price, or (b) total labor costs through G&A and profit, by the number of labor hours (or hours by category in some cases).

APPENDIX B: ACRONYMS

ACO	Administrative Contracting Officer
AP	Acquisition Plan
ATP	Authorization to Proceed
BAFO	Best and Final Offer
BCS	Breakfast Club South
BD	Business Development
BO	Blanket Order
BOA	Basic Ordering Agreement
BOD	Board of Directors
BOP	Business Owners' Policy
B&P	Bid and Proposal
BPA	Blanket Purchase Agreement
BV	Best Value
CAGE	Commercial and Government Entity
CAS	Cost Accounting Standards
CAV	Contractor Assistance Visits
C-CORP	C Corporation
CCR	Central Contractor Registration
CFDA	Catalog of Federal Domestic Assistance
CFR	Code of Federal Regulations
CLIN	Contract Line Item Number
CO	Change Order
CO	Contracting Officer
COBRA	Consolidated Omnibus Budget Reconciliation Act
COC	Certificate of Competency
COGS	Cost of Goods Sold
COR	Contracting Officer's Representative
COTR	Contracting Officer's Technical Representative
COTS	Commercial off-the-Shelf
CPAF	Cost-Plus-Award-Fee
CPARS	Contractor Performance Assessment Reporting System

CPFF	Cost-Plus-Fixed-Fee
CPIF	Cost-Plus-Incentive-Fee
DBA	Doing Business As
DC	Direct Cost
DCAA	Defense Contract Audit Agency
DCID	Director of Central Intelligence Directives
DL	Direct Labor
DLA	Defense Logistics Agency
DM	Direct Materials
D&O	Directors and Officers
DO	Delivery Order
DOD	Department of Defense
DOT	Department of Transportation
DRFP	Draft Request for Proposal
DSS	Defense Security Service
DUNS or D-U-N-S	Data Universal Numbering System
EBITDA	Earnings Before Interest, Taxes, Depreciation and Amortization
EBSA	Employee Benefits Security Administration
EDI	Electronic Data Interchange
EDWOSB	Economically Disadvantaged Women-Owned Small Business
EEOCS	Equal Employment Opportunity Commission
EFTP	Electronic Federal Tax Payment System
EIN	Employer Identification Number
EPLS	Excluded Parties List System
ERISA	Employee Retirement Income Security Act
ERP	Enterprise Resource Planning
eSRS	Electronic Subcontracting Reporting System
FAPIIS	Federal Awardee Performance and Integrity Information System
FAQ	Frequently Asked Questions
FAR	Federal Acquisition Regulations
FAS	Federal Acquisition Service
FBO	Federal Business Opportunities
FCL	Facility Clearance Level
FDPS-NG	Federal Procurement Data System-Next Generation

Appendix B: Acronyms

FEIN	Federal Employer Identification Number
Fedreg	Federal Agency Registration
FFATA	Federal Funding Accountability and Transparency Act
FFP	Firm-Fixed Price
FICA	Federal Insurance Contributions Act
FMLA	Family and Medical Leave Act
FP	Fixed Price
FPR	Forward Pricing Rate
FSA	Flexible Spending Account
FSO	Facility Security Officer
FSRS	FFATA Subaward Reporting System
FSS	Federal Supply Schedule
FSS	Federal Supply Service
FUTA	Federal Unemployment Tax Act
G&A	General and Administrative
GC	Government Contracting (Contractor)
GEOINT	Geospatial Intelligence
GFE	Government Furnished Equipment
GFP	Government Furnished Property
GSA	General Services Administration
GWAC	Government Acquisition Contracts
HRA	Health Reimbursement Account
HSA	Health Savings Account
HUBZone	Historically Underutilized Business Zone
IC	Independent Contractor
IC	Intelligence Community
ICD	Intelligence Community Directives
IDIQ	Indefinite Delivery Indefinite Quantity
IFB	Invitation for Bid
IFF	Industrial Funding Fee
IP	Intellectual Property
IRA	Individual Retirement Account
IRS	Internal Revenue Service
JPAS	Joint Personnel Adjudication System
JV	Joint Venture
KPML	Key Personnel Management List

LI	Line Item
LLC	Limited Liability Company
LLP	Limited Liability Partnership
LOC	Line of Credit
LOE	Level-Of-Effort
LP	Limited Partnership
LPTA	Lowest Price Technically Acceptable
M&A	Merger and Acquisition
MAC	Multiple Award Contract
MAS	Multiple Award Schedule
MEAC	McLean Entrepreneurial Advocacy Council
MEC	Mason Enterprise Center
MIPR	Military Interagency Purchase Request
MMM	Maryland Marketing Meeting
MPIN	Marketing Partner Identification Number
MWOB	Minority or Women Owned Business
NAICS	North American Industry Classification System
NDA	Non-Disclosure Agreement
NGA	National Geospatial-Intelligence Agency
NISP	National Industrial Security Program
NISPOM	National Industrial Security Program Operating Manual
NRO	National Reconnaissance Office
NSA	National Security Agency
NV	Net Value
OCI	Organizational Conflict of Interest
ODC	Other Direct Costs
ORCA	Online Representations and Certifications Application
OSBP	Office of Small Business Programs
OSDBU	Office of Small and Disadvantaged Business Utilization
PASS	Procurement Automated Source System
PBS	Public Building Service
PC	Prime Contractor
PCO	Procurement Contracting Officer
PCR	Procurement Center Representative

Appendix B: Acronyms

PM	Program Manager
PO	Purchase Order
POC	Point of Contact
POP	Period of Performance
PPIRS	Past Performance Information Retrieval System
PR	Purchase Request
PTAC	Procurement Technical Assistance Center
PTO	Paid Time Off
PTO	Patent and Trademark Office
Pwin	Probability of Winning
PWS	Performance Work Statement
QSSS	Qualified Subchapter S Subsidiary
QV	Qualified Vendor
QVL	Qualified Vendors List
RFI	Request for Information
RFP	Request for Proposal
RFQ	Request for Quotation
ROI	Return on Investment
RSS	Rich Site Summary
SADBU	Small and Disadvantaged Business Utilization
SAM	System for Award Management
SAP	Simplified Acquisition Procedures
SBA	Small Business Administration
SBAWG	Small Business Advisory Work Group
SBDC	Small Business Development Centers
SBDC	Small Business Development Consortium
SBIR	Small Business Innovative Research
SBLO	Small Business Liaison Officer
SBPO	Small Business Program Office
SC or S/C	Subcontract
SCC	State Corporation Commission
SCIF	Sensitive Compartmented Information Facility
SCORE	Service Corps of Retired Executives
S-CORP	S Corporation
SDB	Small Disadvantaged Business
SDBU	Small and Disadvantaged Business Utilization
SDV	Service Disabled Veteran

SDVOSB	Service Disabled Veteran Owned Small Business
SEP	Simplified Employee Pension
SIC	Standard Industrial Classification
SIMPLE	Savings Incentive Match Plan for Employees
SIN	Special Item Number
SLIN	Subcontract Line Item Number
SME	Subject Matter Expert
SOO	Statement of Objectives
SOP	Standard Operating Procedures
SOW	Statement of Work
SS	Sole Source
SSA	Social Security Administration
SSC	Source Selection Committee
SSP	Sole Source Procurement
SSP	Source Selection Plan
T&C	Terms and Conditions
TD	Technical Direction
TIN	Taxpayer Identification Number
TM or T&M	Time and Materials
TO	Task Order
UCC	Uniform Commercial Code
UP	Unsolicited Proposal
USGIF	United States Geospatial Intelligence Foundation
UTSA	Uniform Trade Secrets Act
VA	Department of Veterans Affairs
VIM	Virginia Intelligence Meeting
VOB	Veteran-Owned Business
VOSB	Veteran-Owned Small Business
WDOL	Wage Determination Online
WMBE	Women-Owned or Minority Business Enterprise
WOSB	Women-Owned Small Business
WR	Wrap Rate

Made in the USA
Middletown, DE
02 February 2015